ADOBE PHOTOSHOP 2025 GUIDE

Master AI-Powered Tools, Pro Techniques & Next-Gen Design for Stunning Visuals

Sloane Delaney

TABLE OF CONTENTS

TABLE OF CONTENTS III

INTRODUCTION 1

CHAPTER ONE 3

GETTING STARTED 3

New Features of the New Adobe Photoshop 2025 3

Minimum and Recommended Specifications 9

How to Download and Install the New Adobe Photoshop 2025 11

How to Get Acquainted with Adobe Photoshop Workspace 15

Major Components of the Photoshop Workspace 16

Navigating New Features in Adobe Photoshop 2025 19

Customizing the Workspace 20

How to Find and Remove Distractions with the Remove Tool 21

Generative Expand with the Firefly Image 3 Model 23

CHAPTER TWO 27

WORKING WITH THE BASICS 27

How to Reset your Workspace 27

Tips for Maintaining an Organized Workspace 30

How to Understand the Menu Bar 31

How to Know the Toolbar 36

How to Create your First File 44

How to Open Files with the Open Command 46

How to Insert Images Using Drag & Drop 48

How to Insert Files Using Place Embedded 49

How to Insert Files Using Place Linked 52

CHAPTER THREE 54

WORKING WITH LAYERS 54

UNDERSTANDING LAYERS AND LAYER STACKS 54

CREATING, ORGANIZING, AND MANAGING LAYERS 57

    Adjusting Opacity, Blending Options, and Linking Layers 61

CONVERTING LAYERS TO SMART OBJECTS FOR NON-DESTRUCTIVE EDITING 64

    Convert a Layer to a Smart Object in Photoshop 64

HOW TO LOCK AND HIDE LAYERS 65

    Accessing the Layers Panel 65

CHAPTER FOUR 68

MASTERING ADJUSTMENT LAYERS 68

OVERVIEW OF ADJUSTMENT LAYERS: TYPES AND USES OF EACH ADJUSTMENT LAYER 68

    Types of Adjustment Layers and Their Uses 68

    How to Apply an Adjustment Layer 71

USING LEVELS, CURVES, AND COLOR BALANCE 72

    Levels Adjustment Layer 72

    Curves Adjustment Layer 73

    Color Balance Adjustment Layer 75

USING MASKS WITH ADJUSTMENT LAYERS 76

    Adding an Adjustment Layer with a Mask 76

    Refining the Adjustment with the Layer Mask 77

    Mask Areas Using Selection Tools 78

APPLYING AND SAVING CUSTOM ADJUSTMENT PRESETS 79

    Applying Adjustment Layers 79

    Saving Custom Adjustment Presets 80

CREATIVE EFFECTS WITH BLENDING MODES ON ADJUSTMENT LAYERS 81

    Understanding Adjustment Layers 81

    Understanding Blending Modes 81

    Applying Blending Modes to Adjustment Layers 82

    Creative Effects by Using Blending Modes with Adjustment Layers 82

CHAPTER FIVE 83

CROPPING AND TRANSFORMING IMAGES 83

CROPPING FOR COMPOSITION AND SPECIFIC RESOLUTIONS..83

    Cropping to Specific Resolutions...85

USING THE CONTENT-AWARE CROP TOOL..86

    Straightening an Image Using Content-Aware Crop...87

TRANSFORM TOOLS OVERVIEW: FREE TRANSFORM, SKEW, DISTORT, PERSPECTIVE 89

    Free Transform Tool 89

    Skew Tool..90

    Distort Tool...90

    Perspective Tool 91

    Correcting Perspective Distortions 91

HOW TO USE THE PUPPET WARP 93

CHAPTER SIX 97

EXPLORING BRUSHES AND BRUSH SETTINGS 97

SELECTING AND MODIFYING BRUSH TIPS 97

    Understanding Brush Basics in Photoshop 2025 97

    Editing Brush Tips..98

HOW TO USE THE MIXER BRUSH AND SMUDGE TOOL...110

    How to Use Mixer Brush Tool...110

    Advanced Techniques with the Mixer Brush 113

INTRODUCTION TO SMUDGE TOOL 113

    Using the Smudge Tool...114

    Advanced Techniques with Smudge Tool 115

CHAPTER SEVEN 117

SHAPES AND VECTOR TOOLS 117

WORKING WITH SHAPE TOOLS: RECTANGLE, ELLIPSE, POLYGON, AND CUSTOM SHAPE OPTIONS 117

    Accessing the Shape Tools..117

    Transformations and Adjustments with Shape Tool...121

CREATING AND EDITING PATHS: VECTOR-BASED SELECTIONS AND EDITING WITH THE PATH TOOL................122

    Intro to Vector-Based Selections and Paths 122

Converting Selections to Paths and Paths to Selections.. 123

Troubleshooting Common Path Issues 124

RESIZING, ROTATING, AND WARPING SHAPE LAYERS 124

Resizing Shape Layers... 124

Rotating Shape Layers 125

Warping Shape Layers 126

FILL AND STROKE OPTIONS: COLOR, GRADIENT, AND PATTERN FILLS FOR SHAPES 127

Shape Fill and Stroke Options 127

Color Fill 128

Gradient Fill 128

Fill Pattern.. 128

PATH OPERATIONS AND COMBINING SHAPES 130

Setting Up Your Document and Accessing the Shape Tool 130

Using Path Operations through the Options Bar.. 130

Managing Shapes and Paths in the Layers Panel 132

CHAPTER EIGHT 133

BLENDING MODES AND OPACITY 133

DETAILED OVERVIEW OF EACH BLENDING MODE CATEGORY.. 133

PRACTICAL APPLICATIONS OF BLENDING MODES: USING MULTIPLY, SCREEN, OVERLAY, AND MORE 137

Multiply: Darkening Images and Adding Shadows 137

Screen: Lightening Images and Adding Glow 138

Overlay: Adding Contrast and Boosting Color 138

Soft Light: Subtle Contrast and Gentle Effects... 139

Color: Accurate Color Corrections Without Affecting Luminance 140

Difference: Unique Effects and Fine-tuning Alignment.. 140

LAYER OPACITY AND FILL ADJUSTMENTS: DIFFERENCES AND EFFECTS OF OPACITY VS. FILL 141

Advanced Effects with Combined Opacity and Fill... 144

Using Opacity and Fill Creatively in Designs 144

CREATING DOUBLE EXPOSURE AND LIGHT LEAK EFFECTS 145

Double Exposure Using Adobe Photoshop 2025 145

CREATING LIGHT LEAK EFFECTS IN ADOBE PHOTOSHOP 2025 147

LAYERING TECHNIQUES FOR TEXTURE AND TONE BLENDING 149

Setting Up Your Layers for Blending 149

Applying Textures Using Layer Blending Modes 150

Adding Depth with Gradient Maps and Color Fill Layers 150

Texturing with Layer Masks for Precision 151

Experimenting with Texture Blending Using Opacity and Fill 152

Advanced Texturing with Displacement Maps 152

Final Touches with Adjustment Layers 153

CHAPTER NINE 154

WORKING WITH CURVES, LEVELS, AND BRIGHTNESS/CONTRAST 154

CURVES FOR TONE AND CONTRAST CONTROL 154

Understanding Curves: The Basics 154

Adjusting Tone and Contrast with Curves 155

Fine-Tuning Brightness with Curves 156

WORKING WITH COLOR CHANNELS IN CURVES 156

Working with Curves in Photoshop 2025: Some Practical Tips 157

CURVES VS. LEVELS AND BRIGHTNESS/CONTRAST 158

How to Achieve Contrast and Balance 158

Working with Adjustment Layers for Contrast 158

How to Enter the Brightness and Contrast Adjustments 162

How to Change Brightness and Contrast 163

AUTO TONE, COLOR, AND CONTRAST: UTILIZING PHOTOSHOP'S AUTOMATED ADJUSTMENTS 164

Understanding Automated Adjustments in Photoshop 164

When and Why to Use Automated Adjustments 167

Customizing Automated Adjustments 168

USING HISTOGRAMS TO GUIDE ADJUSTMENTS 168

Opening Histograms within Photoshop 2025 169

Interpreting the Histogram 170

Using Adjustment Layers to Modify Histograms 170

Balancing Color Using Histograms *172*

CHAPTER TEN **173**

MASKING TECHNIQUES **173**

UNDERSTANDING LAYER MASKS: BASICS OF MASKING AND TRANSPARENCY CONTROL 173

Creating a Layer Mask in Photoshop 2025 .... *173*

Editing the Layer Mask *174*

Advanced Masking Techniques *175*

Common Use Cases for Layer Masks *176*

USING CLIPPING MASKS: LINKING LAYERS FOR TARGETED EFFECTS 176

Understanding Clipping Masks in Photoshop *176*

How to Set Up a Clipping Mask in Adobe Photoshop 2025 .... *177*

Practical Applications of Clipping Masks *178*

Tips and Tricks for Working with Clipping Masks *179*

MASK REFINEMENT: EDGE DETECTION, FEATHERING, AND ADJUSTING DENSITY 180

Practical Applications of Mask Refinement Techniques *184*

CREATING COMPLEX COMPOSITES WITH MASKS: MASKING FOR MULTI-LAYER COMPOSITES 185

Understanding Masks in Photoshop *185*

QUICK MASK MODE: TEMPORARY MASKING FOR PRECISE SELECTIONS 189

Times to Apply Quick Mask Mode *190*

How to Use Quick Mask Mode in Photoshop 2025 .... *190*

CHAPTER ELEVEN **194**

COLOR BALANCE, HUE/SATURATION, AND SELECTIVE COLOR **194**

COLOR BALANCE FOR TEMPERATURE ADJUSTMENTS 194

Understanding Color Temperature and White Balance *194*

Accessing the Color Balance Tool *194*

Adjusting Color Temperature with Color Balance *195*

New Features in Photoshop 2025 for Color Balance *196*

Practical Temperature Adjustment Tips *196*

ADJUSTING HUE, SATURATION, AND LIGHTNESS 198

Understanding Hue, Saturation, and Lightness *198*

Advanced Tips for Hue, Saturation, and Lightness Adjustments *201*

APPLYING LUTs FOR QUICK COLOR GRADING 205

Applying LUTs in Photoshop 2025 .... *206*

Tips for Effective LUT Use in Photoshop 2025 .... *208*

WORKING WITH GRADIENT MAPS 209

Creating a Custom Gradient *210*

Gradient Types and Presets *210*

Advanced Gradient Map Techniques *212*

Tips for Gradient Maps in Photoshop 2025 .... *212*

CHAPTER TWELVE **214**

THE HEALING BRUSH AND RETOUCHING TOOLS **214**

HEALING BRUSH, SPOT HEALING, AND PATCH TOOL: REMOVING IMPERFECTIONS AND BLEMISHES 214

The Healing Brush Tool *214*

The Spot Healing Brush Tool *215*

ADVANCED RETOUCHING TECHNIQUES: CONTENT-AWARE FILL FOR COMPLEX EDITS 218

Understanding Content-Aware Fill in Photoshop 2025 .... *218*

Setting Up for Content-Aware Fill Success *218*

Using Content-Aware Fill for Complex Backgrounds *219*

Working with Reflections and Shadows *220*

Advanced Workflow Efficiency in Using Content-Aware Fill *221*

CLONE STAMP TOOL: MANUAL CLONING FOR PRECISE CORRECTIONS 222

Understanding Basic Clone Stamp Tool Principles *222*

Tips for Choosing the Right Source Area *223*

Adjusting Brush Settings for Control *223*

Using Clone Sources for Complex Edits *223*

Practical Application of Clone Stamp Tool *225*

FREQUENCY SEPARATION: ADVANCED TECHNIQUE FOR PROFESSIONAL SKIN RETOUCHING 229

Understanding Frequency Separation Layers *229*

Creating Frequency Separation in Photoshop 2025 .... *229*

Retouching with Frequency Separation 230

CHAPTER THIRTEEN **234**

FILTERS AND EFFECTS **234**

INTRODUCTION TO PHOTOSHOP FILTERS 234

Types of Photoshop Filters 235

Applying Filters in Photoshop 2025 236

New Filters Features in Photoshop 2025 237

Tips for Effective Filter Use 237

SMART FILTERS: NON-DESTRUCTIVE APPLICATION OF FILTERS ON SMART OBJECTS 238

The benefit of Smart Filters in Photoshop 2025 238

HOW TO APPLY SMART FILTERS IN PHOTOSHOP 2025 239

Practical Applications of Smart Filters 241

COMMON FILTERS USED IN PHOTOGRAPHY: BLUR, SHARPEN, NOISE REDUCTION 241

Balancing Filters for Optimal Results 245

CREATIVE EFFECTS WITH DISTORT, RENDER, AND STYLIZE FILTERS: EFFECTS FOR DIGITAL ART 245

USING CAMERA RAW AS A FILTER FOR ENHANCED EDITING 249

CHAPTER FOURTEEN **253**

GRADIENT AND COLOR FILL ADJUSTMENTS **253**

WORKING WITH GRADIENTS: LINEAR, RADIAL, AND CUSTOM GRADIENTS 253

Creating Gradient Overlays and Backgrounds 253

WORKING WITH SOLID AND PATTERN FILL LAYERS 256

Understanding Fill Layers in Photoshop 256

Working with Solid Color Fill Layers 257

Working with Pattern Fill Layers 258

APPLYING GRADIENT TO CHANGE LAYER STYLES IN PHOTOSHOP 260

The Role of Gradients in Layer Styles 260

Creating and Saving Custom Gradients 262

Combining Gradients with Other Layer Styles 262

CHAPTER FIFTEEN **263**

USING TYPOGRAPHY AND TEXT EFFECTS 263

WORKING WITH TEXT LAYERS: ADDING, EDITING, AND FORMATTING TEXT 263

Adding Text Effects with Layer Styles 265

Working with Paragraph and Character Panels 266

Saving and Exporting Text Layers 267

TEXT TRANSFORMATION AND WARPING: CREATING DYNAMIC TEXT SHAPES 267

LAYER STYLES FOR TEXT EFFECTS: DROP SHADOWS, STROKES, AND GLOWS 270

Glow Effects (Outer and Inner Glow) 274

Combining Layer Styles for Advanced Text Effects 275

CREATING SELECTIONS FROM TEXT 275

Converting Text to a Selection 276

Saving and Exporting Your Text Selection 278

ADDING DIMENSION AND LIGHTING FOR IMPACT 279

Setting the Foundation with Layers and Smart Objects 279

Using the 3D Lighting Effects Tool 279

Adding Dimension with Gradient Maps 281

CHAPTER SIXTEEN 282

PEN TOOL, PATHS, AND ADVANCED SELECTION TOOLS 282

USING THE PEN TOOL FOR PRECISION SELECTIONS: PATHS, CURVES, AND ANCHOR POINTS 282

Understanding the Basics of the Pen Tool 282

Adding and Removing Anchor Points 284

PATH CREATION AND EDITING: MANIPULATING PATHS AND SHAPES 285

Creating Paths Using the Pen Tool 285

Creating Shapes with Shape Tools 286

REFINE EDGE, QUICK MASK, AND OBJECT SELECTION 289

Working with Channels for Selections 289

Accessing and Navigating Channels 289

CHAPTER SEVENTEEN 293

EXPORTING AND SAVING FILES 293

EXPORTING FOR WEB AND PRINT: CHOOSING FILE TYPES AND OPTIMIZING QUALITY 293

    Understanding Export Needs: Web vs. Print 293

    Choosing the Right File Types 293

    Optimizing Export Settings 295

USING EXPORT AS AND SAVE FOR WEB: EXPORTING FOR DIFFERENT PLATFORMS 297

    The "Export As" Feature 297

    Setting Up Export Options 297

    Multiple Sizes and Formats for Different Platforms 298

    Choosing "Export As" vs. "Save for Web" 299

PRACTICAL TIPS FOR EXPORTING 300

    Exporting for Social Media 300

SAVE AS AND FILE TYPES: PSD, TIFF, JPEG, PNG, AND MORE 300

    Choosing the Right File Format 305

BATCH EXPORT AND AUTOMATION 305

    Understanding Batch Exporting: The Basics 305

    Automating Repetitive Tasks Using Actions 306

    Applying Advanced Automation with Scripts 307

    Working with Droplets of Photoshop for Quick Automation 308

CHAPTER EIGHTEEN 309

ESSENTIAL PHOTOSHOP TIPS, SHORTCUTS, AND WORKFLOW TECHNIQUES 309

ESSENTIAL KEYBOARD SHORTCUTS FOR EFFICIENCY: MASTERING COMMONLY USED COMMANDS 309

USING LIBRARIES FOR ASSET MANAGEMENT: MANAGING COLORS, TEXT STYLES, AND GRAPHICS 313

    Creating a New Library 314

    Managing Colors in Libraries 314

    Organizing Text Styles 314

    Storing Graphics and Logos 315

    Using Adobe Stock and Libraries Together 315

    Synchronizing Assets Across Devices 316

TROUBLESHOOTING COMMON ISSUES (SOLUTIONS TO FREQUENT PROBLEMS AND ERRORS) 317

CONCLUSION 323

INDEX **324**

INTRODUCTION

The Adobe Photoshop 2025 release is here to maintain the status quo as the most powerful image-editing software in the world, applauded for its versatility, power, and precision regarding photo manipulation, digital art, and even graphic design. This new release now builds on the already set concrete foundation laid by previous releases and gives way to more advanced tools and features that will satisfy both the amateur and expert. With the recent developments in the artificial intelligence sphere, Photoshop 2025 reinforces intuitiveness and speed, such as improved object selection, neural filters, and AI-driven adjustments that work together to accelerate workflows and offer full creative control to users. This new version not only lives up to Adobe's standards of quality and performance but raises the bar and extends digital artistry to new confines.

Striking improvements in Photoshop 2025 are improvements to AI-powered editing, crafted to make even the most unwieldy processes significantly easier with phenomenal accuracy. The neural filters within the application have gotten more advanced, with more powerful features: lighting, expression, and color grading at your fingertips with ease. These filters allow users to play creatively with style and mood in a non-destructive way: adjustments can be fine-tuned or removed at any stage without affecting the quality of the original image. This opens perspectives for photographers wanting quick corrections, artists wanting to see a different creative take, or designers wanting to get to a certain aesthetic-all within seconds.

Another major highlight of Adobe Photoshop 2025 is the extended ability to work with 3D objects and augmented reality elements, a feature that comes with a growing demand for immersive and interactive digital experiences. By adding more intuitive 3D modeling tools and AR-friendly design capabilities, Photoshop bridges the gap between traditional 2D graphics and this new age of spatial content. Depth, texture, and realistic light effects can be explored directly in the software, making it far easier to conceptualize and visualize designs that go beyond flat images. The development will be of particular benefit to industries that require realistic prototypes, such as gaming, virtual reality, and product design.

Lastly, the interface of Photoshop 2025 is thoughtfully redesigned with accessibility and customizations in mind. The new layout will also be easy to use with new, simplified menus and contextual toolbars that change depending on the user's workflow to make navigating and working with the application more intuitive. New users will find an improved onboarding flow with greater tutorials and skill-level-targeted in-app guidance to get them up to speed quickly with the basics or into more advanced features. With customizable workspaces and shortcut settings, professionals can easily customize the working environment according to their requirements for photo editing, digital painting, or graphic design. This updated interface will make the usage of Photoshop 2025 more efficient and friendly, combining the full power of Adobe's image processing suite into a wide range of creative areas.

CHAPTER ONE

GETTING STARTED

New Features of the New Adobe Photoshop 2025

Here is a more detailed breakdown of what's new in Adobe Photoshop 2025 and how these additions are expanding creative possibilities and accelerating workflows:

1. **Enhanced Remove Tool Options**

   Photoshop 2025 provides excellent additions that allow the user to get rid of redundant details in pictures without the slightest effort. From merely deleting an object with the tool, the program now uses smart algorithms to immediately identify complex distractions and remove them. These may include wires, street signs, or even people. They will be removed in the blink of an eye.

   - **Smart Identification**: Adobe AI identifies patterns, textures, and shadows for perfect blending of the area after removal.

   - **One-Click Precision**: With this feature, the user needs only to select the part of the image they want to remove, and then Photoshop's AI fills the background with actual content, considering lighting and texture for better results.

- **Bulk Removal Option**: This facility is quite handy for photographers and designers working with more than one image. It enables a designer to facilitate the removal of common objects across a series.

This new Remove Tool will save users' time and give them cleaner results in difficult edits for professional-grade image retouching.

2. **Generate Similar Feature**

A new feature introduced to Photoshop (Generate Similar), enables users to create repetitions of an already edited image or designs created from tools in the likes of Generative Fill and Generative Expand.

- **Efficient Variability:** Users can select a particular style or effect in one image and prompt the software to replicate it across multiple variations.

- **AI-Enhanced Creativity**: It intuitively interprets stylistic cues, making it relatively easy to explore all sorts of different design approaches without having to edit each image manually.

- **Project-Friendly Workflow**: With ease, designers can compare options, and select and make the necessary choices after multiple generations. This is helpful for projects requiring feedback or many revisions.

Generate Similar allows for swift ideation and simplifies the process of going in different creative directions by using the least manual work.

3. **Generate Background**

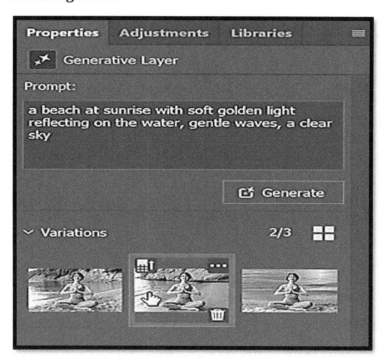

The tool allows users to change the background of an image with AI-generated content that matches the subject in terms of lighting, color scheme, and perspective.

- **Detailed Background Matching**: When creating a new background, Adobe's AI algorithm automatically adjusts lighting and depth, making sure that the subject will look naturally integrated.

- **Personalized Prompts**: A user can input prompts to further detail the background desired, including "**urban skyline at sunset**" or "**forest with soft morning light**."

- **Time-Saving Changes**: Save time doing complex masking to change the background using this one-step tool that will yield polished results suitable for professional presentations.

Generate Background is highly useful for e-commerce and marketing professionals needing fast, high-quality background changes.

4. **Adobe Firefly Image Model 3 Integration**

The integration of Adobe Firefly Image Model 3 into Photoshop 2025 presents a quantum leap in generative AI capabilities. Firefly is a proprietary Adobe AI model developed to generate photo-realistic images with richly nuanced prompt instructions.

- **Photo-realistic Rendering**: The updated model drives higher accuracy and realism where the AI can produce more sophisticated shadows, reflections, and textures.

- **Improved Prompt Processing**: Firefly 3 understands even the most involved and multi-layered prompts, thus allowing users to create images that express very specific artistic directions faithfully.

- **More Advanced Customization Options**: Users are now able to further customize AI-generated images with adjustable parameters that allow for greater precision to their creative vision, including but not limited to light direction, depth of field, and color grading.

This integration massively extends creative capabilities in Photoshop by allowing designers to create AI images that are much more detailed and realistic.

5. **Reference Image Tool in Photoshop Beta**

Still in beta, the Reference Image Tool is going to be a game-changer for designers trying to match or replicate certain styles. Users will be able to choose a reference image, and then Photoshop will take that image as a guide for colors, lighting, and the overall composition of the new work.

- **Style Consistency**: In cases where designers are working within brand guidelines or working on theme-based projects, this tool ensures that the new artwork will align visually with the reference.

- **Fashion and Branding Application**: Since this allows designers to recreate textures, lighting styles, or color schemes, this is ideal for fashion designers and marketers looking for consistency between the shots.

- **Dynamic Adjustments:** The tool automatically adjusts color, contrast, and brightness; further tuning is allowed by the user's artistic discretion.

This adds a layer of creative granularity, enabling users to create highly stylized visuals with few manual changes.

6. **Generative Workspace for Ideation**

The new feature, Generative Workspace, will provide an environment for generating images in bulk with diverse prompts and themes. It is aimed at helping artists and designers during the ideation phase of work.

- **Batch Processing of Ideas**: A user can input a theme or prompt, and Photoshop will generate various options of images that could help in brainstorming sessions.

- **Customizable Settings**: Variables such as color, style, and subject focus can be edited to provide nuances in the fine-tuning of batch generation.

- **Agile Brainstorming of Ideas**: The rapid creation of multiple images enables a designer to brainstorm an idea with others, take feedback, and reiterate their concept much quicker. Needless to say, this very feature is what makes this tool right for your urgent projects.

This workspace will allow designers to flesh out ideas and then easily edit the details where needed.

7. **Substance 3D Viewer**

Adobe re-introduces 3D capabilities in Photoshop through the Substance 3D Viewer, mending a huge gap between the 2D and 3D design spaces. The viewer allows users to import 3D models, manipulate their properties, and place those models into their 2D compositions.

- **Improved 3D Integration**: Users are allowed to add 3D objects directly into Photoshop by positioning them with realistic lighting and shadow effects.
- **Dynamic Adjustments**: Seamlessly rotate, scale, and position 3D objects to take their natural positions in the 2D scene.
- **Real-Time Adjustments**: Change properties like texture, color, and opacity in real time; instantly update how the model looks to ensure a seamless creative process.

The Substance 3D Viewer opens Photoshop further to be a very helpful tool in the working process for a product designer, 3D artist, or anybody who incorporates the work of 2D and 3D elements.

Minimum and Recommended Specifications

The minimum and recommended requirements to run Adobe Photoshop 2025 on your system are as follows:

For Windows:

Processor:

- **Minimum**: Multicore Intel processor with 64-bit support required; 2 GHz or faster processor with SSE 4.2 or later.
- **Recommended**: Intel 11th Generation or newer CPU with Quick Sync, or AMD Ryzen 3000 Series / Threadripper 3000 series or newer CPU.

Operating System:

- **Minimum**: Windows 10 64-bit (version 21H2) or later; LTSC versions aren't supported.
- **Recommended**: Windows 11 64-bit version (version 22H2) or later.

RAM:

- **Minimum**: 8 GB.
- **Recommended**: 16 GB or more.

Graphics Card:

- **Minimum**: GPU that supports DirectX 12, feature level 12_0 or later, 1.5 GB of GPU memory.
- **Recommended**: 4 GB of GPU memory for 4K displays and larger.

Monitor Resolution:

- **Minimum**: 1280 x 800 display at 100% UI scaling.
- **Recommended**: 1920 x 1080 display or greater at 100% UI scaling.

Hard Disk Space:

- **Minimum**: 20 GB of available hard-disk space.
- **Recommended**: 100 GB of available hard-disk space; fast internal SSD for app installation and a separate internal drive for scratch disks.

Internet:

- Internet connection and registration are necessary for required software activation, validation of subscriptions, and access to online services.

For macOS:

Processor:

- **Minimum**: Multicore Intel or Apple Silicon processor with 64-bit support.
- **Recommended**: ARM-based Apple Silicon processor.

Operating System:

- **Minimum**: macOS Big Sur (version 11.0) or later.
- **Recommended**: macOS Ventura, version 13.5.1 or later.

RAM:

- **Minimum**: 8 GB.
- **Recommended**: 16 GB or more.

Graphics Card:

- **Minimum**: GPU with Metal support and 1.5 GB of GPU memory.
- **Recommended**: GPU with Metal support and 4 GB of GPU memory for 4K displays and greater.

Monitor Resolution:

- **Minimum**: 1280 x 800 display at 100% UI scaling.
- **Recommended**: 1920 x 1080 display or greater at 100% UI scaling.

Hard Disk Space:

- **Minimum**: 20 GB of available hard-disk space.
- **Recommended**: 100 GB of available hard-disk space; fast internal SSD for app installation and additional high-speed drive(s) or SSD to set up scratch disks.

Internet:

- Internet connection and registration are necessary for required software activation, membership validation, and access to online services.

For optimal performance, ensure your operating system and GPU drivers are updated. Besides that, Adobe suggests keeping the GPU below 7 years old, updating it from the website of its manufacturer, and updating the display drivers.

How to Download and Install the New Adobe Photoshop 2025

These steps should be carefully followed to download and install Adobe Photoshop 2025. Fortunately, Adobe has made it pretty easy through its Creative Cloud application; it will be a secure and easy installation.

Here are the steps:

1. **Create or Sign In to an Adobe Account**

   - **Step 1:** If you do not already have an Adobe account, you will need to create one for yourself. First, go to adobe.com and click **Sign In** at the top right corner.

   - **Step 2:** Choose "**Create an account**" if you do not have one. Just fill in the necessary information, like your e-mail address and your password. You can also use any account on Google, Apple, or Facebook for ease of registration.

   - **Step 3**: When you log in, make sure your profile information is updated. Adobe may request further verification for downloads, especially if it is for professional purposes.

2. **Download the Adobe Creative Cloud Desktop App**

   Adobe Photoshop, like all Adobe apps, is accessible through the Adobe Creative Cloud Desktop application.

   - **Step 1:** Hover over Creative Cloud on the main navigation menu and then select **Creative Cloud Apps** on the Adobe homepage.

   - **Step 2**: On the page, scroll down; **Creative Cloud Desktop** will appear. Click **Download**.

   - **Step 3:** Follow the on-screen installation and start downloading the application to your computer.

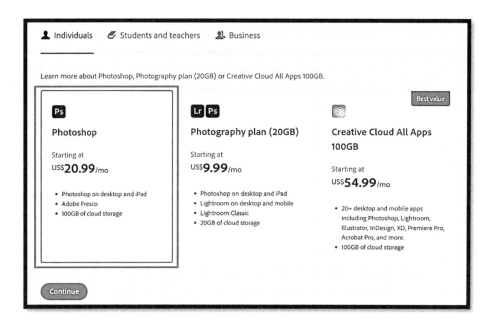

3. **Open and Sign In with Adobe Creative Cloud Desktop**

- **Step 1:** Open the application after downloading it. It will open a window and ask you to sign in with your Adobe account credentials.

- **Step 2:** It will prompt you to log-in; log in using the same account credentials created for Adobe.

- **Step 3:** After logging in, it will open an application dashboard from which you can download various Adobe applications.

4. **Find Adobe Photoshop 2025 in the Creative Cloud**

- **Step 1:** Launch the **Creative Cloud application** and click on the **Apps tab** on the left-hand side.

- **Step 2:** In the All Apps section, scroll down until you see **Adobe Photoshop 2025**. It is usually important to notice that Adobe sometimes names its latest versions with the year. Make sure it displays "**2025**" next to Photoshop.

13

- **Step 3:** If you are unable to view the Photoshop application directly, then select the option for **All Apps**, or you could use the search bar at the top of the Creative Cloud interface.

5. **Download and Install Adobe Photoshop 2025**

   - **Step 1:** Next to Adobe Photoshop 2025, click the **Install option**. The downloading of the application will begin; this may take some time, as it depends upon your internet speed.

   - **Step 2:** Once downloaded, the Creative Cloud application will open itself and start installing the software automatically.

   - **Step 3:** While installation is ongoing, it will ask you to make changes on your device multiple times; make sure you keep clicking **Yes** or **Allow** at the request.

   - **Step 4:** After installation, Creative Cloud will give an Open button beside Adobe Photoshop 2025 and it will be ready to open.

6. **Opening Adobe Photoshop 2025 for the First Time**

   - **Step 1**: Click on Open in the Creative Cloud Desktop app or go to the icon of Adobe Photoshop 2025 on the desktop or application folder.

   - **Step 2**: Launch the application. At once, you will be taken to the **Welcome screen** that you can click through for new features and updates.

   - **Step 3:** Adobe will give you a short tutorial or even tips on how you can use new features. If interested, follow along to understand some of the new features in Photoshop 2025.

7. **Check Your License**

   - **Step 1:** Ideally, Adobe Photoshop 2025 will automatically verify your license if you are signed into an active Creative Cloud subscription.

- **Step 2:** You might need to give your Adobe account credentials because sometimes verification has to be done.
- **Step 3:** If it doesn't go through, then recheck the subscription status from the Account within the Creative Cloud app or through adobe.com.

8. **Update and Manage the Adobe Photoshop 2025**

   Adobe frequently releases updates for Photoshop through Creative Cloud.

   - **Step 1:** Launch the **Creative Cloud Desktop app** and click the **Apps section** to check for updates.
   - **Step 2:** Besides Adobe Photoshop 2025, find **Updates**. If available, click **Update**, then follow through the on-screen instructions to make sure you have the very latest version of the software.

Additional Tips:

- **Subscription Requirements**: Adobe Photoshop 2025 is part of Adobe's subscription model, meaning you will have to have an active subscription. Options go from the Photography Plan, including Photoshop and Lightroom, up to the All Apps plan that opens the door to the full Adobe suite of applications.
- **Free Trial:** Adobe designates new users a free trial for 7 days. You can, therefore, enable this trial via the Creative Cloud Desktop app if you wish to test the program before committing to its subscription.
- **System Requirements:** Adobe Photoshop 2025 has higher system requirements than those of the earlier versions.

How to Get Acquainted with Adobe Photoshop Workspace

The workspace in Photoshop has been organized to easily access various tools and functions for editing photos, designing, and creating digital art. Being customizable, it has flexible features to suit the needs of its users from beginners to pros. The workspace consists of a Menu Bar, Toolbar, Options Bar, Panels, and the area for the Canvas. All of these areas will give you great confidence as you navigate your way around Photoshop.

Major Components of the Photoshop Workspace

They include the following:

1. **Menu Bar**

    At the very top of the screen, the Menu Bar contains different dropdown menus: File, Edit, Image, Layer, Type, Select, Filter, 3D, View, Window, and Help. Each of these menus has options concerning the actions to be taken with images:

    *   **File**: Open, save, and export of projects.

    *   **Edit**: Basic edits, cut, copy, paste, and adjustments of images.

    *   **Image**: Holds options for adjustments, size changes, and image rotation.

    *   **Layer**: To create, duplicate, and merge layers.

- **Type**: Provides options to edit text and manipulate fonts.

- **Select**: To select functions, modify, refine edges, and color range.

- **Filter**: Opens Photoshop's filters for special effects.

- **Window**: Used to open and close panels.

- **Help**: Allows the opening of assistance resources, tutorials, and new feature updates.

2. **Toolbar**

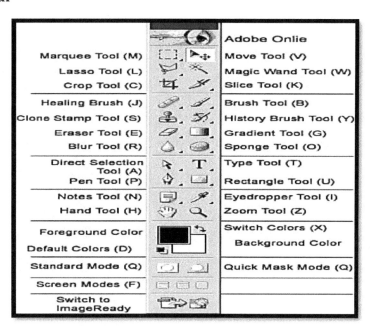

The main toolbar on the left side includes all the main Photoshop tools: selection, crop, painting and retouching, and type tools. Here are some important icons in this toolbar:

- **Move Tool**: Used to move any selection and layer.

- **Selection Tools**: It covers Marquee, Lasso, Magic Wand, and Quick Selection tools.

- **Crop Tool:** Resizes or crops the image.

- **Brush Tool, Clone Stamp Tool, and Eraser Tool**: These three are the major painting and retouching tools.

- **Type Tool:** This tool is used in adding and editing text.

- **Shapes Tools:** To draw shapes, like rectangles, ellipses, and custom shapes.

- **Gradient and Paint Bucket Tools**: Fill areas with gradients or solid colors.

Pro Tip: Run your cursor over each tool for a tool name and quick shortcut key.

3. **Options Bar**

   Just below the Menu Bar, the Options Bar - which changes depending on which tool you have selected - allows you to set options for that tool. For example, when you choose the Brush tool, the Option Bar opens options to set brush size, opacity, flow, and smoothing.

4. **Panels**

   Panels are located on the right of the screen and contain tools for further editing your work:

   - **Layers Panel:** The most critical panel in Photoshop, which comprises work with a layer, blending modes of the layers, opacity, effects, etc.

   - **Properties Panel**: Available options concerning the currently selected tool or current layer.

   - **Adjustments Panel:** Offers various options for non-destructive color and tone adjustments such as Brightness/Contrast, Levels, and Curves.

   - **Color and Swatches Panels**: Choose colors or create a color palette.

   - **History Panel**: Keeps record of recent activity and gives you the option to go back to certain steps that were taken previously.

5. **Canvas and Document Window**

   The image will appear in the area of the canvas. This is where you apply all the edits to your image. This Document Window, surrounds the canvas, documents zoom level, the visibility of layers, and the name of the file. You can adjust the zooming and arranging of the canvas layout here.

Navigating New Features in Adobe Photoshop 2025

The improvements in Adobe Photoshop 2025 are much advanced regarding AI-powered tools and enhancements of selection processes and content-aware editing. They include the following:

1. **AI-Powered Selection Tools**: New AI enhancements make tedious selections easier. For instance, the Select Object tool, which can be found in the Toolbar, now does a better job of identifying the subject of an image, even for those subjects with complicated edges. You can further adjust selections using the options to Select and Mask in the Options Bar.

2. **Content-Aware Fill and Remove Tool**: The "**Remove**" feature in the Content-Aware Fill tool works more with Adobe since one can remove unwanted elements with a single click. Also, after selection, a click on **Edit > Content-Aware Fill** opens up a window whereby selecting the Remove Tool gives great detail about removal.

3. **Neural Filters:** The various AI-powered adjustments in Photoshop 2025 come through the Neural Filters. Some of the other options present within **Filter > Neural Filters** include Smart Portrait, Depth Blur, and Super Zoom. Play with some filters to change things like expressions, lighting, and resolution of an image using realistic effects.

Customizing the Workspace

It can also be very effective to adapt your workspace to the way you work. This will save lots of time. Here's how you can customize the workspace:

1. **Save Workspace Layouts**

   Set up your views, panels, and toolbars as you like, then save the layout by following these steps: Go to **Window > Workspace > New Workspace**. You will be able to easily move across workspace setups designed for photo editing, graphic design, or 3D work.

2. **Docking and Undocking Panels**

   Panels can be either docked (attached) or undocked (floating freely):

   - To dock a panel, simply drag the tab of that panel to dock it beside other panels to undock.

   - Right-click the tab of the panel and select **Close Panel** or **Close Tab Group** if it doesn't need to stay open.

3. **Working with Pre-set Workspaces**

   By default, Photoshop 2025 has different workspaces, depending on your task at hand, including Essentials, Photography, Graphic and Web, Motion, and 3D- if your computer supports it. You can access these under **Window > Workspace** to switch in an instant.

4. **Custom Keyboard Shortcuts**

   You can also create keyboard shortcuts for tools and functions you find yourself using over and over. Go under the **Edit menu**, choose **Keyboard Shortcuts**, then select the function or tool and then create a shortcut. This will greatly help you pick up your speed.

How to Find and Remove Distractions with the Remove Tool

Follow the steps below to find and remove distractions using the remove tool:

Step 1: Open Your Image in Adobe Photoshop

1. Open up Adobe Photoshop 2025.
2. In the menu bar, select **File > Open** or press **Ctrl + O** for Windows and **Cmd + O** for Mac.
3. Take a look at the list of files presented, and click to select your image, then click **Open**.

Step 2: Enable the Remove Tool

1. On the left-hand side of your screen, locate the **Remove Tool** in the Toolbar.
   - Also, right-click on the **Spot Healing Brush Tool** to open up the submenu and reveal the **Remove Tool.**
   - With it selected, at the top, you will see the options available for the tool.

Step 3: Adjusting the Remove Tool Settings

1. Change the Size and Hardness of the Brush depending on where on the image you want to remove a thing. Example:
   - **Brush Size**: Take a little larger than the object you want to remove for a smoother result.
   - **Hardness**: A softer edge works best for blending with the surrounding background because it's harder.
2. Make sure **Sample All Layers** is checked if you're working on a multi-layer document. This option will have the tool analyze all visible layers to make the edit more seamless.

Step 4: Identify Distractions in the Image

1. Carefully scan your image for anything that may distract from the main image. Examples include:

- Unwanted objects, such as litter, unwanted people, and stray objects.
- Blemishes or imperfections like spots or scratches or small elements that catch the eye away from the main focus.

2. In so doing, you must zoom right into the distraction to ensure accuracy. Zoom in by pressing **Ctrl + Plus** (Windows) or **Cmd + Plus** (Mac) and zoom out with **Ctrl + Minus** or **Cmd + Minus.**

Step 5: Utilize the Remove Tool to Erase Distractions

1. With the Remove Tool activated, click and drag over the area one wants to remove. You can cover:

- Whole objects or just parts of them.
- Go slow, ensuring you're covering the unwanted area only.

2. Let go of the mouse when you've covered the distraction. The AI in Photoshop looks at surrounding pixels for a perfect fill of what was taken out-replacing that area with something natural-looking.

Step 6: Refine the Edit

1. After editing with this tool, check the result. Sometimes, it requires a bit of fixing to make the edit realistic.

2. If the removed area doesn't blend in perfectly, you're going to fine-tune it with the **Clone Stamp Tool** or **Healing Brush Tool**.

3. If you are not satisfied, use the **Undo option** (Ctrl + Z) and redo it with less size of brush or changes in settings.

Step 7: Check the Whole Picture

1. Smoothen your edits and check the whole image for longer-notice distractions by zooming out.

2. If you need further editing, repeat the process described above.

Step 8: Save Your Edited Image

1. Save your final image once you're satisfied with it.

   • Navigate to **File > Save As.** or **Ctrl + Shift + S** for Windows, **Cmd + Shift + S** for Mac.

2. Now, select a format that suits your needs, such as JPEG if you want to share it, and PSD if you are going to be editing it further; click **Save**.

Generative Expand with the Firefly Image 3 Model

The Adobe Photoshop 2025 Generative Expand tool uses the most advanced Firefly Image 3 Model, allowing you to fill empty parts of your images or extend an image background more intelligently. With this tool, changes in composition, dimension, and creative elements in photos will be really easy. Here's how you effectively use it:

Step 1: Open the Image and Set Up the Canvas

1. Open Adobe Photoshop 2025 and open the image that you want to enlarge. To do this, click on **File > Open**, then select your image file.

2. To make room for the extended area, select **Image > Canvas Size**. Increase the width or height of the canvas to your liking, but make sure the new open space is at the point at which the extension is to take place. For instance, if you want a top extension for a sky, add the space there.

3. Fill the background color with a color matching any of the edges of the image or leave it transparent to your choice.

Step 2: Enable the Generative Expand Tool

1. With the canvas prepared, highlight where you would like new content to populate. You can then use the Marquee Tool (M) or Lasso Tool (L) to define the vacant area that you have just created in the previous step.

2. Once you have your selection, a **'Generative Fill'** bar should appear at the bottom of your selection. If it does not, you can access Generative Expand manually by going to **Edit > Generative Fill**.

3. In the **'Generative Fill'** input box, you can either leave this empty and let Photoshop generate an image that perfectly fits in with the current content or else specify a prompt such as "**continue the sky with clouds**" or "**add trees and landscape**" to give guidance to the AI model.

Step 3: Customize the Generative Options with Firefly Image 3 Model

1. Enable Firefly Image 3 Model in Adobe Photoshop 2025 for enhanced realism and details. Verify that the model of Firefly Image 3 is turned on in the Generative Fill settings; Photoshop automatically picks the latest model by default.

2. You are also allowed to set some style preferences to match textures, lighting, and depth with the original image. It can be really helpful in smoothly blending problematic areas, like skies, water, or detailed landscapes.

Step 4: Generate the Expanded Content

1. Click **'Generate'** to let the Firefly model analyze and create extended content in Photoshop upon your selected area and prompt.

2. After that, Photoshop takes a few seconds to process the image and then offers, up to three variations for the Generative Fill, which will appear as options in the Properties panel.

3. Click through to preview each variation to see which best matches your image. Every variation can be different in color balance, texture, and other details.

Step 5: Refine the Results

1. Refine it further, if necessary, after getting the best variation. For example,

   - Do slight edge refinements to feather edges with the Clone Stamp Tool.
   - Layer masks can be added optionally if one wants more control over certain areas' blending.

2. If the generative fill is not perfectly aligned, reselect the area and run a Generative Expand with a more specific prompt or adjust the prompt for slightly different results.

Step 6: Finalize and Save Your Work

1. Observe the extended area if it meets your creative vision. Run color, contrast, and other adjustments as needed, so this generative content naturally fits together.

2. Flatten the image in case all edits are complete, especially if the file will live on the web or print since it reduces file size.

3. Save your file in the format you want to save it in, under the **File Menu** by selecting **Save As**. Make sure that you have saved a copy of the layered PSD file, which you can continue editing.

CHAPTER TWO

WORKING WITH THE BASICS

How to Reset your Workspace

Photoshop 2025 has made it easy to reset your workspace by providing easy choices to get you back to the default settings if your tools, panels, or even layout is relatively messy and out of place. Here's how you can reset your workspace effectively:

Step 1: Launch Adobe Photoshop 2025

Before you make changes to your workspace, launch Adobe Photoshop 2025 and navigate to the main workspace area; this is usually where you can see your panels, toolbars, and editing area.

Step 2: Open Window Menu

1. **Navigate to the Top Menu Bar**: This contains the options for File, Edit, Image, and Window.

2. **Click on Window**: The Window option opens a drop-down menu containing other settings related to the workspace when hovered on.

Step 3: Open the Workspace and Choose a Preset

1. **Find the Workspace Options**: The Workspace option should come mid-list in the Window menu, opening a submenu containing custom and reset options for the workspace.

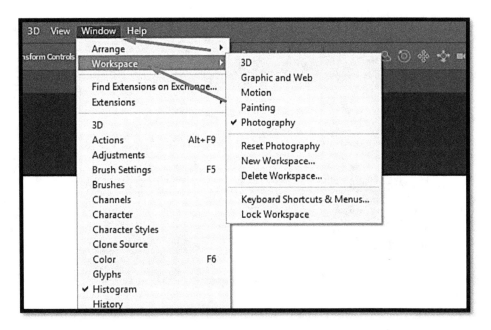

2. **Select a Workspace Preset (Optional):** None, Photography, Graphic and Web, Painting. Click one if you want to initialize the workspace with a specific preset.

    Tip: Presets are meant for tasks; thus, selecting a preset might have your workspace more in tune with your current project needs.

Step 4: Choose Reset Workspace

1. Select the "**Reset Workspace**" by going to the Workspace dropdown menu and then select "**Reset [Your Current Workspace]**" from there. You can think of it in terms of your chosen workspace: if you work under the Essentials, you'll be reset to "**Reset Essentials.**"

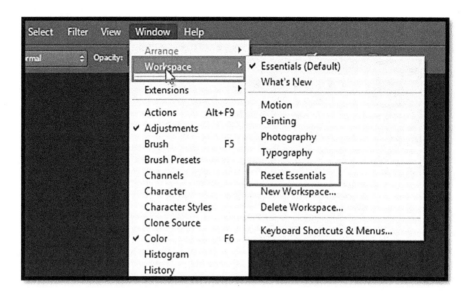

2. Confirm that all the panels, tools, and settings will return to the default positions that were the last time they were placed on a given workspace layout within the Photoshop application.

Step 5: Restore Default Tool Settings (If Needed)

1. **Click a Tool Icon**: While holding the right mouse button (or pressing control-click for the Mac), click on a tool icon in the top Options bar. This will individually reset a tool to its defaults.

2. **Select Reset Tool or Reset All Tools**: Choose either reset just the currently selected tool or reset all tools for a whole overhaul of your toolset settings.

Step 6: Save a Custom Workspace

1. **Navigate to Window > Workspace > New Workspace**: Save it for later use if you've gone and created a certain layout or you have customized tool settings.

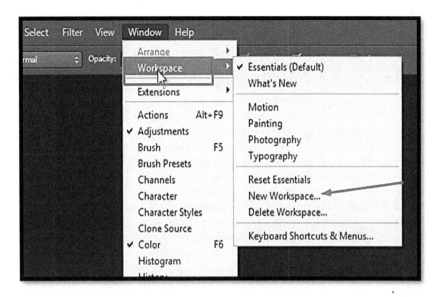

2. **Name and Save your Workspace**: In the dialogue box, name your workspace, i.e., "**My Editing Setup**" and choose what you want to save. This ensures that whenever you need it, you can easily revert to your customized setup.

Step 7: Confirm the Reset

1. **Check Panels and Toolbars**: All panels should be in their default position, and the toolbar will appear with the default arrangement.

2. **Adjust, If Necessary**: If you feel that something still does not look like it should, then you can easily drag or close any panel(s), and repeat the process, if necessary.

Tips for Maintaining an Organized Workspace

- **Use Preset Workspaces**: Adobe has different preset workspaces, each oriented toward another form of an editing workflow. These transitions between photography and graphic design can be done easily by just accessing different workspaces.

- **Save Regularly Used Layouts**: If you frequently work in a particular layout, then saving it as a custom workspace may be helpful because, next time, you will not need to make manual adjustments.

- **Customize Panels for Productivity**: Grab the panels you use regularly and place them in more accessible locations. Close down panels you do not intend to use so that it does not mess up your workplace.

How to Understand the Menu Bar

Adobe Photoshop 2025 brings at your fingertips an extremely user-friendly menu bar that contains everything you need to push your creative process forward faster.

Here is how you can understand the menu bar:

Step 1: Open Adobe Photoshop 2025

1. Open your computer and click the **Photoshop** icon to open Photoshop 2025.

2. Wait for it to load the workspace. You will have a menu bar at the top of the screen. The menu bar is divided by categories; moving from the left side, these start from File to Help on the right.

Step 2: File Menu

The File menu provides you with important commands for opening, saving, exporting, and printing your workpiece.

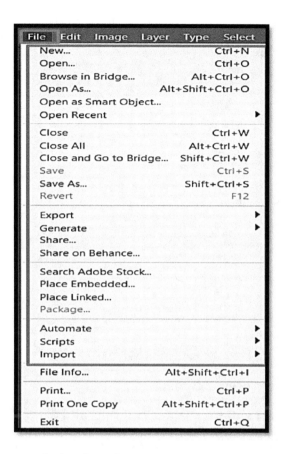

- **New**: This opens a dialog box for you to create a new file. You can adjust the size, resolution, and color mode.

- **Open**: You will see an existing file.

- **Save**: This allows you to save your document.

- **Save As:** You can save under a new name or file format.

- **Export**: This enables exporting your work in different file formats, including JPEG, PNG, and GIF, among others, and using Export As to select quality and file type.

Step 3: Edit Menu

The Edit menu contains functions related to content editing, preferences, and shortcut setup.

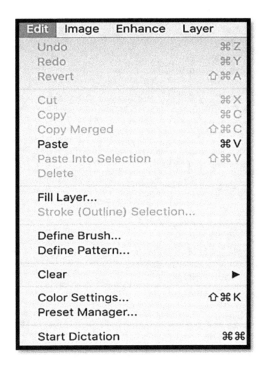

- **Undo**: It reverses recent actions.
- **Transform**: This contains scaling, rotating, and distorting selections.
- **Preferences**: This enables you to change settings such as performance and workspace preferences.
- **Keyboard Shortcuts**: This helps you edit keyboard shortcuts, which is essential whenever you want your work to be a bit more personal and smoother.

Step 4: Image Menu

The Image menu refers to modifications and changes either on the entire image or on selected layers.

- **Adjustments**: It offers settings on brightness, contrast, color balance, and much more. For example, Curves enable you to exercise extreme control over shadows and highlights.

- **Image Size:** This makes an image resize the entire image based on the aspect ratio or modify it.

Canvas Size: Changes the workspace area without changing the size of the content.

- **Mode:** You can select color modes (RGB, CMYK) according to needs regarding various outputs.

Step 5: Layer Menu

The Layer menu is core to Photoshop's non-destructive editing methodology, where you can create and work on layers.

- **New Layer**: Creates a new blank layer above the current one.
- **Layer Styles**: You can add effects like shadow, glow, or gradient to enhance the look of your layer.
- **Adjustment Layers**: Non-destructive layers for color or tonal adjustments.
- **Merge Layers:** Merges selected layers into one.

Step 6: Type Menu

The Type menu is dedicated to text handling. The operations include typography, character settings, and paragraph controls.

- **Font Style and Size**: Select the font, size, alignment, and color of text.
- **Warp Text:** Provides options to distort text into various shapes in arched or wavy ways.
- **Convert to Shape:** Converts text into a vector shape so that you can edit its paths.

Step 7: Select Menu

The Select menu gives you various types of selections you would make. Selections are important whenever you want to focus on particular areas to edit.

- **All (Ctrl+A):** Allows you to select the whole canvas.
- **Deselect**: This clears any active selection.

- **Inverse**: Inverts the selection.
- **Refine Edge:** Also lets you feather the edges of the selection for smooth blending.

Step 8: Filter Menu

The Filter menu allows adding creative effects and processing enhancements to the work. This is where the magic is done.

- **Blur**: Applies different types of blurring, which reduces sharpness and softens out areas.
- **Sharpen**: It enhances the details of an image by making them sharper.
- **Liquify**: This feature reshapes selected parts of an image by pushing and pulling pixels.
- **Gallery**: Includes a set of artistic features, such as Oil Paint and Lens Flare for creative works.

Step 9: 3D Menu (Available only if the 3D features are enabled)

The 3D menu presents options in the features of 3D design, such as shape construction, alteration of depth, and rendering effects.

- **New 3D Layer from File**: This option changes any selected object or layer into a 3D object.
- **Mesh and Material Options**: It manages the structure of the elements in 3D and the surface details of 3D elements.
- **Rendering**: This refines the final look of your 3D object by adjusting lighting and texture quality.

Step 10: View Menu

The View menu controls perspective, zoom levels, and guides.

- **Zoom In/Out**: This controls your view scale.
- **Fit on Screen:** Fits the entire canvas in the workspace.

- **Guides and Rulers:** Turn guides off and on to position pieces with precision.
- **Show/Hide**: Allows showing or hiding extras such as grids, guides, layer edges, etc.

Step 11: Window Menu

The Window menu can be used to change workspace layout and hide or show panels.

- **Workspace**: Save or reset the custom layout of your workspace.
- **Arrange**: Controls window positioning when working with multiple files.
- **Panels**: Toggles the visibility of panels, including Layers, Adjustments, Properties, and many more.

Step 12: Help Menu

The Help menu provides access to Adobe's support resources, tutorials, and updates.

- **Photoshop Help:** Opens the official help documentation from Adobe.
- **Updates**: This ensures that you have the latest features and bug fixes.
- **System Info**: This shows technical information about your Photoshop installation, useful when trying to solve problems.

How to Know the Toolbar

Adobe Photoshop 2025 comprises a toolbar that includes all primary tools to execute most image manipulation, design, and illustration tasks.

Step 1: Locate and Customize the Toolbar

1. **Open Photoshop 2025:**
   - Open **Adobe Photoshop** and find the toolbar, which is often located on the left-hand side of your screen.
   - If you can't find it, go to **Window > Tools** to display the toolbar.
2. **Customize the Toolbar:**

- Right-click on the toolbar or go to **Edit > Toolbar** to display options to customize.

- You can reorder, add, or remove tools to make your workflow better.

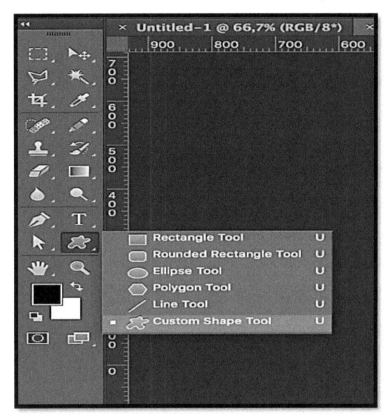

Step 2: Learn Some of Your Most Often Used Tools on the Toolbar

The toolbar is segmented into the type of tool, including **Selection**, **Painting**, **Editing**, and **Navigation tools**. A brief overview of each, by function, is below.

Selection Tools

1. **Move Tool (Shortcut: V)**

- **Purpose**: To move selected pixels, layers, or guides.
- **Usage**: Click and drag to move elements around your canvas.

2. **Marquee Tools (Rectangular, Elliptical) (Shortcut: M)**

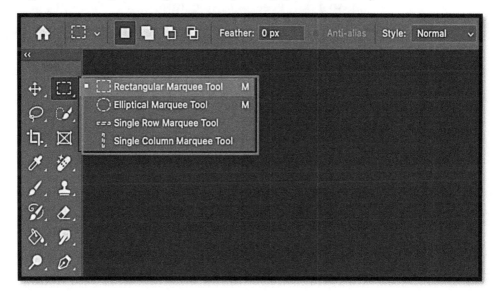

- **Purpose**: To create rectangular or elliptical selections.
- **Usage**: Click and drag over the area you want to select. Hold Shift for perfect squares or circles.

3. **Lasso Tools (Lasso, Polygonal Lasso, and Magnetic Lasso) (Shortcut: L)**

- **Purpose**: Select areas with more precision.
- **Usage**:
  - **Lasso Tool:** Freehand selection.
  - **Polygonal Lasso Tool**: Click around the edges of the area you want to select.
  - **Magnetic Lasso Tool:** Click once and move around the object's edge to have the tool automatically cling to borders.

4. **Quick Selection and Magic Wand Tool Below (Shortcut: W)**
   - **Purpose**: To select areas quickly by color and edge variations.
   - **Usage**: Click inside an area to select like colors. To obtain a finer selection, increase the tool's Tolerance in the options bar.

Crop and Slice Tools

1. **Crop Tool (Shortcut: C)**

- **Purpose**: This is a crop tool that crops the canvas of an image to remove unwanted outer areas of an image.

- **Usage**: Drag a rectangle around the portion of the image you want to keep and then press Enter to crop.

2. **Slice Tool (Shortcut: K)**

- **Purpose**: Splits the canvas into several sections, normally for website design.

- **Usage**: Click and drag across your image, and the slices created can be saved individually.

Retouching and Painting Tools

1. **Brush Tool (Shortcut: B)**

- **Purpose**: Paints with brush strokes, and options to adjust in size, shape, and opacity.

- **Usage**: From the options bar, select one type or size of brush and click and drag on the canvas to paint.

2. **Clone Stamp Tool (Shortcut: S)**

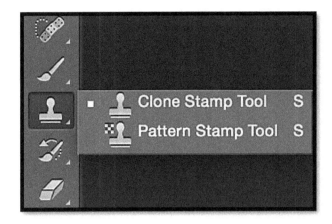

- **Purpose**: Copies pixels from one area to another.
- **Usage**: Hold down **Alt** (Windows) or **Option** (Mac) while clicking to anchor a source point. Brush over an area to be cloned.

3. **Eraser Tool (Shortcut: E)**

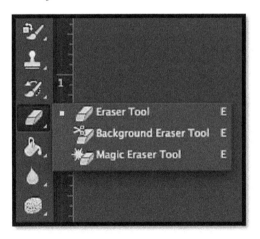

- **Purpose**: Erases pixels in the layer that has been selected.
- **Usage**: Change Size and Hardness and click or drag an area to eliminate.

4. **Healing Brush Tools (Spot Healing, Healing Brush, Patch Tool, Content-Aware Move) (Shortcut: J)**

- **Purpose**: Feathers flaws into surrounding pixels to retouch them.

- **Usage**:

    o **Spot Healing**: Click blemishes to auto-remove.

    o **Healing Brush:** Select **Alt/Option** to set the source point, then brush over flaws.

    o **Patch Tool:** Drag around the area to repair, then drag selection to the area to sample.

    o **Content-Aware Move**: Select the object, then drag the object to a new location on the canvas.

Text and Shape Tools

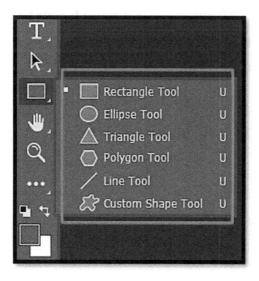

1. **Type Tool (Horizontal & Vertical) (Shortcut: T)**
   - **Purpose**: Layers text onto an image.
   - **Usage**: Click on the image where you want to place your text and start typing. Options such as font, size, and color are changed in the options bar.
2. **Shape Tools: (Rectangle, Ellipse, Polygon, Line, Custom) (Keyboard shortcut: U)**
   - **Purpose:** Creates various vector shapes.
   - **Usage**: After selecting the shape icon, click and drag your cursor across the canvas to create your desired shape. Hold **Shift** to constrain proportions (for example, perfect circle or square).

Adjustment Tools

1. **Dodge, Burn, and Sponge Tools (Keyboard shortcut: O)**
   - **Purpose**: Exposure and Color Saturation Adjustment.
   - **Usage**:
     - **Dodge Tool**: Lightens areas.
     - **Burn Tool**: Darkens areas.
     - **Sponge Tool**: Saturates/desaturates
   - Readjust by clicking and dragging over the desired area.

Navigation Tools

1. **Hand Tool (Shortcut: H)**
   - **Purpose**: Navigate the view without affecting document content.
   - **Usage**: Click and drag to move around the canvas. Works great if zoomed in.
2. **Zoom Tool (Shortcut: Z)**
   - **Purpose**: To view larger or smaller.

- **Usage**: Click for zoom in, hold **Alt/Option** for zoom out, and drag to magnify an area.

How to Create your First File

Follow the steps below to create your first file:

Step 1: Open Adobe Photoshop 2025

1. **Open Photoshop**: Locate and open Adobe Photoshop 2025 from either a desktop shortcut, the applications folder, or the Adobe Creative Cloud application.

2. **Sign in (If Required):** If you do not have experience with Photoshop, you will be prompted to log in using a registered account or to start a free trial if you do not have a subscription.

3. **Check for Update**: Check "**Updates**" in the Creative Cloud app; Adobe does frequent updates.

Step 2: Set Up Your Workspace

Photoshop 2025 allows users to customize their workspace. You can customize your workspace now or later.

1. **Choose Workspace Layout**: Select between the default workspace layouts of Essentials, Photography, or Graphic & Web by going to the **Window > Workspace menu.**

2. **Customize Panels:** On each side of the screen, arrange panels based on your preference (e.g., Layers, Colors, Properties) by dragging. Save a custom workspace by clicking on **Window > Workspace > New Workspace**.

3. **Set Preferences:** Open **Edit > Preference** (for Windows users) or **Photoshop > Preference** (for Mac users) to set the settings of Performances, interfaces, and so on, file handling option.

Step 3: Creating a New File

1. **Open the New Document Window**: Click on the **File menu > New** or simply hit **Ctrl+N** for Windows or **Cmd+N** for Mac to open the window titled "**New Document**".

2. **Choose Preset**: Adobe Photoshop carries a few presets on general mediums like Photo, Print, Art & Illustration, Web, Mobile, and Film & Video. These have the most suitable settings for a medium chosen.

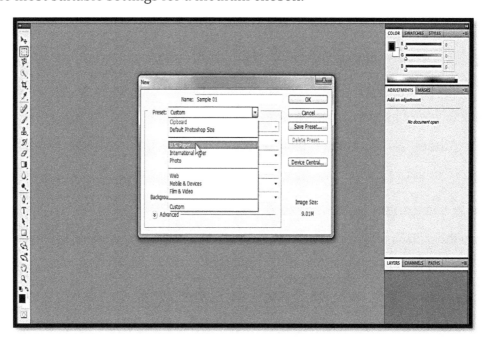

- **Photo**: To be used for digital photographs, presets with sizes similar to 4x6 inches, 8x10 inches, etc.

- **Web**: Presets on web measurements, such as 1080x1080 pixels for social media.

- **Print**: Presets for general size print, like A4 and Letter, at resolution 300 dpi.

- **Mobile**: Screen sizes for devices such as iPhones and Androids.

3. **Custom Dimensions**: If you need a specific size, enter custom dimensions in the Width and Height fields. Choose units (pixels, inches, cm, etc.) according to your project's requirements.

Step 4: Name Your File

1. **File Name**: It is a good idea to name your file for organizational purposes. The field near the top of the New Document window is for naming your file.
2. **Save Location**: Choose where to save the file if you want to save it right away.

Step 5: Creating the Document

1. **Click "Create":** Once the settings are selected, click the **Create** button. A blank open canvas will appear in Photoshop with your preset settings.
2. **Adjust the canvas settings if necessary**: You could go back to **Image > Canvas Size** to make adjustments on the size of the canvas, or **Image > Image Size** to adjust the resolution.

How to Open Files with the Open Command

Step 1: Open Adobe Photoshop 2025

- **Open the App**: The first and foremost thing used in this tutorial is Adobe Photoshop 2025. If using Windows or a macOS device, open it from either your desktop or taskbar or from the Applications menu.
- **Welcome Screen**: By default, when you open Photoshop, you get a welcome screen every time it pops up to give you quick access to recent files, and new projects, among other things.

Step 2: Activating the Open Command

- **Locate the File Menu**: You will find the menu bar at the top left of your Photoshop interface. Click File to drop down a list of options.

- **Select Open**: Next, locate and click the **Open command** from the dropdown menu, or simply use the shortcut **Ctrl + O** for Windows, or **Cmd + O** if you are working in macOS.

Step 3: Choosing Your File

- **File Explorer (Windows) or Finder (macOS)**: The Open command opens a file explorer window on your computer. This window allows you to browse for your intended file to open in Photoshop.

- **Go to the File Location**: Use the directory navigation to find the exact folder containing the file. You can search for a file name or simply scroll through the folders until you come across the image or document you're looking for.

- **Supported File Types:** Adobe supports a variety of file types, including JPEG (.jpg), PNG (.png), TIFF (.tif), and Photoshop files (.psd), among others. Ensure that the file type is compatible.

Step 4: Select and Open the File

- **Click to Select the File**: Once you see your file, click it to highlight it. Alternatively, if you want to select more than one file, hold **Ctrl** for Windows or **Cmd** for macOS and click on each file you want to open.

- **Click Open:** Once you have selected your file(s), click the **Open button** at the bottom left of your file explorer window. Photoshop will now load the file, opening it in a new document tab within the workspace.

Step 5: Check the File in the Workspace

- **Display the Open Document:** The selected document will open as an active tab in Photoshop's workspace. You can check its name on the tab, which would, by default, be exactly as your filename.

- **Multiple Files:** In case you have opened more than one document, each of them is opened in different tabs, and you may switch to any of them whenever you want.

Step 6: Check and Set Document Settings (Optional)

- **Image Mode and Color Settings**: Image mode, including RGB or CMYK, may be viewed from within your open file through the **Image > Mode** dropdown menu on the menu bar. This may help prepare a file for print or web use.
- **Document Properties:** You can also display file information and details by selecting the **Image > Image Size menu**.

Step 7: Save Your Work

- **Save As:** If you opened a file from another format, like JPEG or PNG and you want to edit it, save it as a Photoshop document (.psd) if you want to retain layers. To do that, just go to **File**, click **Save As** locate the Photoshop format, and click **Save** in your desired location.

How to Insert Images Using Drag & Drop

Drag and drop is the easiest way to insert images into Adobe Photoshop 2025 and amp up your workflow efficiency. Here's how you can do it:

1. **Open Your Photoshop Document:** Open Adobe Photoshop 2025, then open the document where you want to insert the image.
2. **Find the Image File**: Using your operating system's file explorer, in other words, via File Explorer in Windows, or Finder in macOS, navigate to the folder that contains the image you want to insert.
3. **Drag and Drop Image:**
   - Click and hold onto the image file.

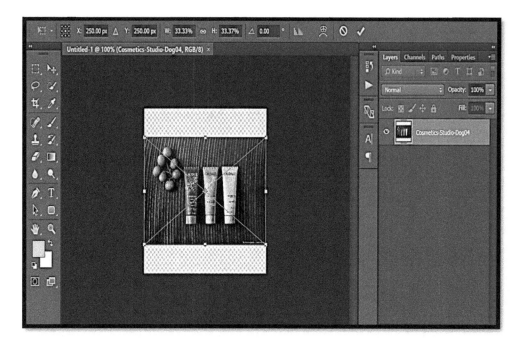

- Drag it onto the open window of your Photoshop document.
- Let go of the mouse button, dropping the image into the document.

4. **Position and Resize the Image:**

- When you drop, it creates a new layer and is immediately set to Free Transform mode.
- Scale the image by dragging any of the corner handles while holding the Shift key to constrain the proportion.
- Position the image in your document.
- Hit **Ctrl+Enter** (Windows) or **Command+Return** (mac) to confirm the placement.

How to Insert Files Using Place Embedded

Adobe Photoshop 2025 lets you insert external files as Smart Objects into your document using Place Embedded. This maintains the original integrity of the content for non-destructive editing. Place Embedded can be applied using the following steps:

1. **Open Your Photoshop Document**: Open your document in Photoshop where you want to place the external file.

2. **To access the Place Embedded command**:
    *   Go to the top menu and click on **File > Place Embedded**.

3. **Select the File to Place**:
    *   In the open dialog box, navigate to where the file is located that you want to place.
    *   Highlight the file and click **Place**.

4. **Position and Transform the Placed File:**

- The placed document will open in your document in a bounding box.

- To move the item, click inside the bounding box and drag it to where you want it.

- To scale the file, drag any of the corner handles of the bounding box. If you hold the Shift key while dragging, the proportions are constrained.

- To rotate, move your cursor just outside a corner handle until it changes to a curved arrow; then click and drag to rotate.

5. **Confirm Placement:**

- Once satisfied with positioning and transformation, hit **Enter** for Windows or **Return** for Mac to confirm and set the file in place as a Smart Object.

Embed files as Smart Objects, and you will be able to edit in a non-destructive fashion: rescale, rotate, and apply filters without losing any quality in the original image.

How to Insert Files Using Place Linked

Place Linked in Adobe Photoshop 2025 enables you to add external files to your project as Smart Objects, creating a dynamic link to the source. This ensures that should the source file change, so will your Photoshop document. To do so:

1. **Open Your Photoshop Document**: Open up Photoshop and then open the document where you want to place the external file.

2. **Open the 'Place Linked' Command:** From the top menu, click **File > Place Linked**.

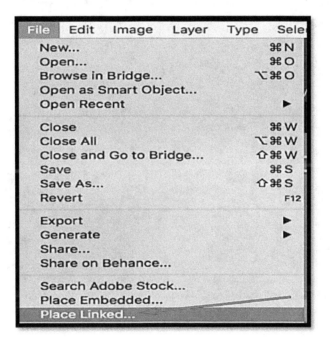

3. **Choose a File to Place:**

    • In the opened dialog box, select the file you want to place into your document.

    • Highlight the file you want and click **Place**.

4. **Position and Transform the Placed File:**

    • The placed file opens in your document inside a bounding box.

    • You can move, scale, or rotate the file appropriately.

- When positioned as desired, press **Enter** [Windows] or **Return** [Mac] to set.

Using "**Place Linked**," the placed file will remain linked to its source. If the source file is edited, Photoshop will automatically alert you that there is an update for the linked Smart Object, and this can be updated within your document. This is crucial when updates need to be made frequently or when working for/with others.

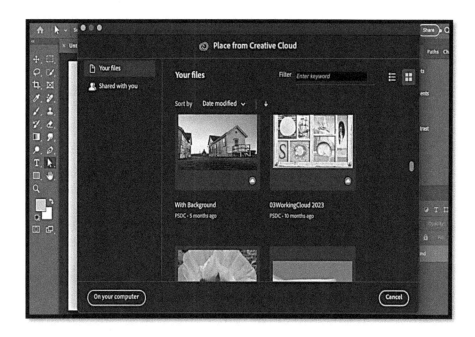

CHAPTER THREE

WORKING WITH LAYERS

Understanding Layers and Layer Stacks

In Photoshop, the general fundamentals are layers, which allow you to construct and edit images in a non-destructive way. Each layer is like an individual sheet that is laid over or under other layers and that allows working on individual elements without affecting the rest of the image. This structure provides flexibility in editing, compositing, and applying effects.

Understanding Layers:

- **Create and Manage**: New layers are added, and already- added ones can be duplicated or grouped. This helps in managing complicated projects.

- **Visible/Opacity:** Every layer has controls for visibility (the eye icon) and opacity for showing, concealing, or making elements semi-transparent.

- **Blending Modes**: Layers can interact with other layers with blending modes that define how the pixels in a layer will blend with the underlying layers.

Working with Layers:

1. **Creating a New Layer:**
    - Move to the Layers panel.
    - Click the "**Create a new layer**" icon button at the bottom of the panel.
    - Alternatively, you can choose **Layer > New > Layer** from the top menu.

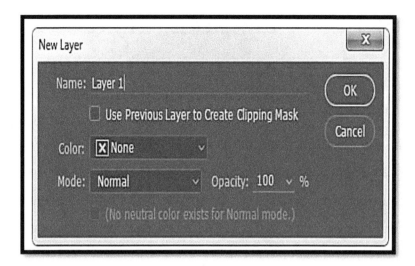

2. **Organize Layers into Groups:**

    • To select more than one layer, press the **Ctrl key** (Windows) or **Command key** (Mac) while selecting other layers.

    • Right-click and choose **Group from Layers**, or hit **Ctrl+G** (Windows) or **Command+G** (Mac).

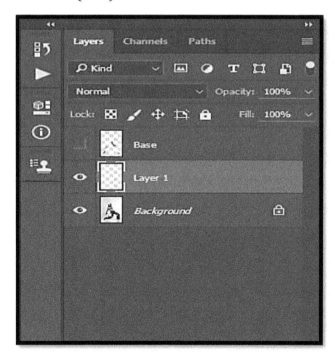

3. **Adjusting Layer Opacity:**
    - To adjust a layer's opacity, highlight that layer.
    - Locate your Layers panel and move the Opacity slider until you achieve your required transparency for that particular image.

Layer Stacks:

Layer stacking refers to the hierarchical structure of layers in the Layers panel. In a stacking order, layer order defines how layers will appear in the image, whether it overlaps above another layer or partially hides a layer: top most layer shows up in front of all other layers; the bottommost layer will be behind all other layers.

By dragging the layers up or down in the Layers panel, you will be able to reorder the layers. This feature is crucial in making a composite of images, which allows you to decide what should be in the front or at the rear.

Managing Layer Stacks

1. **Reordering Layers:**
    - Click your mouse and hold on the layer you want to move in the Layers panel.
    - Drag the said layer up or down to wherever you want it to end.

2. **Merging Layers**:

   - To merge layers, highlight all of the layers you would like to merge.

   - Right-click and choose **Merge Layers**, or use the hotkey **Ctrl + E** on your PC and **Command + E** on your Mac.

3. **Flattening an Image:**

   - To flatten an image into one background layer simply highlight **Layer > Flatten Image**.

   - Flattening will delete any separation between the layers so save a copy of your image before flattening.

Creating, Organizing, and Managing Layers

Think of layers as transparent sheets placed on top of one another with different parts of your image on each layer. This makes it possible to change a layer without affecting the other layers in the file. You can keep track of your layers using the Layers panel. To display this panel, choose **Window > Layers** or press **F7**.

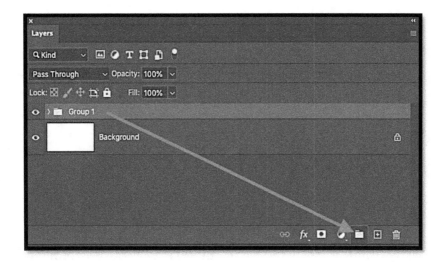

Creating New Layers

You'll need to create new layers to construct detailed images. To create a new layer:

- Click the **Create a New Layer button** at the bottom of the Layers panel.

- Or, choose **Layer > New > Layer** via the Menu Bar.

- To name a layer, set options (or for added control), click the **Create a New Layer button** while holding **Alt** (Windows) or **Option** (Mac OS) to open the New Layer dialog box.

Organizing Layers with Groups

This will keep things clear as your project builds up:

- To select multiple layers, add a command and hold **Shift** for contiguous layers or **Ctrl** for Windows / **Command** for Mac OS and click the layers you want, right-click on the selected layers, choose **Group** from Layers, or simple **Ctrl+G** for Windows / **Command+G** for Mac OS.

- To ungroup layers, select the group and choose **Layer > Ungroup Layers**.

Working with Layer Visibility and Opacity

Hiding and showing layers, and modifying their opacity are the basic skills that every person working in Photoshop should master:

- Click the eye icon beside a layer in the Layers panel to make the layer invisible/visible.
- To set the Opacity of a layer: select the layer and drag the Opacity slider at the top of the Layers panel.

Adding Layer Effects and Styles

Add the following effects to your layers:

- Select a layer, and at the bottom of the Layers panel click the **Add a Layer Style icon**.
- Click **Drop Shadow, Inner Glow,** or **Bevel and Emboss** among others.
- In the Layer Style dialog box drag the controls until the effect is the way you want.

Performing Non-Destructive Editing with Adjustment Layers

Adjustment layers allow you to perform color and tonal adjustments without touching the original image data:

- Click the **New Adjustment Layer button** at the bottom of the Layers panel.
- Choose an adjustment type, such as Levels, Curves, or Hue/ Saturation.
- In the Properties panel, adjust the settings for the adjustment.

Linking and Aligning Layers

You can link layers and manipulate them in conjunction; to do this:

- To link layers, highlight the layers to be linked.
- Click the **Link Layers icon** at the bottom of the Layers panel.
- To align layers, select them and use the alignment options in the options bar with the Move Tool active.

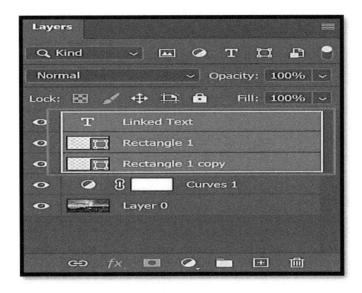

Merging and Flattening Layers

To decrease file size or lock an image, you may want to merge or flatten layers:

- **Merge Layers**: With your desired layers selected choose **Layer > Merge Layers**.

- **Flatten Image**: To flatten an image means to merge all layers into one background layer. To do this, go to **Layer > Flatten Image**. **Note**: By flattening, you will lose all your layer information. You might want to save a copy of your image in its layered state before flattening.

Rasterizing Layers

Most operations can be performed only after rasterizing vector-based layers:

- Select the vector layer that you want to work with, for example, the text or shape layer.

- Select **Layer > Rasterize > Layer**. Remember that to rasterize means to convert information to pixels hence, it is resolution-dependent and will not be as flexible for future edits.

Adjusting Opacity, Blending Options, and Linking Layers

The layer opacity, blending options, and the ability to link layers together are key resources in creating complex and visually appealing compositions in Adobe Photoshop 2025. Being able to make subtle adjustments to how the layers of an image can work with each other enables the creation of complex effects and seamless integrations.

Changing Layer Opacity

The opacity of an image, or any item in a layer, is the measure of how see-through it is. Changing this property affects how it merges or blends into lower layers. This section shall explain how to change the opacity of a layer.

1. **Select the Layer**: Click on the layer whose opacity you would like to adjust within the Layers panel.

2. **Adjusting Opacity:**

   - The Opacity slider is available at the top of the Layers panel.

   - To decrease opacity and increase transparency, click and drag the slider to the left, while dragging it to the right will do the opposite: increase opacity and decrease transparency.

   - Alternatively, click the percentage value beside the slider and type a specific opacity percentage.

   Note: A 0% opacity means a layer is completely transparent, and a 100% opacity indicates that it is fully opaque.

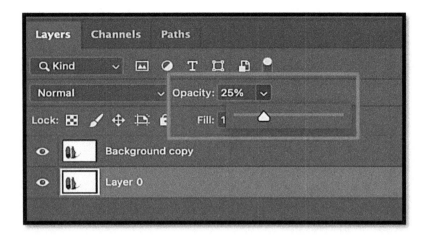

Applying Blending Modes

Blending modes are ways a layer's pixels merge with pixels on underlying layers, thus applying a range of effects.

1. **Select Layer**: In the Layers panel, click to select a layer you want to work with.

2. **Choose a Blending Mode**:

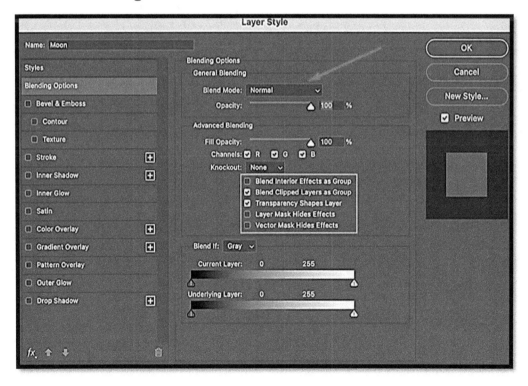

- At the top of the Layers panel, find the Blending Mode drop-down menu, the default setting is "**Normal**."

- Click the drop-down and observe several blending mode options appear: Multiply, Screen, and Overlay, among others.

- Hover over each in turn to quickly visualize what each does to the layer.

- Click to apply the blending mode of your choice.

  Tip: You can achieve unique visual results by trying different blending modes for a layer.

Linking Layers

Linking layers allows you to move or transform multiple layers at once, keeping their relative positions.

1. **Select Layers to Link**:

   - Click the first layer in the Layers panel that you want to link.

   - To add more layers to your selection, hold **Ctrl key+click** (Windows) or **Command key+click** (Mac).

2. **Link the Layers:**

   - With your selected layers, click the **Link Layers** icon at the bottom of the Layers panel.

   - Alternatively, right-click one of the selected layers and choose **Link Layers** from the pop-up menu.

Note: When you have layers linked together, they all move and transform as one. To unlink linked layers, select the linked layers and click the **Link Layers icon** again, or select **Unlink Layers** from the context menu. By effectively manipulating opacity, applying blending modes, and linking layers, you will go one step further with your enhancement in Photoshop and get professional, striking results.

Converting Layers to Smart Objects for Non-Destructive Editing

Smart Objects are layers that contain image data from raster or vector images, such as Photoshop or Illustrator files. They preserve an image's source content with all its original characteristics, enabling you to perform non-destructive editing to the layer.

Convert a Layer to a Smart Object in Photoshop

1. **Open Document**: Open Adobe Photoshop 2025 and open the document containing the layer to be converted.
2. **Select the Layer:** In the Layers panel, highlight one of the layers you want to turn into a Smart Object.
3. **Convert to Smart Object:**
   - Right-click on the selected layer and select "**Convert to Smart Object**" in the pop-up menu.
   - Or, with the layer selected, on the top menu select **Layer > Smart Objects > Convert to Smart Object**.

   After conversion, a Smart Object icon appears in the lower-right corner of the layer thumbnail, indicating that this layer has now been made a Smart Object.

Editing a Smart Object

To edit the contents of a Smart Object:

1. **Open the Smart Object**: Double-click the Smart Object layer thumbnail in the Layers panel.
2. **Edit the Content:** A new window opens containing the content of the Smart Object. Perform your desired edits in this window.
3. **Save and Update:** After editing, save and close the Smart Object window. The changes will immediately appear in the original document.

Applying Filters to Smart Objects

If you apply filters on a Smart Object, they become Smart Filters-non-destructive and editable, such as:

1. **Select the Smart Object Layer:** Click on the **Smart Object layer** in the Layers panel.

2. **Apply a Filter: At** the top menu, select **Filter** then choose the filter you want to apply to it.

3. **Adjust Filter Settings:** A pop-up window opens with the filter settings, adjust accordingly and click **OK**.

   The added filter is visible in the layers panel below the Smart Object layer. You can come back here to double-click this layer to adjust the settings or to turn it off.

   Additional Tips:

- **Returning to its Original State**: To change a Smart Object into a normal layer select the Smart Object layer, right click and choose "**Rasterize Layer.**" Note this will delete the non-destructive benefits of the Smart Object.

- **Linked vs. Embedded Smart Objects**: Photoshop has both linked and embedded Smart Objects. Linked Smart Objects link to external files; embedded Smart Objects are saved within the document. To replace an embedded Smart Object as a linked Smart Object, select the **Smart Object** layer, then choose **Layer > Smart Objects > Convert to Linked**.

How to Lock and Hide Layers

Accessing the Layers Panel

The Layers panel is the default control center for all activities involving layers. To open it:

1. Along the topmost menu bar, click **Window > Layers**.

2. The Layers panel opens, displaying for you all the layers in the currently active document.

Locking Layers

When a layer is locked, it cannot be edited in any way, thus offering some protection against an object being accidentally altered or moved. To lock a layer:

1. In the Layers panel, select the layer you want to lock by clicking on it.

2. You will see several options at the top of the Layers panel to lock:

   • **Lock Transparent Pixels**: Allows editing only to the opaque parts of the layer.

   • **Lock Image Pixels**: No modification of the content of the layer's pixel is allowed.

   • **Lock Position:** The layer content can't be moved but you can allow all other edits.

   • **Lock All:** Finally, completely locks the layer for changes.

To lock all properties of a layer:

   • Click the **Lock All** icon at the top of the Layers panel

   A padlock icon will appear beside the layer name.

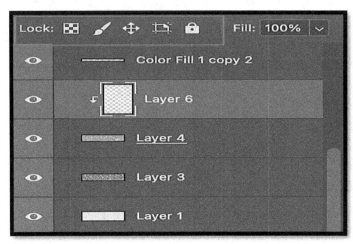

Unlocking Layers

To unlock a layer and recommence editing:

1.   In the Layers panel, highlight the layer that is locked.

2.   Click the **padlock icon** beside the layer name to turn off the padlock.

Hiding Layers

Hiding layers allows you to focus on parts of your project without other elements distracting you. To hide a layer:

1.   In the Layers panel, select the layer you want to hide.

2.   After the layer name, click the **Eye icon**. The layer will disappear from view on the canvas, and the Eye icon will be replaced by a blank area, signifying that the layer is hidden.

Showing Hidden Layers

To make visible a hidden layer:

1.   In the Layers panel find the layer that you would like to see and click on the empty box where the eye icon had been in.

2.   The eye icon will re-appear along with the layer becoming visible on the canvas.

CHAPTER FOUR

MASTERING ADJUSTMENT LAYERS

Overview of Adjustment Layers: Types and Uses of Each Adjustment Layer

The adjustment layer in Adobe Photoshop 2025 is an advanced utility that enables color and tone editing of images in a non-destructive manner. Hence, while working with adjustment layers, one can edit images without permanently changing the original pixel data, gaining more flexibility and control over the editing process. Each of these adjustment layer types serves a specific purpose; for enhancements in photos precisely.

Types of Adjustment Layers and Their Uses

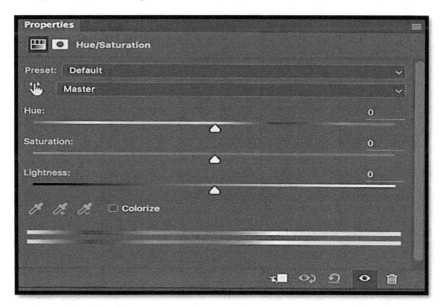

1. **Brightness/Contrast:**
    *   **Purpose**: It gives the possibility of modifying lightness/darkness and the contrast between light and dark areas of the image.

- **Usage**: When in need of making basic tonal adjustments in an image to improve the overall exposure, it's best used here.

2. **Levels**:
   - **Purpose**: Light and dark areas are manipulated by controlling shadows, midtones, and highlights.
   - **Usage**: Improves imbalanced tonality and enhancement of image contrast is best done through the use of the levels tool.

3. **Curves**:
   - **Purpose**: The feature allows for fine control over the adjusting of tones by moving points on a curve to adjust brightness and contrast.
   - **Usage**: Allows for detailed adjustments in local ranges of tones, enabling fine-tuning of image contrast and color balance.

4. **Exposure**:
   - **Purpose**: The feature enables adjustment of the exposure, offset, and gamma correction of the image to fix overexposed or underexposed images.
   - **Usage**: Perfect for exposure correction in an image where it helps to improve details.

5. **Vibrance**:
   - **Purpose**: It desaturates colors, having as a target less-saturated colors so as not to oversaturate.
   - **Usage**: Increase color without affecting skin tones or areas that color a lot.

6. **Hue/Saturation:**
   - **Purpose**: Changes hue, saturation, and lightness for an entire image or colors of a chosen range.

- **Usage**: Good for changing specific colors, de-saturating images, and using color effects.

7. **Color Balance:**
   - **Purpose:** Change the color balance for shadows, midtones, and highlights to rectify color casts.
   - **Usage**: This is helpful to adjust color imbalances and achieve certain color tones.

8. **Black & White:**
   - **Purpose**: Turns a color image to grayscale but allows for some creativity with how colors are converted.
   - **Usage**: Creative control during the grayscale conversion can also improve contrast and detail.

9. **Photo Filter:**
   - **Purpose**: Colorizes an image using colored glass filters mimicking traditional glass filters on the lens.
   - **Usage**: Warm up or cool down an image, or apply creative color effects.

10. **Channel Mixer:**
    - **Purpose:** Adjust color channels for creating custom color work or converting images to grayscale.
    - **Usage**: Allows sophisticated color mixing and is widely used in producing high-quality black-and-white images.

11. **Invert**:
    - **Purpose**: Reverses the colors of an image for a negative effect.
    - **Usage**: Done mostly when special effects are needed or during the analysis of the tonal values.

12. **Posterize:**

- **Purpose**: This controls the number of tonal levels in an image to achieve a poster-like effect.

- **Usage**: It is used for artistic effects, or when preparing images for screen printing.

13. **Threshold:**

  - **Purpose**: Converts an image to high-contrast black and white by designating a threshold level above or below which all pixels will be black or white.

  - **Usage**: Useful for making masks or analyzing the tonal distribution.

14. **Selective Color:**

  - **Purpose:** Allows you to adjust the amount of process colors (cyan, magenta, yellow, and black) in specific primary color components.

  - **Usage:** Allows for quite precise color adjustments when doing print work.

How to Apply an Adjustment Layer

1. **Open Your Image**: To get started, open **Photoshop** and open an image you'd like to work with.

2. **Access the Adjustments Panel**: To access the Adjustments panel, go to **Window > Adjustments**.

3. **Choose a Type of Adjustment Layer:** Click the icon in the Adjustments panel for the adjustment you'd like to apply - Levels, Curves, etc.

4. **Adjust Settings**: The properties panel will display the controls of the selected adjustment. Make settings to suit the desired effect.

5. **Exploit Layer Masks for Selective Adjustments**: Each adjustment layer has a layer mask associated with it. White, black, and gray shades are used to paint

on the mask for the showing, hiding as well as partial transparency of an adjustment in selected areas.

6. **Edit or Delete Adjustments:** To modify the adjustment, double-click the adjustment layer icon in the Layers panel. To delete it, select the layer and press **Delete**.

Using Levels, Curves, and Color Balance

Levels Adjustment Layer

The Level adjustment edits the tonal range and color balance by adjusting the intensity levels of shadows, midtones, and highlights.

Creating a Levels Adjustment Layer:

Via Adjustments Panel

1. In Photoshop, open your image.
2. Click the **Adjustments** panel.
3. Click the **Levels icon** that resembles a histogram.

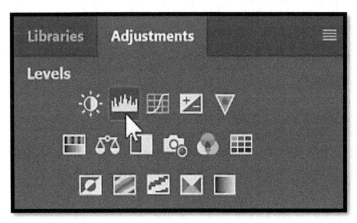

Via the Layers Panel:

1. Click the **Create new fill or adjustment layer icon** in the bottom right of the Layers panel.
2. Select **Levels** from the dropdown.

Via the Menu Bar:

1. Click **Layer > New Adjustment Layer > Levels**.

2. A dialog will come up; name the layer and click **OK**.

Adjusting Tonal Range:

1. You will notice, in the Properties panel, a histogram showing you the range of tones.

2. Move the Input Levels sliders:

    -   **Black slider (left):** It selects the black point and darkens the shadows upon being dragged to the right.

    -   **Midtone slider (middle):** The gamma controls, brightening midtones via dragging to the left or darkening midtones via dragging to the right.

    -   **White slider (right):** It sets the white point and thereby lightens highlights while dragging to the left.

3. Adjust the **Output Levels sliders** to compress the tonal range:

    -   **Black Output slider (left):** Moving this slider to the right will result in brightening the shadows.

    -   **White Output slider (right):** When it is moved to the left, it darkens the highlights.

Curves Adjustment Layer

The Curve adjustment enables you to have exacting control over tonal adjustments as you can manipulate points throughout the tonal range.

Creating a Curves Adjustment Layer:

Via Adjustments Panel:

1. Open the image in Photoshop.

2. Go to the **Adjustments panel**.

3. Click the **Curves icon** as indicated by the curve graph.

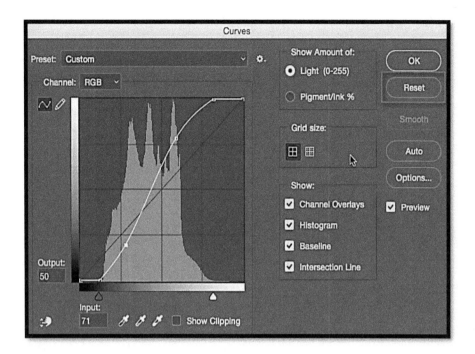

Via Layers Panel

1. In the Layers panel go to the **Create new fill** or adjustment layer icon.

2. Select **Curves** from the drop-down menu.

Via Menu Bar

1. Click **Layer > New Adjustment Layer > Curves**.

2. In the dialog box that opens, name the layer and click **OK**.

Curve Adjustment

Follow the steps below:

1. In the Properties panel, there is a diagonal line representing the tonal range.

2. Click along the line to add control points in:

   - **Shadows**: Near bottom-left to lighten the dark areas.

   - **Midtones**: In the center for mid-tones.

   - **Highlights**: Near top-right to lighten bright areas.

3.   **Drag the points to**:

- **Upward**: Lighten the selected tonal range.

- **Downward**: Darkens the selected tonal range.

4.   For finer adjustment, the On-image adjustment tool can be used:

- Click the hand icon in the **Properties** panel.

- Alternatively, click directly on the image area you want to adjust and pull up or down.

Color Balance Adjustment Layer

The Color Balance adjustment changes the color balance of the image to correct color casts or creatively grade the colors of the image.

How to Create a Color Balance Adjustment Layer:

1.   Open your image in Photoshop.

2.   Go to the Adjustments panel.

3.   Click the **Color Balance icon**, indicated by a set of scales.

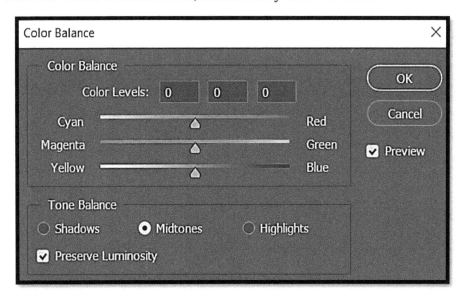

Using Masks with Adjustment Layers

An adjustment layer is a kind of layer that performs an edit targeted to brightness, contrast, hue, saturation, etc., without touching the original image pixels. By default, every adjustment layer is bound to a layer mask; you can see it as a white thumbnail next to the layer thumbnail in the Layers panel. This mask allows controlling the visibility of the adjustment effect on any given part of an image:

- **White areas** of the mask display the adjustment completely, and the underlying areas of the image are fully influenced by it.

- **Black areas** of the mask conceal the adjustment, allowing the underlying image to come through in those areas.

- **Gray areas** of the mask display the adjustment partially. The lighter the gray, the more the adjustment comes through.

Adding an Adjustment Layer with a Mask

1. **Choose the Layer**: Click the image layer in the Layers panel that you want to adjust.

2. **Add an Adjustment Layer:**
   - At the bottom of the Layers panel, click the "**Create new fill or adjustment layer**" icon.
   - Choose from the pull-down menu what type of adjustment you want to make to your image: Hue/Saturation, Levels, and Curves.

A new adjustment layer will be added above the layer that is highlighted in the Layers panel and will also be paired with a white layer mask thumbnail.

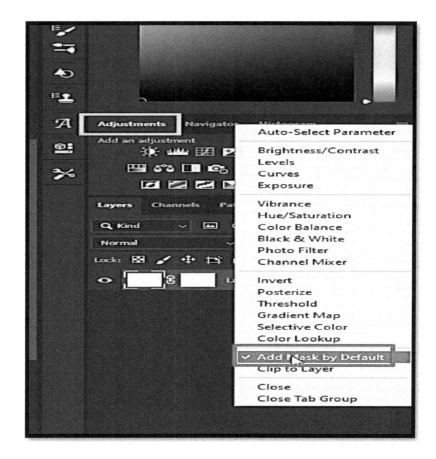

3. **Adjust Adjustment Settings:**

  • The Properties panel will display controls relevant to.

  • Adjust the settings as desired; these are chosen to have a universal effect on the image.

Refining the Adjustment with the Layer Mask

To allow the adjustment to act on selected areas only:

1. **Enable the Layer Mask**: Click the layer mask thumbnail in the adjustment layer to ensure it is enabled.

2. **Choose the Brush Tool:**

  • Access the Brush tool via the toolbar or press **B** on your keyboard.

- Ensure the foreground color is set to black, which will be used while painting to mask out/reduce the visibility of the adjustment effect.

3. **Paint on the Mask:**
   - To mask the adjustment in parts of the image, paint over the image area using the black foreground color.
   - To unmask the adjustment in previously hidden areas, change the foreground color to white and paint over the hidden areas.
   - For partial adjustments, use gray shades of color to produce a partially transparent area.

Mask Areas Using Selection Tools

You can also use selection tools to define an area to be adjusted:

1. **Make a Selection:** Apply the Quick Selection Tool, or the Lasso Tool, and select an area where you want to make adjustments.

2. **Adding an Adjustment Layer:**
   - With your selection active, add a new adjustment layer as guided earlier.
   - Photoshop will instantly create a layer mask from your selection and allow the adjustment to take effect only in the selected area.

Editing the Layer Mask

To refine the mask:

1. **Access the Properties Panel**:
   - With the layer mask selected, Properties provides options for **Density** and **Feathers**.
   - **Density** reduces the mask's opacity and allows more of the adjustment to pass through.

- **Feather** softens the mask edges and delivers a softer transition between the adjusted and non-adjusted areas.

2. **Refine Mask Edges:**
    - Click the "**Select and Mask**" button in Properties-the workspace for refining mask edges opens.
    - Refine Edge Brush amongst other tools, will help you increase the accuracy of your mask.

Saving your Work

Save your document in a format that supports layers to keep your adjustment layers and masks for future editing.

By learning how to work with masks and adjustment layers, you'll achieve accurate, non-destructive editing to enhance the quality and flexibility of your projects in Adobe Photoshop.

Applying and Saving Custom Adjustment Presets

Applying Adjustment Layers

By using an adjustment layer, edits can be made to an image without permanently changing the original pixels. At any time, the adjustments layer can be double-clicked to edit all of the settings or the layer can be deleted which completely removes all of the edits from the image. This is very powerful.

1. **Open Your Image:** First, open Photoshop and open an image that you want to edit.
2. **Activating the Adjustments Panel**: To open the Adjustments panel select **Adjustments** under the Window menu.
3. **Select Adjustment Type**: On the Adjustments panel, click to select the adjustment you want to make. The options include Levels, Curves, and Color

Balance, among others. For instance, if you want to make changes to brightness and contrast, click the **Brightness/Contrast** icon.

4. **Make Adjustments**: After selecting the adjustment type that you want to make, the Properties panel opens showing various controls applicable to adjusting. Make adjustments by moving the sliders or keying in values to achieve your desired effect.

5. **Apply with Layer Mask:** Each adjustment layer is equipped with a layer mask to selectively apply adjustments. Click the mask thumbnail in the Layers panel and use painting tools to indicate where the adjustment should be applied.

Saving Custom Adjustment Presets

Once you have created an adjustment layer and configured it as desired, you can save it as a preset so you can reuse exactly that same adjustment using the same settings on other images.

1. **Create the Adjustment Layer:** Apply and refine an adjustment layer according to the instructions in the previous steps.

2. **Save the Preset:**
    *   In the Properties panel, click the **Preset Options icon**.
    *   Under the Preset Options icon, select **Save Preset** from the drop-down list.
    *   In the opened dialog box, name your preset descriptively.
    *   Click **Save** to save the preset.

3. Apply Preset to Other Images:
    *   Open a new image.
    *   Add the corresponding adjustment layer type (e.g., Curves, Levels).
    *   In the Properties panel, click the **Preset Options icon**.
    *   Select from the list your saved preset to apply these settings.

Manage Presets

Photoshop allows you to manage your presets for organization and efficiency.

- **Access the Preset Manager**:
  - Go to **Edit** > **Presets** > **Preset Manager**.
  - In the Preset Manager dialog box, select the preset type you want to manage from the dropdown menu.

- **Organize Presets**:
  - To rename a preset, select it and click **Rename**.
  - To delete a preset, select it and click **Delete**.
  - To load additional presets, click **Load**, navigate to the preset file, and click **Open**.

Creative Effects with Blending Modes on Adjustment Layers

Understanding Adjustment Layers

The adjustment layers provide color grading and tonal adjustments to your image without permanently affecting the original pixels. It gives flexibility in this non-destructive approach whereby one can at any time in the future go back and revise or remove the adjustments. The most frequently used adjustment layers are: Levels, Curves, Hue/Saturation, and Color Balance.

Understanding Blending Modes

Blending modes are a means of specifying how the pixels in a layer will interact with the ones in the underlying layers. Each blending mode represents a different formula for combining pixel values, for a range of various effects. Different blending modes are available within Photoshop under a host of categories, including Darken, Lighten, and Contrast, among many others.

Applying Blending Modes to Adjustment Layers

To apply a blending mode on an adjustment layer, do the following:

1. **Create an Adjustment Layer**: At the bottom of the Layers panel, click the "**Create new fill or adjustment layer**" icon and select your adjustment type, such as Levels or Curves.

2. **Select the Adjustment Layer:** Ensure the adjustment layer is selected in the Layers panel.

3. **Set Blending Mode:** At the top of the Layers panel, click the drop-down that already says "**Normal**" and select from any of the other blending modes listed.

4. **Adjust the Opacity if Necessary**: Click in the Opacity slider beside the blending mode menu to adjust the intensity of the effect.

Creative Effects by Using Blending Modes with Adjustment Layers

Combining an adjustment layer with an appropriate blending mode can result in some creative effects:

- **Soft Light with Curves Adjustment**: Insert a **Curves adjustment layer** and set its mode to Soft Light to enhance the contrast and saturation, hence giving an image a more dramatic look.

- **Multiply with Levels Adjustment:** Adding a Levels adjustment layer, and changing the blending mode to Multiply will darken the layer, giving it a lot more depth and mood.

- **Screen with Hue/Saturation Adjustment**: Add a **Hue/Saturation adjustment layer**; change the blending mode to Screen. This will lighten the layer, enabling better color vibrancy.

CHAPTER FIVE

CROPPING AND TRANSFORMING IMAGES

Cropping for Composition and Specific Resolutions

Cropping and transforming images in Adobe Photoshop 2025 is a basic skill that is very crucial to enhance composition and reach specific resolutions.

1. **Cropping Images for Composition**

   Cropping allows you to remove unwanted areas, highlight key elements, and further improve the overall composition of an image.

   Selecting the Crop Tool:

   - In the Tools panel, click to select the **Crop Tool** (hotkey: C).

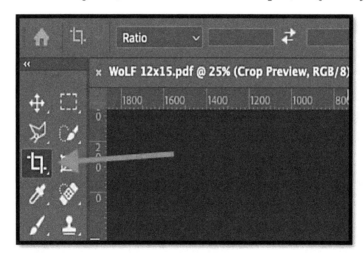

   - Crop borders will show up around your image.

   Editing the Crop Area:

   - To define an image area, click and drag the corner or edge handles of the crop border.

   - To preserve the aspect ratio of the original image, hold the **Shift key** while resizing.

Setting the Aspect Ratio:

- **Select in the Options bar:** From the image, preset aspect ratios, or your dimensions.

- **Some common GUI presets:** 1:1, 4:3 and 16:9

Straightening the Image:

- To straighten a tilted image, drag the cursor a little bit outside a corner handle until it changes to a curved arrow, and then drag it to rotate.

- Alternatively, click the **Straighten button** in the Options bar and drag a line along an element that should be horizontal or vertical; Photoshop will rotate the image according to that.

Apply the Crop:

- Press **Enter** on Windows, or **Return** on Mac to apply the crop.

- In case you want to cancel, press **Esc**.

Cropping to Specific Resolutions

Cropping images for specific resolutions is useful when you are creating images that may be printed or viewed on the web.

To set the Crop Tool to specific dimensions:
- With the Crop Tool activated, in the Options bar, enter the width, height, and resolution you want.
- For example, to prepare an image for a print in the size of 4x6 inches at 300 dpi set the width to 4 in, height to 6 in, and resolution to 300 pixels/inch.

Resizing the Crop Area:
- Take the drag of crop handles for modifying the area. Photoshop will constrain the proportions based on whatever dimensions you have entered.

Apply the Crop:
- Press **Enter** or **Return** to apply it. Photoshop will resample the image to meet the specified dimensions and resolution.

Transforming Images

Transformations such as scaling, rotating, skewing, and distorting are performed to change the appearance of elements in an image.

Free Transform Command:
- Select the layer or object you want to transform.
- Then go to **Edit > Free Transform**, or **Ctrl+T** for Windows, or **Command+T** for Mac.
- You will see a bounding box with handles around your selected item.

Scaling:
- Drag any of the corner handles to resize.

- To maintain the aspect ratio, ensure that the **Maintain Aspect Ratio** (Link icon) is activated in the Options bar.

Rotating:
- Drag the cursor outside a corner handle until it becomes a curved arrow and drag to rotate.
- Holding Shift will constrain the rotation in 15-degree increments.

Skewing and Distorting:
- Right-click inside the bounding box and select **Skew** or **Distort.**
- Drag the handles to slant or stretch the image as required.

Apply the Transformation:
- Press **Enter** or **Return** to complete the transformation.

Using the Content-Aware Crop Tool

The Content-Aware Crop tool within Adobe Photoshop 2025 steps up your game another notch when cropping and straightening images, filling in intelligently any gaps that may result from such adjustments. This proves very helpful while rotating or extending the canvas area since this fills in with the surrounding information seamlessly.

Enable the Content-Aware Crop Tool:
1. **Select the Crop Tool**: Tap the **Crop Tool** from within the Toolbar, or use the shortcut: (C).
2. **Activate the Content-Aware Option**: Put a check in the box for Content-Aware in the Options bar at the top to turn this on.

Straightening an Image Using Content-Aware Crop

1. **Activate the Crop Tool:**

   • Once the Crop Tool is activated, a crop boundary will appear around your image.

2. **Rotate to Straighten:**

   • Position your cursor just outside a corner of the crop boundary and, when it changes to a double-pointed, curved arrow, click and drag to rotate the image.

   • Use the overlay grid as a guide to align elements within the image, such as the horizon or architectural lines.

3. **Apply the Crop:**

- Press **Enter** (Windows) or **Return** (Mac) to commit the crop. If rotating this image has resulted in some empty areas, then Photoshop will automatically fill the area with content matched from the surrounding parts.

Changing the Aspect Ratio with Content-Aware Crop:

1. **Choose Aspect Ratio**: In the Options bar, click on the **Aspect Ratio** dropdown menu and then click on your desired ratio, such as 1:1(Square).

2. **Adjust Crop Boundary**: Click inside the crop boundary and drag to move the subject within the frame. To extend the crop boundary outside the image bounds, drag one of the corner or edge handles outwards. This will produce blank areas in the canvas.

3. **Apply the Crop:** Press **Enter** on Windows or **Return** on Mac to commit the crop. Photoshop will fill the newly empty areas with similar content to the rest of the picture using intelligent filling.

Additional Tips:

- **Non-Destructive Cropping**: By default, cropping in Photoshop is non-destructive, meaning the pixels are preserved if cropped. Just in case, make sure the Delete Cropped Pixels box is unchecked in the Options bar.

- **Using the Straighten Tool:** To straighten precisely, click the Straighten icon in the Options bar, and click-drag a line along an element in the image that should be perfectly horizontal or vertical.

Transform Tools Overview: Free Transform, Skew, Distort, Perspective

Free Transform Tool

The Free Transform tool offers a general option of all of the transform options by offering the reshaping, rotating, flipping, and skewing of an image or layer.

How to Use Free Transform:

1. **Select the Layer:** Highlight the object layer or the object to be transformed in the Layers panel.

2. **Activate Free Transform:** Simply press **Ctrl + T** for Windows and **Cmd + T** for Mac, or get this done through the menu at **Edit > Free Transform**.

3. **Resize/Scale:** To scale the layer, pull any of the corner handles. With Shift held down during the drag, the proportionality is maintained.

4. **Rotate:** Just position your cursor a little offset from a corner handle. When it turns into a curved arrow, click and drag to rotate.

5. **Skew and Distort:** To access additional transform options, right-click (Windows) or Control-click (Mac) on the object. From this menu, choose **Skew** or **Distort**.

6. **Confirm Changes:** Press **Enter** or click the checkmark in the options bar to commit the transformation.

Skew Tool

The Skew tool will allow you to slant or tilt an object in your image and can be used to simply adjust perspective.

How Skew Works:

1. **Choose the Layer:** Select the layer or object that you want to skew.

2. **Launch Free Transform:** Click **Ctrl + T** (Windows) or **Cmd + T** (Mac) to switch to Free Transform mode.

3. **Select Skew**: Right-click (Windows) or Control-click on Mac.

4. **Skew Adjustment:** Click and drag any side or top handles to skew the image horizontally or vertically.

5. **Apply the Transformation**: Click **Enter** or hit the checkmark.

Distort Tool

The distort tool allows the stretching of an image along any part of a direction by manipulating the corners individually. It will be appropriate to create realistic perspectives or reshape things.

How to Apply Distort:

1. **Choose the Layer**: Choose your layer to distort.

2. **Activate Free Transform:** Press **Ctrl + T (Windows)** or **Cmd + T (Mac)**.

3. **Select Distort:** Right-click (Windows) or Control-click (Mac) and choose **Distort** from the menu.

4.   **Move Corners Independently**: Click and drag any of the corner handles to stretch the image. The key difference between Skew and Distort is that with Distort each corner can be adjusted independently.

5.   **Apply Changes:** Hit **Enter** or click the checkmark to commit.

Perspective Tool

The Perspective tool is used to align images to the viewpoint or angle of other elements in the scene. Many times, this is used to make an image appear to be receding into the distance.

How to Use Perspective:

1.   **Select the Layer:** Select the layer that you want to change.

2.   **Activate Free Transform**: Press **Ctrl + T** or, if you're using a Mac, use **Cmd + T**.

3.   **Select Perspective**: Right-click and select Perspective or, for Mac users, Control-click to select **Perspective**.

4.   **Perspective Change:** Click any of the corner handles and pull. Pulling a corner in will automatically push a corner out and create perspective.

5.   **Confirm Transformation**: Hit **Enter** or click the checkmark.

These tools offer the possibility of enhancing the compositions, making angle corrections, and manipulating images to fit various visual contexts. Feel free to ask if you need more details on any of the features or tools!

Correcting Perspective Distortions

Step 1: Open Your Image in Photoshop

- Open Adobe Photoshop 2025.

- In the menu, click **File > Open**, then select your image to be corrected.

- When opened, make sure in the Layers panel your image layer is unlocked; if it is locked, simply double-click on the layer to unlock it.

Step 2: Activate the Crop Tool

- To do this, click the **Crop Tool** situated in the toolbar on the left side or press C on your keyboard.

- When active, a cropping boundary will appear on your image, with handles at each corner and midpoint.

Step 3: Enable the Perspective Crop Option

- Check the box in the Options bar at the top that says Perspective-newer versions may have a Distortion Correction dropdown.

- This will let you drag each corner of the crop boundary independently to correct perspective distortions.

Step 4: Adjust Crop Handles to Correct Perspective

- Drag each corner handle until the edges of the area you want to correct are matched. For example, the crop handles align with the four corners of the building or object in the image that appears distorted.

- Ensure lines that in real life should be perfectly vertical or horizontal are as close to the crop frame as possible.

Step 5: Apply the Crop

- Once the boundary of your crop matches the correct perspective, hit **Enter** or click on the checkmark in the Options bar.

- Photoshop will automatically adjust the perspective to match your adjustment. This adjustment will help straighten and align objects in the frame as intended.

Step 6: Further Transformations with the Transform Tool

- If you need to make further adjustments, go into **Edit > Transform > Perspective**.

- When the crop was original, and it didn't fully correct the distortion, use the corner handles to adjust the perspective. Dragging a corner handle will, in Perspective mode, automatically adjust the opposing corner so that the transformed perspective is maintained.

Step 7: Fine-Tune with the Warp Tool [Optional]

- When more refined control is needed, select the option **Edit > Transform > Warp**.
- The best part is that this will allow you to manipulate different parts of the image individually by dragging either grid points or lines. Ideal for when you need just a little tweaking here and there after adjusting for perspective.

Step 8: Distortion Check and Saving

- Zoom allows you to have a closeup of the corrected image and check if the lines and proportions are natural.
- If satisfied, then go ahead under **File > Save As** and save your corrected image in your desired format, such as JPEG, PNG, or PSD.

How to Use the Puppet Warp

The Puppet Warp tool is a mighty tool in Photoshop, which allows users to transform and manipulate parts of an image with minute detail and accuracy. It differs from other transformation tools because it creates a mesh over the selected object to have control over parts of the image to make adjustments that are necessary while maintaining its object-natural look.

How to Use Puppet Warp in Adobe Photoshop 2025:

1. **Open Your Image in Photoshop**
   - Launch Adobe Photoshop 2025 and open any image you want to manipulate.

- Ensure the layer containing the image is unlocked; to do so, simply double-click on it and rename it if necessary.

2. **Create a Selection (Optional)**
   - If you want to apply **Puppet Warp only** to a portion of the image, make a selection around the area.
   - Select the area to be manipulated using one of the Quick Selection Tool, Lasso Tool, or Pen Tool. Once the selection is made, right-click and select **Layer via Copy** to work on an isolated layer outward.

3. **Convert the Layer to a Smart Object**
   - Right-click on the layer for non-destructive editing and select Convert to Smart Object. This allows one to go back and edit later, and not affect the original image taken.

4. **Enable the Puppet Warp Tool**
   - With the layer selected, at the top menu, go to **Edit** and select **Puppet Warp**.

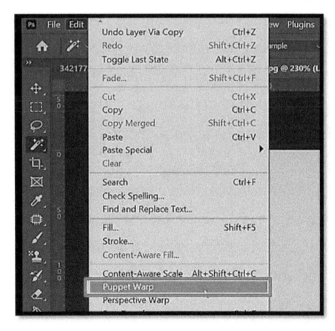

- A mesh will appear over the selected object or layer, highlighting control points, which you can now adjust.

5. **Adjust the Puppet Warp Settings (Optional)**

- **Mode**: Choose one from Rigid, Normal, or Distort depending on how flexible you want the transformation to be.
  - **Rigid**: Keeps more of the structure intact.
  - **Normal**: Standard flexibility.
  - **Distort**: Allows for extended adjustment.

- **Density**: More Points is for finer details, while Fewer Points is for broader adjustments.

- **Expansion**: Increase/decrease the area around the mesh. Will provide allowance for transformations that are closer to the edge of the selected object.

6. **Add Pins for Control Points**

- Click on parts of the image where you want to set Pins. Each pin is an anchor point; it holds a portion of the image either in place or it moves.

- Set pins along the lines of areas you want to remain stationary to avoid warping when you are manipulating other parts.

7. **Apply Transformation of the Image with the Pins**

- Click and drag on a pin to move it, warping the image. For example, when adjusting the arm of a subject, place pins down the arm and gradually pull them to move into position.

- Move the pins slowly for subtle adjustments: the more movement done, the more distortions there will be. Optimize strategic pin manipulation to achieve the desired shape and flow.

8. **Rotate the Object Using Puppet Warp**
   - To rotate part of the image, hold **Alt** (for Windows) or **Option** (for Mac) and drag your cursor close to any pin until you see the circular arrow show up.
   - Click and drag to rotate what's selected around that pin, giving you control over the angle of transformation.

9. **Refine the Transformation**
   - Tweak the pins and mesh to get the desired result. You can add more pins to manipulate other regions of the object.
   - To delete a pin that's placed inaccurately, highlight it and click **Delete**. Reposition when needed.

10. **Apply the Puppet Warp Transformation**
    - Once you have what you want with your manipulations, hit Enter or click the checkmark at the top of the workspace to apply the Puppet Warp transformation.

11. **Finalize Your Image**
    - If your layer has been converted to a Smart Object, you can at any time re-edit the Puppet Warp effect by double-clicking on it under the layer.
    - Perform other touch-ups, cropping, and refinements in completing your transformation.

CHAPTER SIX

EXPLORING BRUSHES AND BRUSH SETTINGS

Selecting and Modifying Brush Tips

In Adobe Photoshop 2025, brushes have grown to be more flexible and editable within the newest feature options an artist, designer or photographer can employ to achieve a texture, stroke, or effect with precision.

Understanding Brush Basics in Photoshop 2025

Before adjusting brushes, it's important to first learn how one selects a brush, explores the Brush Settings panel, and does some basic adjustments to shape and size.

1. **Opening the Brush Tool**

    - Step 1: Select the **'Brush'** tool from the toolbar or use hotkey (**B**) on the keyboard.

    - Step 2: Just click the icon for the **'Brush Preset Picker'** in the **'Options'** bar at the top; immediately, a pop-up menu lists the available brush presets.

2. **Selecting a Brush Tip**

    - **Step 1:** While having the **'Brush'** tool selected, open the **'Brush Preset Picker'**, and there it shows the list of brush presets that are available by default, including soft round, hard round, and natural brushes.

    - **Step 2:** To select a brush, click any brush thumbnail. Below the icons for brush presets are the Size and Hardness sliders; use these to make quick adjustments.

3. **Creating a New Brush**

    - **Step 1:** To open the Brush Settings Panel, go to **Window** and select **Brush Settings**.

- **Step 2:** Adjust Shape Dynamics, Scattering, and Texture to create the custom brush.

- **Step 3**: Having customized it, click the **+** icon in the Brush Preset Picker and save the new brush. Give it a name and check Capture Brush Size in Preset if the size is important for your brush.

Editing Brush Tips

Photoshop 2025 has introduced a few new edits to the brush tip, making the creation of dynamic and personalized brush strokes much easier.

Brush Settings Panel

- **Step 1:** Click on **Window > Brush Settings**.
- **Step 2:** Within the Brush Settings, you will find several settings entitled Tip Shape, Shape Dynamics, Scattering, and Dual Brush. These are all the settings that will define the overall characteristics of the brush tip.

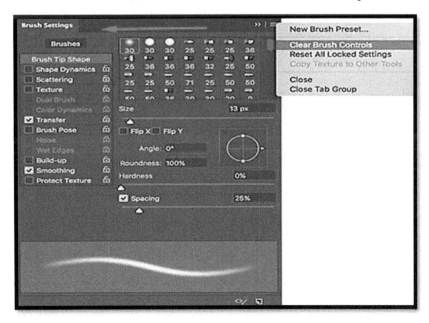

Adjusting the Shape of the Brush Tip

- **Step 1:** Within the panel of settings for the brush, select the Brush Tip Shape option. The bottom presents the preview of your brush stroke.

- **Step 2:** To change the size of the brush, slide the Size slider, and to rotate the tip of the brush, slide the Angle slider. These two bring a variation of effects in the brush.

- **Step 3:** The Spacing slider contains the distance between each stamp of the brush included in the stroke. The lower values give smoother strokes, whereas the higher values are likely to give dotted effects.

Using Shape Dynamics

- **Step 1:** Enable Shape Dynamics via the Brush Settings panel. Shape Dynamics will change the shape of your brush depending on pressure, angle, and direction throughout a stroke.

- **Step 2:** Now increase the Size Jitter to make each brush stamp randomly different in size. You can then make use of a Pen Tablet for varying the pressure.

- **Step 3:** You can further create organic variations for every stroke by playing with Angle Jitter and Roundness Jitter.

Scattering

- **Step 1:** Click the Scattering in the Brush Settings panel to introduce randomness into the position of the brush stroke.

- **Step 2:** Move the Scatter slider to distribute brush stamps along the path of the stroke, which produces a scattering effect. Additionally, use the Count to set the number of stamps in one stroke.

- **Step 3**: Select **Both Axes** to scatter the brush in several directions.

Adding Texture Brush

- **Step 1:** Click on the **Texture** in the panel of the Brush Settings, and add a texture overlay to the brush.

- **Step 2:** To make your brush textured look, click on the **Pattern Picker** and after that select a pattern. For this example, it will be much more useful for creating realistic effects, such as chalk or charcoal.

- **Step 3:** Scale, Depth, and Mode settings will let you set how much of the texture should be visible. You can also try Depth Jitter to have the texture change in intensity from stroke to stroke.

Saving and Managing Custom Brushes

Once you edit your brush, you will want to save your settings and use them in other projects.

Saving Your Custom Brush

- **Step 1:** First, open the Brush Preset Picker and click the **+** icon.

- **Step 2:** Give your custom brush a name and check any options you wish, which may include the Include Tool Settings box if you want to save specific settings for your brush.

- **Step 3:** Click **OK** to close and add your new brush to the library.

Organizing Brushes

- **Step 1:** To access the Brush Preset Manager, go under **Window > Brushes**.

- **Step 2:** Here, in this, you can make new groups; rename, duplicate, or delete them to organize your library.

- **Step 3:** Drag and drop brushes into groups to categorize them by project or type.

Advanced Tips for Brush Customization

Using Dual Brush

- **Step 1:** Open the Brush Settings panel and then choose the **Dual Brush option**. It will join two brush tips for a special effect.

- **Step 2:** Choose any secondary brush tip and, in turn, alter a few settings such as Size, Spacing, and Scatter to allow proper blending of the two brushes.

- **Step 3:** Now, try out the brush on your canvas, as each combination may work out differently according to the blending mode chosen.

Setting Smoothing for Accuracy

- **Step 1**: In the Options bar, check **Smoothing**. By checking this option, it smoothes the brushstrokes and is convenient in inking and when precision is required.

- **Step 2:** Slide the **Smoothing Percentage** to the right to increase the amount that Photoshop will smooth your stroke, or to the left for more free-form strokes. The higher the value, the steadier your line.

- **Step 3:** Experiment with Pulled String Mode and Catch-Up on Stroke End under Smoothing options for changing how Photoshop handles an intricate or rapid stroke.

Creating and Saving Custom Brushes

Custom brushes in Photoshop grant artists and designers a great deal of latitude. From simple shapes to intricate textures, the ability to create custom brushes lets you personalize your work.

Understanding Brush Basics

- **Accessing Brush Settings**: Open the Brush Settings panel by going to **Window > Brush Settings**.

- **Exploring Default Brushes**: Take note of some of the default brushes available to you within Photoshop's Brush Preset panel, as many shapes, textures, and effects are covered.

Creating a New Brush from Scratch

Step 1: Open a New Document

- Open a new document; select **File > New**. Set a canvas size to your liking for your intended brush, e.g. 500x500 px.

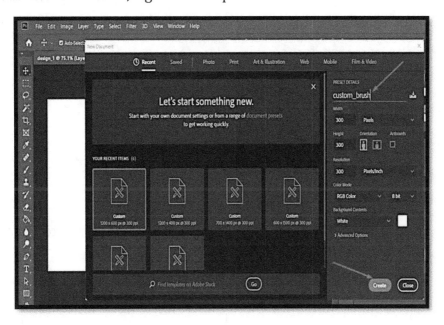

Step 2: Define Brush Shape

- Using any of the shape drawing tools in Photoshop, like the Brush Tool (B), the Pen Tool (P), or the Custom Shape Tool (U), draw an outline or a design that you want to be your brush.
- You can also create textures and patterns and even shapes composed of text.
- Adjust the Opacity and Hardness of your design to control how it will appear when used as a brush.

Step 3: Convert to a Brush Tip

- Once you have your desired shape or design, select using **Ctrl+A** for Windows or **Cmd+A** for Mac to select all the canvas.

- Go to **Edit > Define Brush Preset**.

- Name your brush in the dialog box that opens and click **OK**.

Step 4: Refining Brush Settings

- Enter into the Brush Settings panel to edit your newly created brush. Now in the Brush Settings, you can play with settings such as Shape Dynamics, Scattering, and Transfer.

- Press any settings to produce an effect, such as responses to pressure or texturing.

Exploring Key Brush Settings

Each one of these brush settings enables further customization. Following is a description of the most influential settings involved:

- **Shape Dynamics:** Controls size, angle, and roundness jitter of the brush stroke.

- **Scattering**: It controls how the brush shapes would be scattered around on the canvas.

- **Texture**: Adds texture to the brush to achieve special effects.

- **Transfer**: Controls opacity and flow jitter for a natural stroke-like feel.

- **Dual Brush**: Allows combining two brush tips for complex shapes.

- **Brush Tip Shape**: Allows adjusting the spacing, angle, and roundness of a brush tip.

Saving Custom Brushes

Step 1: Open the Brushes Panel

- Open the Brushes panel by going to **Window > Brushes,** which is where you'll save and manage your new brushes.

Step 2: Save Brush Preset

- Click the **Create New Brush icon** at the bottom of the Brushes panel, or select **Brush Settings > Create New Brush Preset** with your brush selected.

- A dialog box opens in which you get to name your brush and choose options to include-size, for example, and color dynamics.

- Click **OK** to save your brush.

Step 3: Organizing Brushes

- Drag and drop your newly created brush into Groups within the Brushes panel so that your brushes are organized.

- You can also export your brush as a .abr file by selecting **Export Selected Brushes** in the menu of the Brush Settings. This file can be imported later or shared with others.

Using Your Custom Brushes

- To use your brush, select the **Brush Tool** via (**B**) then locate your brush saved via Brushes.

- Add all settings with **Size** and **Opacity** to what will work for you with each project.

- Try tuning brush settings, such as **Flow** and **Smoothing** for more detailed strokes.

Dual Brush, Scattering, And Texture Usage in Realism

Getting Started with Brush Settings

To access the advanced options of brushes in Photoshop 2025, follow these steps: Click to select the Brush tool in the toolbar or select it using the keyboard hotkey **B**. It will open the Brush Settings Panel on the right-hand side; if you can't see it, go to **Window > Brush Settings**.

Dual Brush: Creating Complex Brush Textures

The Dual Brush allows you to incorporate two different brushes in one, creating a much more subtle layering effect that is very good for adding realism to textured objects such as foliage, fur, or skin. Here's how to set it up:

1. Open the **Brush Settings Panel** and choose your base brush.

2. Under the Brush Settings menu, tick the box marked Dual Brush; this opens extra options for customizing.

3. **Choose the Secondary Brush**: Below your primary brush, you will need to choose a secondary that complements your primary brush. Experiment with different combinations of brush shapes to obtain authentic texture.

    *   The soft round brush and the rough texture combine to create soft and irregular edges, which are perfect for an organic shape.

4. **Choose your Blend Mode**: Choose the blend mode available under Dual Brush settings that determine how the two brushes interact. The three most common modes are:

    *   **Multiply**: Darkens the texture effect to give depth.
    *   **Overlay**: Highlights edges and textures, perfect for detailed work.

5. **Scale and Spacing**: Under Scale, use the **Size slider** to set the size of the secondary brush in relationship to the primary brush; use the Spacing slider to adjust the frequency of the pattern.

Application Tip: Use the Dual Brush to apply foliage by choosing a dispersed, textured secondary brush. Adjust **Size Jitter** and **Angle Jitter** for strokes that are more organic and that vary.

Scattering: Adding Organic Randomness to Brush Strokes

Scattering spreads the brush strokes within an area of a selected size, giving the appearance of the strokes occurring randomly. This can be used to achieve patterned designs such as grass, leaves, or even starry skies.

1. **Enable the Scattering option from within the Brush Settings Panel:** Click the **Scattering** checkbox.

2. **Set the Scattering Quantity**: The Scattering slider determines how much your particles will scatter from the stroke. High values of Scattering will spread the particles apart, while low values will have them closer together.

3. **Count**: Determines how many copies the brush will make with one stroke.

4. **Count Jitter**: Adds a random fluctuation to the number of particles created per stroke so that each stroke with a brush will be different.

5. **Control Dynamics by Pen Pressure (Optional):** If you have a pressure-sensitive tablet, under the Control section check the box next to Pen Pressure. It will scale the amount of scattering depending on how hard you press. This adds a great extra level of control.

Application Tip: For snow or falling leaves, use high Scatter and Count Jitter. For finer details, such as adding freckles or dust, a low Scatter value and close-together particles do the trick.

Texture: Adding Realistic Surface Detail

The Texture feature allows you to add surface details to brush strokes-a very important feature when painting skin, stone, or wood.

1. **Enable the Texture option in the Brush Settings Panel:** In the menu option for Texture, choose a pattern from its drop-down list.
   - Photoshop 2025 has several pre-set textures. To load your custom textures, go to **Settings > Import Texture**.
2. **Scale the Texture**: This Scale slider will adjust the size of the texture. The bigger its scale, the more pronounced the texture will be, and a smaller scale adds subtlety.
3. **Depth**: The amount of Depth regulates how deeply the texture should show up on the brush. High depth adds contrast, while lower values create soft textures.
4. **Blend Mode**: To see how the texture merges with the color of the brush, choose a way of blending. For realistic textures:
   - **Multiply** works wonders when the purpose is to add shadows and depth.
   - **Overlay** can be used to give textures a slight 3D pop effect.
5. **Depth Jitter**: Introduces randomness into the depth of the texture, useful for faking irregular surfaces.

Application Tip: To paint skin textures, choose a subtle skin pore texture and set Depth and Scale low. For stone or rough surfaces, bump up Depth and switch to Multiply mode for more pronounced texture.

Brush Tool Settings: Flow, Opacity, Smoothing, and Pressure Sensitivity
Flow

Flow in Photoshop essentially sets the amount of paint that is being applied to the canvas as airbrushing would. By lowering the Flow setting, softer easier strokes ensue-building up colors after multiple strokes.

Usage:

1. Select the **Brush Tool (B)** from the toolbar.

2. On the top toolbar, you'll find the **Flow** setting beside Opacity.

3. Adjust Flow either by typing a value in its field or using the slider.

4. **Exercise**: Set Flow very low, say 10-20%, and paint several strokes in a single spot. Watch how the paint builds up into a soft layered appearance.

Tips:

- For smooth feathered blending, low Flow, and Opacity.

- The highest Flow works best for solid, completely opaque strokes, while lower values give more control in detailing.

Opacity

Opacity sets the level of transparency for each stroke and, therefore, how much of the background will be visible. Lower opacity creates lighter, more transparent strokes.

Usage:

1. With the Brush Tool active, find the Opacity setting in the top toolbar.

2. Either pull the slider or key in a number from 0% completely transparent to 100% fully opaque.

3. **Exercise**: Put Opacity between 30-50% and paint anywhere on the canvas with multiple strokes over each other. You will notice that it is semi-transparent since the applied color allows some shade to be noticeable.

Tips:

- Low values of Opacity are used for subtle shadowing and highlighting.

- Mix Opacity with the variation of Flow to achieve smooth transitions, and blending - this may be useful in Digital Painting and image retouching.

Smoothing

Smoothing keeps your lines clean and controlled by reducing jitter in hand-drawn strokes. That's useful if you draw with a tablet or freehand.

Usage:

1. Select the **Brush Tool** and click the top toolbar for Smoothing (it's represented by a percentage).

2. To change the Smoothing percentage from 0% to 100%, click it to set the amount of stabilization Photoshop will apply to your strokes.

3. **Exercise**: Try drawing a curved line with a Smoothing set to 0%, and then draw one with a Smoothing set between 50% - 70%. You will be able to tell that the steadiness and flow of the line is different.

Tips:

- Smoothing at a high setting is great for inking and creating very detailed line work.

- Click on the icon of the gear to open the Preferences menu. You can modify Pulled String Mode for even smoother paths and Catch-Up settings for better line accuracy.

Pressure Sensitivity (for Pen Tablet Users)

It allows the responsiveness of brush settings to pressure applied on a tablet pen, especially in creating strokes that simulate natural media, like pencil and ink.

Usage:

1. Connect and calibrate your pen tablet (e.g., Wacom, Huion) to Photoshop.

2. After selecting the Brush Tool, open **Brush Settings** via **Window > Brush Settings**.

3. Enable **Shape Dynamics** and, under Size Jitter, enable **Control** to Pen Pressure. Here, the size of the brush will vary with pen pressure.

4. Then check **Transfer** [Other Dynamics] to have it controlled with pen pressure for either **Opacity** or **Flow**.

5. **Exercise**: With your pen start painting lightly and with continuously increasing pressure on your pen, notice how brush thickness and opacity change.

Tips:

- Experiment with **Minimum Diameter** under Shape Dynamics to control the minimum size of your brush when light pressure is applied.

- Combine Pressure Sensitivity with Flow and Opacity gives a more traditional feel to the painting, especially useful in digital art and retouching.

These settings give you pretty good control over the active behavior of the brushes, making it easier to get all kinds of different effects-from smooth shading to dynamic, expressive strokes.

How to use the Mixer Brush and Smudge Tool

The Mixer Brush Tool in Photoshop truly mimics the real-life mixing of paints. As you stroke your virtual brush across the canvas, colors mix. In this way, it gives a relaxed feel to traditional painting and has hence become popular among digital artists since it creates a real look. Mixer Brushes enable wetness, paint load, and mix control that spans from heavy strokes to delicate blending effects.

How to Use Mixer Brush Tool

1. **Choose Mixer Brush Tool**: Launch Photoshop and select **Mixer Brush Tool** from the menu of Brush Tools in the toolbar.

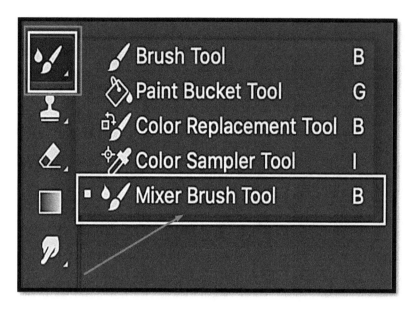

2. **Adjust Brush Settings:** Go to the **Options** bar where you'll find a set of options dedicated to Mixer Brush:

- **Wet**: This sets how much paint the Mixer brush will pick up and mix. The higher you go with the value, the more liquid the brush will be and your stroke wet and mixed.

- **Load**: Choose how much paint there would be on your brush when you start making a stroke.

- **Mix**: Controls the ratio of the canvas color against the color of the brush. That is, a high mix uses more canvas color, while a low mix relies more on the brush color.

- **Flow**: This controls the opacity of paint, as it does for other brush tools.

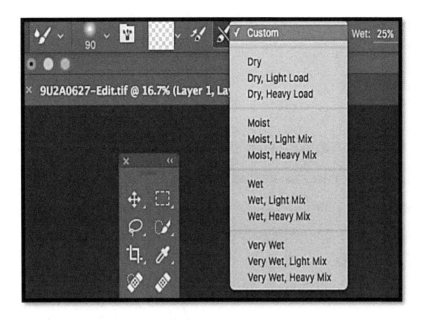

3. **Adapter Brush Tip Shape and Hardness:**

- Click to select a preferred size and shape of the brush you will use. You will see options under the panel of "**Brush Settings**" which can be opened via **Window > Brush Settings**.

- Adjust **Hardness** for a softer or more defined edge.

4. **Choose Blending Options**:

- **Sample All Layers**: Check this box if you want the Mixer Brush to consider the contents of all visible layers, not just the current layer.

- **Load Solid Colors Only**: If enabled, this prevents varied colors from being picked up with the brush; this is useful if you want to paint with only one color.

5. **Begin Painting:**

- Click and drag on the canvas to start mixing colors. Experiment with different Wet and mixed values to see how colors blend and/or interact.

Tip: Permit more subtle blending of colors at lower Mix and Wet settings.

6. **Reload Color**:

- By default, the Mixer Brush will sustain your paint load until you pick up a new color. To reload the color, you will check **Load Brush After Each Stroke** in the Options Bar.

Advanced Techniques with the Mixer Brush

1. **Blending for Realistic Skin Tones:** Apply the base color first, then select a lighter and a darker tone for a blending palette. Mixer Brush set to **low Wet** will allow tone blending for skin shading to be smooth and realistic.

2. **Create Painterly Effects:**

   - To simulate oil or acrylic paint effects, use high **Wet** and high Load **settings** and make broad, texturally-rich brush strokes.

   - Experiment with **Brush Tip Shape** to introduce some variability into brush strokes. You could try some of the textured brushes in the Brush Library to give a more 'painted' feel.

3. **Color Mixing on Palette**: Create a blank layer to use as a palette. Load colors onto this layer and, with the Mixer Brush loaded, mix and custom color before picking up to apply to the main artwork.

4. **Using Layers for Non-Destructive Painting**:

   - Place each color or effect on a new layer to adjust or erase without affecting the whole artwork.

   - Set each layer blending mode to Multiply or Overlay to create depth.

Introduction to Smudge Tool

The Smudge Tool allows you to create an effect as though you were dragging or smearing paint on a surface. This tool offers a smooth, flowing way to blend or distort areas. Unlike the Mixer Brush, it doesn't add or mix paint; it pushes pixels around. It comes in handy for wispy effects, softening edges, or creating soft transitions between colors.

Using the Smudge Tool

1. **Select the Smudge Tool:** Find the Smudge Tool in the Tools panel (Shortcut R). It's grouped with the Blur Tool and Sharpen Tool.

2. **Choose a Brush:**
   - Open the Brush Settings via **Window > Brush Settings**, then select a brush tip for the desired effect.
   - Adjust the Size and Hardness settings to control the size and definition of the smudge effect.

3. **Adjust Strength Settings:**
   - In the Options Bar, you have Strength. The higher the strength, the more radical will be the smudging of pixels and vice versa. This may sound too technical, but briefly, a high strength will give more extreme or dramatic results, while a low one will provide very subtle ones.

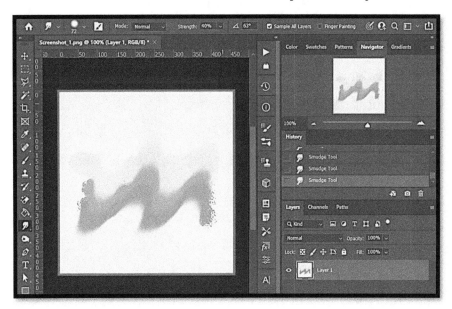

- **Tip**: It's best to first work with a low strength, 15-20%, in smooth, controlled smudges, and then increase if you feel like you want a more intense effect.

4. **Enable Sample All Layers**: By checking this option in the Options Bar, you will be able to drag pixels onto other layers (the Smudge Tool) from any layer. This is of particular use when it comes to composite artwork.

5. **Use Finger Painting**: Enable this to allow the Smudge Tool to add color to the smudge effect. If enabled, the foreground color will be applied at the start of every stroke-perfect for creating light sources or giving hints of color within the smudge.

6. **Begin Smudging:**
    - Click and drag to perform the smudging in your image. Shorter strokes allow tight control, while longer strokes will give sweeping effects.
    - Experiment with different pressures on your tablet to achieve a variation in the smudge intensity.

Advanced Techniques with Smudge Tool

1. **Blending Edges of Digital Paintings:** For lower strength settings, the Smudge Tool will blend the hard edges in digital portraits, landscapes, or abstract art into smooth transitions and soft focus.

2. **Add Motion and Speed Effects**: Use the Smudge Tool in fast swipes over an object to indicate speed or motion blur. This works well on backgrounds or for special action effects.

3. **Smoothing and Texturing Details**: Once textures or patterns have been added, it is possible with a small brush, at medium strength, to make use of the Smudge Tool in blending or softening regions to render natural looks with textures of hair or fabrics.

4. **Creating Ethereal and Dreamy Effects**: By smudging the edges and details of the highlights or bright areas, you get to have a glowing or dreamy effect around the subjects.

CHAPTER SEVEN

SHAPES AND VECTOR TOOLS

Working with Shape Tools: Rectangle, Ellipse, Polygon, and Custom Shape Options

Accessing the Shape Tools

1. **Location:** The shape tools are located in the Toolbar to the left of the workspace.

2. **Dropdown Selection**: Click and drag on the **Rectangle Tool icon**, or select **U** on your keyboard to access the shape tool options including Rectangle, Ellipse, Polygon, Line, and Custom Shape.

3. **Selecting a Shape Tool:** Any of these tools can be selected based on requirements in design.

Rectangle Tool

Creating a Rectangle:

*   In the toolbar, select the **Rectangle tool**.

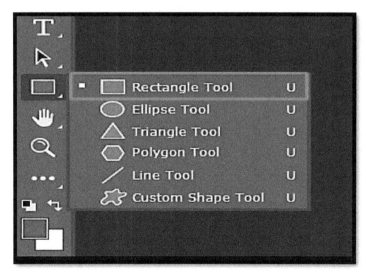

- Click and drag anywhere in the canvas to draw a rectangle shape.
- To draw a perfect square, hold the **Shift key** down while dragging.

Customizing Rectangle Properties:

- **Fill and Stroke**: By using the Options Bar available at the top of the screen, you can change the fill color and stroke (border) color.
- **Size and Proportions**: Exactly define width and height values under the Properties Panel for full control over rectangle dimensions.
- **Rounded Corners**: Adjusting for corner radii is now in real-time in Photoshop 2025. Adjust the corner radius directly from the shape or by inserting values via the Properties Panel.

Ellipse Tool

Creating an Ellipse:

- Click the **Ellipse Tool** in the Toolbar.
- Click anywhere in the canvas and drag to draw an ellipse.
- To draw a perfect circle, hold **Shift** while dragging.

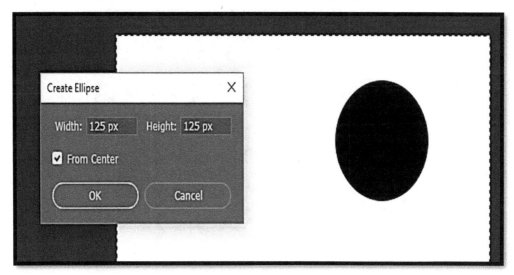

Customizing Ellipse Properties:

- **Fill and Stroke:** Fill and stroke can be edited from the Options Bar to change color and outline.

- **Proportions**: Accurate width and height can be specified in the Properties Panel.

- **Blending Options**: Outer glow, inner shadow, and pattern overlays are just some of the Layer Styles that can be used with the shape.

Designing Tips for Precision:

- **Center the Shape**: With **Alt** (Option on Mac), click and drag on the canvas to draw from the center out.

- **Mask with Ellipses**: Draw an ellipse as a clipping mask over photos or text for interesting design effects.

Using the Polygon Tool

Creating a Polygon:

- Access the **Polygon Tool** via the Toolbar.

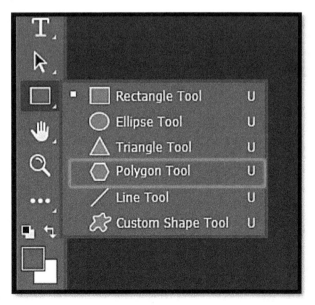

- In the Options Bar, input the number of sides for the polygon. A minimum of 3 sides can be used.

- Click and drag to draw the polygon. Hold **Shift** to constrain symmetrically.

Editing Polygon Properties

- **Fill and Stroke**: For fill and stroke settings, the Options Bar is where you want to go.

- **Corner Radius:** Live corner rounding of polygons is supported in Photoshop 2025. To edit these, use the Properties Panel or drag the handles at the corners of the shape.

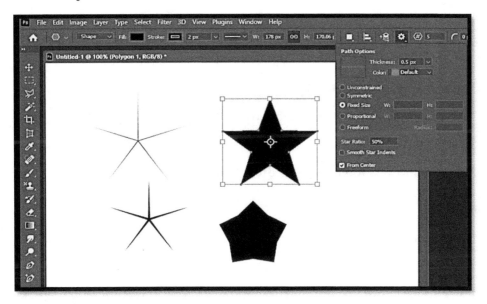

Advanced Techniques for Polygons

- **Star Shapes:** To create star polygons, enter a star ratio via the Options Bar.

- **Align and Distribute:** Use alignment properties in the Properties Panel to evenly distribute multiple polygons on the canvas.

Using the Custom Shape Tool

Creating a Custom Shape:

- The Custom Shape Tool is available through the Toolbar.

- The Shape Picker is available in the Options Bar which shows a list of custom shapes.

- Select one of them and click-and-drag on the canvas to draw the shape.

Editing Custom Shape Properties:

- **Shape Library**: By default, Photoshop 2025 has a set of loaded custom shapes, including arrows, icons, and symbols.

- **Fill and Stroke**: In the Options Bar, you are allowed to edit the fill and stroke colors.

- **Resizing and Transformation**: Once drawn, one can use **Ctrl + T**, **Command + T** for Mac, to transform the shape into resizing, rotating, or skewing it.

Adding New Custom Shapes:

- **Import Shapes:** To import new custom shapes into the menu, go to **Window > Shapes > Settings Menu** and click on **Import Shapes**.

- **Save as a Custom Shape:** You can create any unique path you want and save it as a custom shape through **Edit > Define Custom Shape**.

Uses of Custom Shapes:

- **Icon Design**: The ability to handle and work with custom shapes makes creating icons very easy when one is working on web and app design.

- **Pattern Making**: Repeating customized shapes in design can make up unique patterns or backgrounds.

Transformations and Adjustments with Shape Tool

1. **Free Transform Mode**: Pressing **Ctrl + T** while having any shape layer selected will take you into a Free Transform mode. You can scale, rotate, or distort the shape.

2. **Working with Warp Options:** Upon going into the Free Transform mode, you'll find an option bar for warp settings to reshape a selected shape.

3. **Layer Masks with Shapes**: Use shape layers as masks over images by right-clicking and selecting **Create Clipping Mask** to start creating soft-edged photos within geometric frames.

Creating and Editing Paths: Vector-Based Selections and Editing with the Path Tool

Intro to Vector-Based Selections and Paths

- **Overview of Paths:** Unlike pixel-based selections, paths are vector-based, thus never suffering from quality degradation when scaled.
- **Why Use Paths:** Paths come in useful when highly detailed selections are required, like object isolation, clipping paths, and other complex shapes.
- **Primary Tools for Paths:** There are several ways to work with paths inside of Photoshop 2025; the most key tools are the Pen Tool, the Direct Selection Tool, and the Path Selection Tool.

Setting Up the Workspace

- **Create New Document**: Select **File > New**, select canvas size and make sure it is fit for vector work.
- **To Access Path Panel**: Select **Window > Paths**, to open the **'Paths'** panel where you'll manage and store your paths.

Creating Paths with the Pen Tool

To Use the Pen Tool:

- Click on the pen tool icon on the toolbar or just press **P**.
- Make sure in the top options bar the selection says Path and not Shape.

Basic Path Creation Steps:

1. **Click to Add Anchor Points**: When clicked, each click adds an anchor point that creates a straight segment.

2. **Drag for Curved Segments:** On clicking and dragging, it creates a control handle that adjusts the curvature of the path.

3. **Ending the Path:** Close a path by hovering over the starting point until it shows a little circle, then select it.

Editing Anchor Points:

- Individual points can be selected using the **Direct Selection Tool (A).**

- To alter curvature, move the handles of the anchor points

4. **Editing Paths with Path Selection and Direct Selection Tools**

    Path Selection Tool (Black Arrow): Similar to the **'Move'** tool it will select the path as a whole or multiple paths at once.

    - **To move paths:** Just click and drag any path anywhere over the canvas.

    - **To transform the paths:** Go to **Edit > Free Transform Path** by which you can scale, rotate, or even skew your path.

Direct Selection Tool (White Arrow): Allows for highly detailed changes in moving the location of an anchor point or handle.

- **Modifying Curves and Segments:** Click an anchor point and adjust its control handles to fine-tune the curve's shape.

- **Adding/Deleting Points:** Right-click on the path, and choose **Add Anchor Point Tool** or Delete Anchor Point Tool to refine the path.

Converting Selections to Paths and Paths to Selections

Create a Selection from a Path:

1. Choose any of the selection tools; for example, Lasso or Marquee tools.

2. Go to **Select** and select **Make Work Path**; set a Tolerance Amount (the higher the more general the path will be).

Making a Selection from a Path:

- In the Paths panel, right-click on your path and select **Make Selection**. A path that has been turned into a selection useful in editing an image where you want to isolate part of the image from the rest.

Saving and Managing Paths

- **Saving Paths:** Working in the Paths panel, you will double-click this Work Path name because if you do not save it, Photoshop will discard it when you create a new path.

- **Creating Multiple Paths:** If you want to work with multiple paths, you need only create a new path in the Paths panel. You then can turn any of these sets on or off.

Troubleshooting Common Path Issues

- **Path Not Visible:** Check that Path is turned on within the settings of the Pen Tool. Additionally, check layer visibility and opacity.

- **Misaligned Anchor Points:** Use Snap To settings under View to align precisely with guides or grid lines.

- Difficulty Creating Smooth Curves: These are made by adjusting the length and angles of the handle in the Convert Point Tool or the Direct Selection Tool.

Resizing, Rotating, and Warping Shape Layers

Resizing Shape Layers

Scaling shapes in Photoshop is done by scaling which changes the size without loss of quality. Shape layers retain a clear, crisp edge even if size changes have been imparted due to the vector nature that they exhibit.

The steps:

1. **Identify the Shape Layer**: In the Layers panel, click through to the shape layer you want to resize.

2. **Activate the Transform Controls**: Press **Ctrl + T** (Windows) or **Cmd + T** (Mac) to invoke the Free Transform bounding box around the shape.

3. **Resize the Shape**: With any of the corners of the bounding box, click and drag to scale the shape proportionally. While holding down Shift allows you to freely scale it without maintaining the aspect ratio.

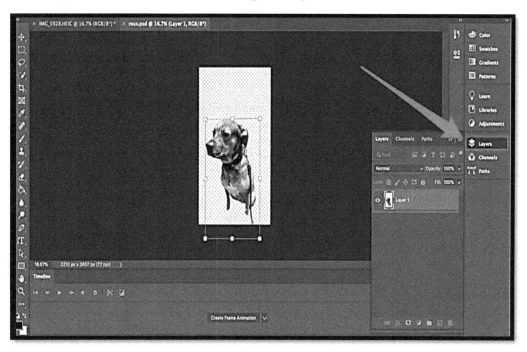

4. **Confirm the Resize**: Confirm the resize by hitting **Enter** on Windows or **Return** on Mac.

Hint: If you need the dimensions to be specific, you have the option to specify the exact width and height in the Properties Panel using the visible settings for Transform.

Rotating Shape Layers

Rotating shapes can add energy, style, or orientation to your design, which especially comes in handy when you're working with logos, icons, and other purely decorative elements.

Rotation Steps:

1. **Select Shape Layer**: Click to select the shape layer that you want to rotate from the Layers Panel.

2. **Enable the Transform Tool:** Select **Ctrl + T** for Windows users or **Cmd + T** for Mac users and this would engage the Free Transform tool.

3. **Rotate the Shape**: Hover just outside a corner of the bounding box until you see a curved, double-headed arrow. Click and drag to rotate the shape to whatever angle you want.

4. **Set a Specific Angle**: If you want a precise angle, you can set it through the Options Bar at the top by specifying a certain angle within the rotation field.

5. **Apply the Rotation**: Tap **Enter** or **Return** to confirm.

Pro Tip: You can also right-click (or Control-click) on the shape with the transform controls activated and choose **Rotate 90° Clockwise, Rotate 90° Counterclockwise**, or **Flip Horizontally/Vertically** for quick rotations.

Warping Shape Layers

Warping shapes offer the flexibility to create unique distortions that will enable you to mold a shape to fit a particular design or to add creative flair.

How to Warp Shapes:

1. **Select and Activate Free Transform**: Once the shape layer is selected, the short cut for Free Transform in Windows is **Ctrl + T**, while on Mac, it is **Cmd + T**.

2. **Enable Warp Mode**: With the transform box enabled, right-click anywhere within the box and, from the context menu, choose **Warp**.

3. **Change Warp Controls**: It overlays the shape with a grid with handles at each corner and the center of every side. Pull these to stretch, bend, or otherwise warp the shape.

4. **Use Warp Presets**: Up in the top Options Bar, there's a dropdown menu listing several warp presets including Arc, Bulge, Flag, and several others. Click to select one, then adjust the Bend percentage to see it from mild to wild.

5. **Custom Warp Adjustments**: For complete control, click and drag individual points in the grid, or make use of the Split Warp option in the Options Bar for even more precise manipulations.

6. **Confirm Warp Adjustments**: Once satisfied, hit **Enter** or **Return** to apply the warp.

Expert Tips:

- **Reset Warping**: Need a fresh start? If so, click the **Reset Warp button** in the Options Bar, and the shape returns to its original form.

- **Refine with Liquify**: If you want more subtle distortion, you can also use the Liquify Filter on top of warping for subtle adjustments.

Fill and Stroke Options: Color, Gradient, and Pattern Fills for Shapes

Shape Fill and Stroke Options

Step 1: Create or Select a Shape

- Open your project or start a new file in Photoshop.

- Select **Shape Tool** from the toolbar, and select one of the options of shapes that you will create.

- Click and drag on your canvas to draw your shape.

- While the shape is still selected, go to the **Properties Panel** on the right.

Step 2: Access the Fill and Stroke Options

- You will find options for **Fill** and **Stroke** in the Properties Panel.

- The Fill box opens up the options for Fill when clicked.

- You'll find the Stroke box, where you can also apply colors or patterns to the stroke of your shape.

Apply Fill Options

Color Fill

- To fill your shape with a solid color fill, click **Color** in the Fill Options panel.
- A color picker will open; you can either choose a color or use the color code to achieve accurate coloring using RGB, HEX, etc.
- Click **OK** to fill it with color.

Gradient Fill

1. In the Fill options, click the box beside **'Gradient'**.
2. A preview of the gradient will be shown in the form of a default gradient - click on that to open the **Gradient Editor**.
3. In the Gradient Editor:
   - Click to pull up the Gradient menu, where you can select a default gradient or create a custom one by clicking and dragging the color stops at either end of the gradient bar.
   - Click on each color stop to edit the color of that gradient stop or add color stops by clicking anywhere along the gradient bar.
   - Change the **Angle** of the gradient to specify the direction in which your shape will fill.
   - Scale adjusts the size of the gradient inside your shape.
4. Once you are satisfied with your gradient, click **OK** to apply the gradient.

Fill Pattern

1. In the Fill options, select **Pattern**.
2. A sample of the pattern will appear - select the drop-down to view pattern preset options.

3. Choose one of the numerous patterns provided or select **Custom Patterns** to import additional patterns.

4. The Scale slider will enlarge and reduce the size of the pattern within your shape. Smaller percentages will reduce the size of the pattern and repeat it more; larger ones will increase the scale.

5. Click **OK** to fill your shape with the pattern.

Apply Stroke Options

Stroke Color

1. In the Stroke box, select **Color**.

2. In the color picker, decide on a filling color for your stroke or even type in a color code if you need it more accurate.

3. Click **OK** to set the stroke color.

Gradient Stroke

1. In the Stroke options, choose **Gradient**.

2. Click the preview of the gradient to edit it. You can adjust the gradient colors and angle just as you have done for the fill gradient.

3. Click **OK** when complete.

Pattern Stroke

1. In the option for Stroke, select **Pattern**.

2. Choose a pattern in the list or, if available, use custom patterns.

3. In the pattern scale adjust the scale to match the stroke size.

4. Click **OK** to set the pattern stroke.

Stroke Settings Adjustment

1. **Size**: From Stroke settings, the Size slider is available to adjust the stroke's thickness.

2. **Position**: Set the stroke position inside, center, or outside according to the outline of the shape.

3. **Blend Mode**: Choose other blend modes for creative effects of how the stroke will interact with either a fill color or a background.

4. **Opacity**: Make your stroke transparent using the Opacity slider.

Path Operations and Combining Shapes

Setting Up Your Document and Accessing the Shape Tool

1. Open Photoshop 2025, then create a new document by going to **File > New** or **Ctrl+N**.

2. Set your document size, resolution, and background color to your liking, then click **Create**.

3. Select the **Shape Tool** from the Tools Panel, located on the left side-the default shortcut is **U**. In this set, Photoshop has Rectangle, Ellipse, Polygon, Line, and Custom Shape.

Creating Basic Shapes

1. Select the **Shape Tool** that you want to use, such as Rectangle.

2. Click and drag on the canvas to draw your shape. To create a perfect square or circle, hold down **Shift**.

3. If needed, refine the **Fill** and **Stroke** settings in the Options Bar at the top.

Using Path Operations through the Options Bar

If you have drawn at least two shapes, proceed to unite them using Path Operations.

1. In the Layers Panel, click to select one of your shape layers.

2. With the Shape Tool still selected, go up into the top Options Bar, where you will find Path Operations:

    - Combine Shapes (Add)
    - Subtract Front Shape

- Intersect Shape Areas
- Exclude Overlapping Shapes

3. Select a **Path Operation** based on your desired outcome.

Combining Shapes (Add)

1. Make the Shape Tool active and be on a shape layer.

2. Over your first shape, draw your second shape.

3. In the Options Bar, select **Combine Shapes**. The two shapes will now combine into one path.

Subtracting Shapes

1. Activate your **Shape Tool** and make sure you are on the shape layer you want to modify.

2. With the new shape overlapping the old, select **Subtract Front Shape** in the Options Bar.

3. It would remove the area of the new shape from the old one.

Intersecting Shapes

1. Have your shape layer selected and draw a second shape over it.

2. Under the Path Operations in the Options Bar, click on the option labeled **Intersect Shape Areas**.

3. Only the intersection part between the two shapes will remain.

Excluding Overlapping Shapes

1. With the shape layer active, click to create a new intersecting shape.

2. In the Path Operations area select **Exclude Overlapping Shapes**.

3. This will delete any overlapping portions, leaving just the 'negative space.'

Managing Shapes and Paths in the Layers Panel

1. Once shapes have been merged, the resulting new combined shape will be represented in the Layers Panel as one single shape layer.

2. To edit the individual paths, you'll need to select the shape layer and then choose the **Path Selection Tool** to move or adjust the individual paths.

3. Right-clicking on the shape layer in the Layers Panel and choosing **Convert to Smart Object** will retain the shape combination but still allow for edits.

Stroke and Fill Adjustment

1. You can adjust the **Fill** and **Stroke** of combined shapes by selecting the combined shape layer.

2. In the Properties Panel, you can edit:

   - **Fill Color** to define the color of the main color of the shape.
   - **Stroke Color** and **Width** if you want an outline for your shape.

Saving and Exporting Your Combined Shapes

1. Once you have combined shapes to your liking, open the **File Menu** and select **Save As** to save your document as a PSD for future edits.

2. To export your merged shapes as an image, go to **File > Export > Export As**, then select the file format you want to save it as, such as PNG or JPEG.

CHAPTER EIGHT

BLENDING MODES AND OPACITY

Detailed Overview of Each Blending Mode Category

1. **Darken Blending Modes**

   These modes finally darken the overall image. They perform by comparing the base and blend color and maintaining the colors with the darker color.

   How to Use Darken Blending Modes Steps

   1. Open your image in Photoshop 2025.
   2. On top of your base layer, create a new layer with the color or effect that you want to blend.
   3. Select the new layer, then in the Layers panel choose the Blending Mode drop-down menu.
   4. Choose any mode in the Darken group:
      - **Darken**: This mode retains only the darkest pixels of the two layers.
      - **Multiply**: Darkens, creating a rich effect as it multiplies the sum of the top pixel for darker shadows and tones.
      - **Color Burn**: Wanting luminance, the base layer darkens with added contrast.
      - **Linear Burn**: Brightness is reduced for an effect of deeper darkening beyond what Color Burn can achieve.
      - **Darker Color**: Only the darker color will appear.

5.   Adjust the layer opacity if needed to lighten the effect.

2. **Lighten Blending Modes**

These modes lighten the image by preserving the lighter of the base and the blend of colors.

How to Use Lighten Blending Modes

1.   Create a new layer with a light-colored gradient above your base layer.

2.   Apply the Lighten Blending Mode to the new layer:

- **Lighten**: Keeps the lightest pixels of the two layers.

- **Screen**: The overall lightens the image giving it a soft glow.

- **Color Dodge**: Operates through the brightening of the base color and adds contrast. Ideal for highlights.

- **Linear Dodge (Add):** Stronger brightening compared to Color Dodge.

- **Lighter Color**: Shows the lightest color.

3.   Adjust **Fine-tune the opacity** of the layer to control the intensity of the lightening effect.

3. **Contrast Blending Modes**

In these modes, the contrast is increased by darkening the darker regions while lightening up the lighter areas.

Steps to Apply Contrast Blending Mode

1. Duplicate the main image layer or create a new adjustment layer for applying any contrast effect.

2. Apply a Contrast Blending Mode:

   - **Overlay**: Probably the most standard default to add some kind of contrast.

   - **Soft Light**: This is similar in function to overlay, but it produces an extremely soft and often unobtrusive effect on contrast.

   - **Hard Light:** More contrasting than Soft Light, this might be good for saturation enhancement.

   - **Vivid Light**: It enhances the contrast, especially through darkening the shadows and brightening the highlights.

   - **Linear Light:** Stronger compared to vivid light.

   - **Pin Light:** Applies only dark or light pixels and discards midtones.

   - **Hard Mix**: A high contrast effect giving a posterized feel to an image.

3. To soften the effect more, reduce the opacity or fill with modes such as Hard Mix.

4. **Inversion Blending Modes**

These are a set of modes that allow the creation of special effects by inverting the colors.

How to Work with Inversion Blending Modes

1.   Add a new layer and fill it with a solid color or gradient.

2.   Select an Inversion Blending Mode:

- **Difference**: It compares the colors of layers and inverts them so that a peculiar effect can be achieved.

- **Exclusion**: Almost like Difference but with a more subtle effect, so very suitable for fancies of surreal or dream effects.

- **Subtract**: The blend layer is subtracted from the base, which results in a darker look.

- **Divide**: The base color is divided by the blend color, often the result is lighter looking.

3.   By using opaqueness, it is also possible to experiment to regulate the intensity of the effect.

5.   Component Blending Modes

These modes will allow you to alter individual color properties such as hue, saturation, or brightness.

How to Apply Component Blending Modes

1.   Click on the **'New adjustment layer'** or select an additional layer with a desired color effect.

2.   Select **Component Blending Mode**:

- **Hue**: Hue of the base layer gets replaced by the hue of the blend layer.

- **Saturation**: It keeps the saturation from the blend layer.

- **Color**: Results in retaining the luminosity of the base layer but its hue and saturation are changed.

- **Luminosity**: This preserves the hue and saturation of the base but then applies the blend's luminosity.

3.   Adjust layer opacity to soften the overall effect.

Practical Applications of Blending Modes: Using Multiply, Screen, Overlay, and More

Blending modes are powerful features that will enable Adobe Photoshop 2025 users to control how layers will interact with each other. You will be able to make dynamic compositions by adjusting the way colors blend, enhance lighting, add texture, and manipulate images in almost any way you can imagine. So, here we go:

Multiply: Darkening Images and Adding Shadows

Of all the darkening modes that blend a top layer with the underlying layer, perhaps one of the most used is indeed Multiply. Multiply multiplies the base color by the blend color, which always results in a darker color.

Practical Applications:

- **Darken Images**: Apply a Multiply layer to underexposed images, or for moodier scenes.
- **Adding Shadows**: Duplicate your image, put the top layer to Multiply, then mask in where you want shadows.
- **Making Richer Tones**: Lay color swatches over top to deepen and enrich color schemes in a photo.
- **Adding Depth to Textures**: Use Multiply to layer textures over an image for a grungy, vintage look of some sort.

You can combine Multiply with adjustment layers, like Levels, to control the intensity of the effect.

Screen: Lightening Images and Adding Glow

The Screen blending mode lightens the image by inverting the base and blending colors, multiplying them, and then inverting the result again. Thus, it is ideal for lightening images without losing their contrast or detail.

Practical Applications:

- **Lightening Dark Images**: If your image comes out too dark, adding a duplicate layer set to the Screen will bring out the highlights.
- **Adding Glow Effects**: The screen is great for adding glows around things such as light bulbs, fireflies, or any kind of magical effect.
- **Adding Lens Flare or Sun Effects**: Create a new layer with a circular gradient and make sure its mode is set to Screen. Then adjust the opacity to get a natural sunlight effect.
- **Portraits**: Place a Screen layer over an image of skin to give it a soft, glowing appearance.

Always use a low opacity of Screen layers to maintain that natural look, especially if you shoot portraits.

Overlay: Adding Contrast and Boosting Color

The overlay is a blend mode that introduces further contrast by darkening the dark areas and lightening the light ones. This is useful for when you want detail to pop, or for adding texture and depth to your image where a simple color shift isn't enough.

Practical Applications:

- **Landscapes with Accentuated Contrasts:** Use Overlay to develop a high-contrast landscape and give richness to the shadows and highlights.
- **Textures with Overlay Applied:** Adding a high-contrast grunge or paper texture at an Overlay blending mode is a real creative effect.

- **Vivid Color Adjustments**: This works pretty well for enhancing color tone, creating a wider dynamic range in flat images.
- **Dramatic Skies Added**: If you have duplicated the sky layer, everything gets an overlay blend mode here with opacity adjusted for dramatic and contrastive skies.

The overlay is quite strong, so mostly it gets softened by adjusting opacity levels or by masking off areas you want to retain in their original form.

Soft Light: Subtle Contrast and Gentle Effects

The soft light is similar to overlay but is subtler; it is great for portraits or areas where a touch-up is required. That is what you need when you want subtle, less-intense effects on the contrast.

Practical Applications:
- **Soften Highlights of Portraits**: Duplicate the portrait layer, apply Soft Light and mask areas that you want to retain soft.
- **Adding Subtle Shadows and Highlights:** You can add subtle controlled shadows and highlights with a low-opacity black or white brush to a Soft Light layer.
- **Dreamy Aesthetics:** Soft Light is pretty much used in wedding or portrait photography because it gives off that soft, dreamy look and does not over-saturate colors.
- **Subtle Texture on Surfaces**: Adding a low-opacity texture to a Soft Light layer enhances surfaces without overpowering the original image.

Set the opacity to get the right softness for the image and try to have the effect barely visible to retain a more natural look.

Color: Accurate Color Corrections Without Affecting Luminance

The Color blending mode sets the hue and saturation of the blend layer to the base layer, but it maintains the luminance of the base layer. This blending mode is perfect whenever color adjustments need to be performed without affecting light and shadow.

Practical Applications:

- **Colorize Black and White Photos**: Color a monotone photo on layers set to Color for realistic colorizing.

- **Tinting and Toning Images**: Progressively and subtly tint an image with a range of colored tints, including sepia tone, without affecting the shadows and highlights.

- **Correcting Skin Tones:** Apply a Color layer selectively to correct skin tones in portrait shots without overexposing the rest of the image.

- **Changing Object Colors**: Click on an object; add a Color layer and paint over it with a new color. This way, the object changes its color but does not lose its texture or shade.

Use a soft brush and carefully feather it around the edges for natural color change.

Difference: Unique Effects and Fine-tuning Alignment

Difference is often employed to achieve creative effects and becomes useful when you want to align layers by matching colors. Where the colors of both layers match exactly, Difference mode will produce black, so that misalignment is easily noticeable in a composition.

Practical Applications:

- **Checking Alignment**: Use Difference to align complicated elements, using a copy of the original on top of the edited version.

- **Abstract Art**: Using Different layers with duplicates creates a variety of psychedelic effects, especially when combined with gradients.

- **Stylized Photography Effects:** Apply Difference to parts of your image for an inverted-color effect. This works especially well in portraits, yielding surreal, and often artistic, results.

- **Contrasting Textures and Patterns:** Apply Difference to layered textures as a means of exploring dynamic contrasts along with interesting and often unpredictable combinations.

The Difference blend mode shines when used experimentally. Layer it over other modes of blending for various outcomes.

Practical Workflow Tips

- **Layer Masking:** Add layer masks with blending modes to effects only where necessary.

- **Blend If:** Use the **"Blend If"** sliders within Layer Style to target the highlights or shadows for added control.

- **Adjustment Layers**: Insert adjustment layers above or below blend layers to enable fine color, contrast, and exposure adjustments.

- **Opacity and Fill:** Do not forget to make use of opacity and fill settings for subtlety. Quite often, less is more.

Layer Opacity and Fill Adjustments: Differences and Effects of Opacity vs. Fill

Mastering the subtleties of Layer Opacity versus Fill in Adobe Photoshop 2025 will help you achieve the special effects you may want and give you finer control over how elements in your design look. Although both are under the Layers panel, Opacity and Fill controls have different purposes and will perform differently in your artwork.

First, let's explore the nature of both the Opacity and Fill adjustments, along with some practical examples of how best to utilize each.

The Basics: What are Opacity and Fill?

Opacity means the transparency of an entire layer refers to its content (canvas pixels, shapes, or images), as well as any layer styles applied to that layer, such as drop shadows, strokes, or outer glows.

Fill also controls transparency, but only for the content of the layer without affecting the layer styles applied to the layer. It means you can adjust the visibility of your main content independently of the visibility of the effects that you added using layer styles.

Although these two options are somewhat similar, their effects substantially diverge depending on the type of layer with which someone is working and the desired result. Knowing how each of them works will help you make better choices toward your goals of either a detailed or an eye-catching visual output.

Opacity Adjustment: Full Transparency Control

The Opacity slider is at the top of the Layers panel, allowing you to set a layer's overall opacity from 0% (fully transparent) to 100% (fully opaque). It applies both to the actual pixels or vectors on a layer, but also to any of its layer styles.

For example, consider this text layer with a drop shadow applied:

- 50% Opacity makes both text and drop shadow 50% visible.
- When it is at 0%, both text and drop shadow become fully transparent, thus disappearing completely.

This is useful when you want to uniformly degrade the layer's transparency along with all the effects applied to that layer. You may want to make such an adjustment in creating subtle overlays, softening images, or layering textures without overpowering other design elements.

When to Use Opacity Adjustments:

- **Texturing Background Layers**: If you want a layer not to compete visually but rather to subside into the background, using reduced Opacity will help it blend in.

- **Overlays and Effects:** Low Opacity on duplicated layers creates a soft ghosted effect perfect for enhancing photographic elements or composite.

- **Full Layer Effects**: In case of a layer having more than one style attached to it, such as shadow and bevel effects, and you want everything to fade at the same time, then you need to use Opacity.

Using Fill: Content-Only Transparency Control

While Opacity affects everything on the layer, Fill controls the visibility of just the main content of the layer (the pixels or shapes), without affecting the appearance of layer styles at all. It is that particular behavior that gives you more freedom to be creative because, most of the time, you want the effect styling to remain visible even after the primary layer content turns transparent.

To explain further: suppose you have a shape layer that has a stroke effect applied to it:

- It will also mean that, when you bring the Fill down to 0%, the actual shape disappears and only the stroke effect shows up.

- This does indeed allow for a sort of **'hollow'** or **'outlined'** shape type of effect where, in design, only the stroke appears.

This can come in handy when you want a text or a shape to show an effect, such as an Outer Glow, Stroke, or Shadow, with the original object hidden. That gives you some pretty cool visual effects that are simply impossible to get by using only Opacity.

When to Use Fill Adjustments:

- **Outlined Text Effects**: Filling up 0% on a text layer with a stroke applied creates an outlined text effect, which is in wide use in graphic design and logos.

- **Custom Glow or Shadow Effects**: If you want the glow or shadow to appear but not the content of the layer itself, lowering the Fill is pretty straightforward.

- **Layer Style Effects**: The Fill property is ideal for situations where the layer styles are predominant in the effect viewed. For instance, halo effects, illusions of frames, or patterns using styling above the base for visibility.

Advanced Effects with Combined Opacity and Fill

The magic happens when Opacity and Fill adjustments are used together. Balancing both sliders against each other offers the ability to create complex layering effects where a layer's content and the applied effects can have different levels of visibility. That way, you have fine-grained control over how each layer presents itself by being able to emphasize or de-emphasize various elements in your design.

To take a common example, consider a logo with multiple layer styles:

- This will set the fill of the logo to 0%, which means the logo itself won't be seen, but the glow, shadow, or stroke is visible outside. This can then be used for decoration purposes on your logo without the main text or shape visible.

- You can manage the opacity and fill so that the main element becomes semi-transparent and the shadow becomes fully viewable to show depth without overwhelming the rest of the composition.

Using Opacity and Fill Creatively in Designs

- **Play around with Styles of Layers**: In some of the effects, like bevel and emboss or outer glow, setting Fill at 0% might lead to an extraordinarily good and special look. For example, such adjustment might provide for so-called embossed or engraved effects in digital art or textured backgrounds.

- **Layer Mask Synergy**: Combine the use of Opacity with layer masks for subtle transparency applications that require parts of the layer to be retained while the rest are faded.

- **Smart Objects and Groups:** Remember that if working with smart objects or grouped layers, adjustments through Opacity and Fill apply to the whole group or object, thereby making it easier with complex designs.

Creating Double Exposure and Light Leak Effects

Double exposure and light leak effects have been leading trends in the worlds of digital art, photography, and graphic design. Thanks to Adobe Photoshop 2025, both these effects are more accessible than ever with advanced layer tools, advanced options for blending, and non-destructive editing.

Double Exposure Using Adobe Photoshop 2025

Double exposure involves merging two or more photos into one for a dramatically striking combination of details. This can range from overlaying a landscape within the subject's portrait to combining textures with shapes for artistic results. Let's explore making a simple double-exposure effect.

Step 1: Open and Prepare Your Images

1. **Select Your Base Images:** You will need to select two high-resolution images; for the first layer, preferably a portrait, while for the secondary layer, it could be a landscape or texture.

2. **Opening Images in Photoshop:** Choose **File > Open** > Select each file in a different tab.

Step 2: Set Up Your Layers

1. **Combine Images into a Single Document:** Drag one image onto the other image's canvas, or use **Select > All** and then **Edit > Copy** and **Edit > Paste,** bringing it onto the portrait layer.

2. **Convert Layers to Smart Objects:** Right-click on each layer then select **Convert to Smart Object.** Smart Objects will allow you to make edits to the placement and blending mode of the image non-destructively, affording you a bit more wiggle room as you're working.

Step 3: Change Blending Modes

1. **Experiment with Blending Modes:** Select the topmost layer, go to the Layers panel, and choose a blending mode. For a traditional double exposure try blending modes such as Screen, Overlay, or Multiply. Results will vary depending on the brightness and contrast of the images, and each blending mode will interact differently.

2. **Adjust Layer Opacity:** The topmost layer has to be given a lower Opacity value so that the two images blend smoothly. At the top of the Layers panel, move the Opacity slider to adjust the strength of the effect.

Step 4: Use Layer Masks Accurately

1. **Add a Layer Mask:** Having selected the topmost layer, click the **Add Layer Mask** button at the bottom of the Layers panel.

2. **Brush with the Brush Tool:** With the Brush Tool selected, choose a soft, round brush at opacity and flow settings that will work together in creating a smooth blend. Over the layer mask, use black to hide parts of the top layer where desired, allowing the bottom layer to show through.

Step 5: Refine the Effect with Adjustment Layers

1. **Black & White Adjustment:** If it needs further refining, go to **Layer > New Adjustment Layer > Black & White** to turn both layers black and white. This

will render a harmonious picture because the attention will all be focused on the textures and not on color.

2. **Contrast with Curves**: Go to a Curves adjustment layer and make provision for the contrast between the images. It will give more drama to your double exposure effect. One only needs to drag the curve up or down depending on how much one wants to increase or decrease the contrast.

Creating Light Leak Effects in Adobe Photoshop 2025

Light leaks are brilliant bursts of light on film, generally caused by the film being exposed to light when the camera is opened accidentally. It is a bright and colorful shine. With Photoshop, you can simulate this effect in an analog manner and apply it to any photo to give it a retro feel.

Step 1: Open Your Image

1. **Choose Image**: Images with darker backgrounds give better results because the light will show up way more brightly.

2. **Open in Photoshop:** Open the selected image by clicking on **File > Open**.

Step 2: Adding a Gradient Overlay for the Light Leak

1. **Add New Layer:** Create a new layer via **Layer > New > Layer**, and name it **"Light Leak."**

2. **Choose the Gradient Tool:** From the Gradient Tool, your gradient will be Radial, and you want to choose colors that are associated with light leaks, like orange, pink, red, or yellow.

3. **Apply Gradient:** With the new layer, click and drag the gradient across to achieve the light effect. Feel free to experiment with the gradient placement until you get an effect that works.

Step 3: Set Blending Mode for Realism

1. **Screen Blending Mode:** With the light leak layer selected, switch the blending mode to Screen via the Layers panel to make colors in this layer naturally blend with the photo to give a realistic glow.

2. **Adjust Opacity and Fill**: If the effect is too strong, lower the opacity, or duplicate the layer if you need to amplify it.

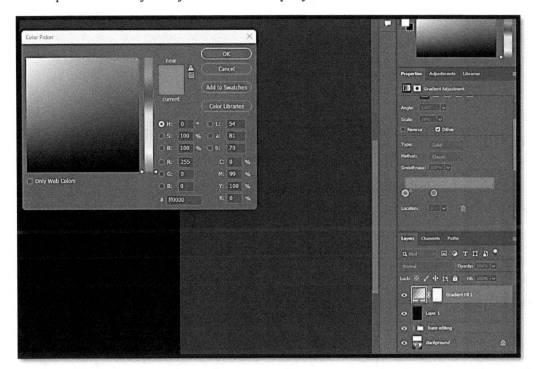

Step 4: Adding Blur and Adjustments

1. **Apply Gaussian Blur:** This will soften the gradient so that it fades naturally. Go to **Filter > Blur > Gaussian Blur**. The radius is usually between 20-50 pixels, depending on your image resolution.

2. **Apply Hue/Saturation Adjustments:** Enhance the colors of the light leak by going to **Image > Adjustments > Hue/Saturation**. You can change the color tone by using the Hue slider or adjusting Saturation for vibrancy.

Step 5: Refine Light Leak with Vignette and Additional Gradients

1. **Enable Vignette**: To create a vignette, go to **Filter > Lens Correction**. Under the Custom tab, click on the Vignette section, then lower the Amount slider to darken the edges and draw attention toward the light leak area.

2. **Add Extra Gradients for Dimension:** Try adding several more gradient layers in various colors and modes to achieve that multi-leak look. Adjust the opacity and mode of each of the gradient layers separately until it looks good to you.

Final Touches

If you've completed both effects, you might want to merge your layers into a single Smart Object. That will let you easily resize, transform, or add filters across all the layers without quality loss.

Export Your Image: Under **File**, select **Export**, then **Export As**..., and choose your desired file format. PNG and JPEG are common file formats that will keep the high-quality effects of your work.

Layering Techniques for Texture and Tone Blending

Setting Up Your Layers for Blending

Laying the groundwork for a great blend means organization of your layers. Compose your image elements in individual layers, and keep your backgrounds, textures, and subjects separate. Then organize your layers into groups to manage groups of related layers more easily. If you're adding texture to a portrait, for instance, you'll want to put the subject, background, and texture layers in their groups for easier adjustment.

Photoshop 2025 introduces AI-powered "**Smart Groups.**" The AI looks at your layers and then logically groups them. For example, it'll gather all the layers related to textures or all the color adjustments so that you can more easily toggle their visibility or change their opacity.

Applying Textures Using Layer Blending Modes

Blending modes unify the transition of textures with base images. In Photoshop, it helps in texturing, especially when using Overlay, Soft Light, and Multiply blending modes.

1. **Overlay and Soft Light**: Both of these layer modes increase contrast while applying textures without drastically changing the color balance. Overlay serves best for high-contrast texture blending when gritty or grungy textures are incorporated into an image, whereas Soft Light yields a much more subtle effect. This is great for skin textures on portraits or atmospheric backgrounds.

2. **Multiply and Screen**: Multiply works well to darken textures, adding shadow generally, while Screen lightens the textures, which is useful for applying glow effects or softening dark areas.

   The new blending modes panel in Photoshop 2025 allows you to see on-the-spot previews by hovering over each option, making choosing the right blending mode for what you are doing a lot easier.

Adding Depth with Gradient Maps and Color Fill Layers

The Gradient Maps and Color Fill Layers are worth their weight in gold for tonal blending. Gradient Maps change the tonal range of an image according to selected colors and are great for setting up mood and atmosphere. For instance, if you want a vintage or warm result, then choose a Gradient Map with sepia tones. Gradient Maps prove especially useful when textures involving high color contrast are combined because they harmonize the tone between layers.

1. **Using Gradient Maps**: Put a Gradient Map layer over your texture and move its colors toward the mood you want to express. Blend with Soft Light or

Overlay to subtly infuse tones throughout your texture layers without overpowering the original image.

2. **Color Fill Layers:** Add a **Color Fill layer** over the texture by selecting Soft Light or Overlay modes in the menu. Adjust its opacity to either soften or strengthen the tone to your preference. This is helpful when trying to give cohesive colors in multiple layers of work, where one could be working with different textures that need to come together.

The Color Harmonizer tool in Photoshop 2025 expands on the previous iteration by taking into account the colors of your image and suggesting complementary hues within Photoshop. This is particularly useful for choosing gradient or color-fill tones that do not clash with the original image.

Texturing with Layer Masks for Precision

Layer masks are crucial for selective texturing. You will want to control the region where textures will show up on an image. If you are applying texture to only a portion of a subject, for example, clothing in a portrait, a layer mask will let you paint in texture only where you need it.

1. **Create a Layer Mask:** Click the **Layer Mask icon** with the texture layer selected, and then with a soft brush of variable opacities, show or hide parts of the texture. These work great for things like crack, grunge, or grain effects that have to appear organic.

2. **Refine Mask Edges:** The Edge Refinement tool is more advanced in Photoshop 2025, which enables the mask edges of a layer mask to be smoother and more accurate. It's especially helpful when you deal with small details, like hair in portraits, to ensure that your textures naturally blend in without any hard lines.

Using layer masks together with blending modes multi-dimensional textures can be achieved to appear integrated into the subject rather than pasted on top of them.

Experimenting with Texture Blending Using Opacity and Fill

Using Opacity and Fill Opacity and Fill settings are those often-forgotten yet important adjustments one needs to make when trying to balance out the intensity of the textures.

- **Opacity**: The opacity adjusts the transparency of the entire layer. This way you can make textures that are too loud a little softer. If your textures are going to be very subtle, natural ones, reduce the opacity of the texture layer to about 40-60%.

- **Fill**: Unlike Opacity, Fill affects just the layer's contents and does not affect any applied effects, like shadows or strokes. This comes in handy in cases where you want a soft texture but still want visible shadow effects.

  The Opacity Panel in Photoshop 2025 has quick-access opacity options right on the layer thumbnail so you will be able to adjust opacity without going into the layer properties, hence saving time during editing.

Advanced Texturing with Displacement Maps

Displacement maps produce the apparent wrapping effect around objects that depends on the contours of the objects and are hence excellent in providing real-life, textured effects, like draping fabric onto clothes or rough skin texture.

1. **Creating a Displacement Map**: Save a copy of your base layer as a grayscale file and then apply a Gaussian Blur to soften the details. Go back to **Filter > Distort > Displace** and it will ask you to select the grayscale file as its displacement map. This will distort the texture layer to follow the contours of the original image so that it looks more realistic and embedded.

2. **Masking with Layer Masks**: Rely on a layer mask to mask the displacement effect well so that the depth will only appear where it should. This way, a fabric texture can be confined to particular regions of the attire and exclude skin or background elements.

Final Touches with Adjustment Layers

The adjustment layers, like Curves, Brightness/Contrast, and Hue/Saturation, are all micro-adjusting textures and tones on every layer. Throw these to the top of your stack and make a global unification of a look without fiddling with every single layer.

Dynamic Adjustments in Photoshop 2025 will give these adjustment layers the power of automatic adaptation to what lies beneath them. As it happens, this is extremely useful in blending tones across complex textures to make sure adjustments will look and feel natural and cohesive.

CHAPTER NINE

WORKING WITH CURVES, LEVELS, AND BRIGHTNESS/CONTRAST

Curves for Tone and Contrast Control

Adobe Photoshop 2025 is equipped with features that give photographers and designers much-needed control over images. Among them, the basic adjustments include Curves, Levels, and Brightness/Contrast for tone, contrast, and brightness. While all three differ in their unique advantages, the Curves tool seems to use a really strong operation in adjusting both tone and contrast smoothly. In this paper, we will go deep into explaining the functionality of Curves and explore how you can use it to effectively enhance your images.

Understanding Curves: The Basics

Essentially, the Curve adjustment in Photoshop affects the image's tonal range. A graph showing the curves has the shadows, midtones, and highlights of an image on an x-y axis. The horizontal axis plots the original brightness values from black to white, while the vertical axis plots the output brightness. An advantage of this curve adjustment is that it offers more control in general contrast, brightness, and color balance in an image with more precision than other tools.

To get started using the Curves adjustment in Photoshop 2025, follow the directions below:

1. Select **Image > Adjustments > Curves** in the top menu or by pressing **Ctrl + M**, or **Cmd + M** on Mac.
2. You will see the Curves dialog opening with a graph; there is a diagonal line running from the bottom left to the top right-the "**curve**". This line, by default,

describes a linear relationship, which by default does not apply any adjustments.

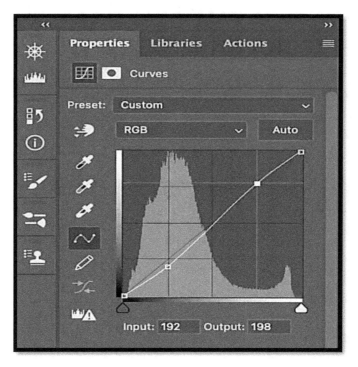

3. By adjusting the points on this curve, you can remap the tones of the image, so you can manipulate shadows, highlights, and everything in between directly.

Adjusting Tone and Contrast with Curves

To enhance the tone and contrast of an image, you will want to create an S-curve in the Curves dialog. This S-curve is very popular for adding depth to images because it greatly increases the contrast:

1. **Add Points to the Curve:** To add points, simply click anywhere on the diagonal line. Each point decides any particular tonal range in the image (shadow, mid-tone, or highlight).

2. **Creating the S-Curve**:

    •   Click on the lower part of the line and pull it down slightly; this will deepen the blacks by darkening the shadows.

- Now, click near the upper part of the line and pull it up slightly to brighten your highlights.

3. As you build the S-curve, the image starts to develop some contrast. This automatically stretches between pure black and pure white to give a natural boost to contrast without losing the midtones.

Sometimes you want something a bit more subtle. So, you make a light adjustment to a curve. Not a huge adjustment, but just a slight one. In this way, the brightness of your image increases by improving contrast without overwhelming it. The more you increase the S-curve, the greater the contrast will be.

Fine-Tuning Brightness with Curves

Aside from contrast, Curves also has room for adjustment to the overall brightness. The midpoint of the curve is where midtones fall. The steps to make an image brighter include:

1. Click near the center of the line and drag upwards. This makes the image brighter while maintaining details in both shadow and highlight areas.

2. To make an image darker, pull the mid-tone point down.

The elegance of the Curves tool is that you can make these adjustments without overblowing the highlights or losing detail in the shadows, as long as you stay away from extreme curve adjustments.

Working with Color Channels in Curves

In Photoshop 2025, Curves allows you to adjust each color channel (Red, Green, Blue) individually. This feature is extremely useful for color correction and for color grading:

1. **Channel Selection**: At the top of the Curves dialog box is a pull-down menu that lets you choose between selecting RGB by default or either one of the color channels: Red, Green, and Blue.

2. **Color Curves Manipulation**: If you want to slightly remove the blue hue from an image, you click with the Blue Channel in midtones and pull down. It will reduce the blues and warm it up.

3. You can give coolness by uplifting the Blue Channel curve.

   Color effects can be achieved color cast correction can be done, and even an accurate white balance adjustment can be done by working with individual color channels with the least effect on other tones.

Working with Curves in Photoshop 2025: Some Practical Tips

1. **Use the Target Adjustment Tool:** The newer versions of Photoshop, such as 2025, provide an inbuilt Target Adjustment Tool when you open the Curves dialog. You can click on any area of your image that you want to adjust. Photoshopping will place points on the curve that correspond to the tones in that particular area, which enables easy adjustments to specific parts of the image.

2. **Use the Histogram for Guidance**: The underlying histogram behind the curve graph is used for reference in the Curves dialog in Photoshop 2025. This will give you a real-time preview to guide your adjustment based on the tonal distribution. Avoid over-clipping the shadows or highlights, as this will lead to a loss of information.

3. **Adding More than One Point for Precision**: You are not confined to one or two points on the curve. If there is an image that requires multiple tone adjustments, you can simply add more points to create a custom curve shape. Just be careful not to overdo it-too many points introduce a jagged, unnatural appearance. Try instead for smooth, gradual curves that should end in a polished result.

4. **Play with Presets:** Preset Curves come in Photoshop 2025 to easily adjust. While presets will not replace manual adjustments, they are good starting

points. Experiment with the different presets to get an idea about how they influence tone and contrast; then readjust them manually as necessary.

Curves vs. Levels and Brightness/Contrast

Although both Levels and Brightness/Contrast also perform tone adjustments, neither offers the precision or flexibility of Curves. Levels have limited applications, best used in setting black and white points, and for performing simple contrast adjustments. Brightness/Contrast, as its name suggests, offers basic brightness control. For nuanced tonal control (particularly color correction and selective contrast, adjustment), Curves are the tool of choice.

How to Achieve Contrast and Balance

Understanding Contrast and Balance

Before opening Photoshop, let's define what contrast and balance are in design.

- **Contrast** refers to the differences between elements that depend on color, brightness, or texture. High contrast will make areas pop by amplifying their differences; low contrast can result in a more uniform look.

- **Balance** is defined as the way the artistic elements' visual weight is distributed in a picture. Symmetrical balance provides stability and calmness, while asymmetrical balance creates a dynamic, visually interesting composition without the "**heaviness**" on one side.

Finding just the right mix of contrast and balance will make your designs more engaging and professional-looking.

Working with Adjustment Layers for Contrast

Adjustment layers offer a non-destructive way to adjust contrast in Photoshop. Let me show you how to use a couple of adjustment layers to bring out the contrast in your images.

Curves Adjustment Layer

1. Open your image and go to the **Layers** panel.

2. To start, go up to **Layer > New Adjustment Layer > Curves**. The Curves tool allows you to make brightness and contrast adjustments by creating a custom curve.

3. Along the Curves panel, pull the lower-left part of the curve down to lighten the shadows and pull the upper-right part up to brighten the highlights. This is another **"S-curve"** technique that works wonders on enhancing contrast.

Contrast/Brightness Adjustment Layer

1. Choose **Layer > New Adjustment Layer > Brightness/Contrast**.

2. In the panel, move the Contrast slider to the right to increase or to the left to decrease contrast.

3. If you need to balance out the exposure after adjusting the Contrast, select the **Brightness slider**.

Levels Adjustment Layer

1. Go to **Layer > New Adjustment Layer > Levels**.

2. The Levels panel is going to show a histogram. You drag the black slider to the right to add some shadow and drag the white slider to the left to enhance the highlight.

3. The middle-gray slider may help you adjust your midtones to have a good contrast with not too much aggressiveness.

Enhance Color Contrast

Color is one of the strong ways to achieve contrast. With Photoshop 2025, there are various ways to work with color contrast.

Selective Color Adjustment

1. Go to **Layer > New Adjustment Layer > Selective Color**.

2. In the panel, you can adjust the colors. For example, if the image is too green, you can decrease that while increasing its complementary colors (like reds).

3. Experiment with adjustments to boost the key colors, to make them pop, yet not overpower the image.

Adjusting Color Balance

1. Select **Layer > New Adjustment Layer > Color Balance**.

2. Move the Shadows, Midtones, and Highlights sliders to achieve the desired color balance.

3. This is another amazingly powerful tool that can be used to create mood. For instance, adding blue to the shadows creates a cooler, more dramatic contrast, while the addition of yellow can warm up the highlights.

Blending Modes for Added Contrast

Blending modes allow you to merge layers in a way that creates great contrast and adds depth to your layers.

Overlay Blending Mode

1. Duplicate your image layer.

2. In the Layers panel, set the blending mode of the duplicated layer to Overlay.

3. Overlay increases the contrast by boosting the darks and lights. If it's too much, reduce the Opacity for more subtle outcomes.

Soft Light Blending Mode

1. Duplicate the layer again but this time set this new layer's blending mode to Soft Light.

2. Soft Light does enhance contrast too, but in a much subtler manner. So, it is perfect for portraits and soft textures.

Feel free to experiment with these modes along with Hard Light and Vivid Light to see what works best for the contrast in your image.

Creating Balance Through Composition

The principle of balance can be achieved by the strategic placement of elements within your design. In Photoshop, several tools and techniques can be used in aid of this.

Rule of Thirds and Guides

1. To turn the grid on, go to **View > Show > Grid**, or use the Guides feature.
2. Using the Rule of Thirds, place the points of interest along the intersection of grids to achieve a balanced composition.

Aligning and Distributing Elements

1. Select more than one element using the Move Tool and align them, using the options in the top toolbar for spacing objects evenly.
2. If you're working with text or graphic elements, this can help them be balanced out so they don't appear cluttered, yet remain visually interesting.

Fine-Tuning with Dodge and Burn Tools

These tools let you lighten and darken parts of the image selectively to give you total control over contrast.

1. For brightening areas, select the **Dodge Tool** from the toolbar, then select its range either to Midtones or Shadows, and set its Exposure to a low value, about 10 to 15%.
2. If you want to dark areas of this picture, you can make use of the Burn Tool. Similar settings apply here. Low exposure will allow you to work with the picture more gradually and naturally.
3. Use these tools rarely to avoid an unnatural look they may create; they do an excellent job of enhancing facial features and adding depth to shadows and highlights in landscapes.

Using Smart Filters for Non-Destructive Edits

Smart Filters enable you to perform contrast adjustments non-destructively for easy editing or removal.

1. Convert your layer into a Smart Object by right-clicking the layer and choosing **Convert to Smart Object**.

2. Apply any filter, such as Camera Raw Filter, under **Filter > Camera Raw Filter**, which provides you with advanced contrast and clarity edits.

3. Since this is a Smart Filter, you can always re-edit the settings of the filter simply by double-clicking the filter.

Composing Your Image with Global Adjustments

Before exporting your image, it's often a good idea to make some global adjustments that will complete your image.

1. Click the **Gradient Map Adjustment Layer icon** in the Layers panel for some subtle color grading. You might find this ties all the tones together and gives a slight contrast boost.

2. Last but not least, look into the **Vignette Effect**. Go to **Filter > Lens Correction**, then select Custom; move the Vignette slider to darken the corners, therefore subtly drawing the viewer's eye toward the center.

How to Enter the Brightness and Contrast Adjustments

1. **Open Your Image:** First, open Adobe Photoshop 2025, then open an image you want to work on by clicking on **File > Open**, then select your image.

2. **Locate the Brightness/Contrast Tool**: You can access the Brightness/Contrast adjustment from either the Adjustments panel or from the top menu by going to **Image > Adjustments > Brightness/Contrast**. The Adjustments panel is especially useful, as it provides an easy way to add adjustments in a non-destructive manner by creating an adjustment layer.

Such an adjustment layer can easily be double-clicked later for editing or removal.

3. **Create an Adjustment Layer**: If you are working non-destructively, which is encouraged to maintain original image quality, click the **Brightness/Contrast icon** in the Adjustments panel. A new adjustment layer is created that will then apply changes in brightness and contrast without touching your image data. Additionally, the use of an adjustment layer also permits you to make fine-tuned changes while still working on other elements.

How to Change Brightness and Contrast

Now you have opened the tool, and basically, there are two major sliders in the Brightness/Contrast panel: the Brightness and Contrast. Here is how to make effective adjustments to each of them:

1. **Adjust Brightness**

   - **Brighten things up first:** Take the brightness control to the right to lighten the image or to the left to darken it. The results can be dramatic; therefore, move the slider slowly.

   - **Shadows and Highlights:** A slight increase in brightness should be added just enough to reveal details in the shadows or dark areas without over-lightening the image to the point that the highlights get washed out. The balance between **+10** and **+20** offers a good effect in most images without over-influencing either the highlight or shadow areas.

1. **Set the Contrast**

   - **Adjust Contrast:** The contrast can be increased to give depth to the image. If the contrast slider is moved towards the right, then it increases the difference between light and dark by adding intensity and a spot of visual interest.

- **Subtlety is Key**: Be wary of too high a contrast, as it can yield stark divides and an unnatural feel in the images. A decrease in contrast may come in handy for those images that require a softer and more smoothened effect, such as portraits. A contrast of about **+15** to **+25** is usually good to highlight the details with no overemphasis.

2. **Preview for Change Tracking**
   - As you move each slider, note the Preview checkbox. With this selected, you can instantly see the results of your changes. Sometimes clicking the **Preview option** on and off will help you determine if your edit is enhancing or degrading the image.

Saving Your Edited Image

Once satisfied with your adjustments, it is time to save your image:

- **Save as PSD for future editing:** Save your work as a .PSD to retain all your layers and settings so you can revisit them later without a loss in quality.

- Export for Web or Print: To finally export for web or print, from the **File menu**, choose **Export** and select the **Export As**... option to save copies in formats such as JPEG or PNG. Choose settings suitable for the intended use-higher quality for print, lower for the web.

Auto Tone, Color, and Contrast: Utilizing Photoshop's Automated Adjustments

Understanding Automated Adjustments in Photoshop

Automatically adjusting tone, color balance, and contrast in Photoshop carries out an analysis of the image, then makes corrections based on information in its pixels to smoothen out the overall general look of an image. In this sense, these adjustment tools are ideal for exposure, color balance, and tonal range to quickly yet effectively modify without making complex manual edits. They're particularly useful when working with images that lack contrast, have off-color balance, or simply appear dull. Each of these automatic adjustments is oriented to another aspect:

1. **Auto Tone** automatically adjusts the tonal range and contrast by balancing the highlights, midtones, and shadows.

2. **Auto Color** makes color correction by eliminating color casts to provide a natural color balance.

3. **Auto Contrast** allows enhancement of the contrast without affecting the colors. It is suitable for black-and-white images where color shifts should not occur.

   Let's examine each of these tools in detail to understand precisely how they work and how to use them optimally.

Auto Tone: Let Depth Loose

Auto Tone automatically adjusts the image brightness and contrast by balancing highlights, midtones, and shadows. The operating process includes a redistribution of the image tones to bring out the details and give more life to the image.

To use Auto Tone in Photoshop:

1. Open your image in Photoshop.

2. Go to **Image > Auto Tone**. Alternatively, use the shortcut **Shift + Ctrl + L** for Windows or **Shift + Command + L** for Mac.

Auto Tone seeks the brightest and darkest points within an image and then stretches these out over the tonal range to improve contrast. This works especially well with images that may appear "flat" due to low contrast or poor lighting. Applied, this can help separate the subject from the background and give a three-dimensional-like appearance through adjusted contrast of different areas.

Remember that while Auto Tone is an excellent starting point, it is a general adjustment. You may need to manually refine the tonal range using adjustment layers in the form of **Levels** or **Curves**, particularly for images that require subtle, specific changes in contrast.

Auto Color: Adjusting Color Balance

Auto Color will try to remove any unwanted color casts in your image that may occur because of different lighting conditions, especially fluorescent and tungsten lights. Color casts can give unnatural scenes in images. This tool balances the colors in seconds for a more natural look.

Steps to use Auto Color:

1. With your image open go to **Image > Auto Color** or **Shift + Ctrl + B** (Windows) or **Shift + Command + B** (Mac).

    Photoshop analyzes the colors within your image and removes color imbalances by neutralizing any single predominant color that's skewing the overall look. If, for example, an image is too warm because the lighting is yellowish, Auto Color will attempt to balance it with the introduction of cooler tones.

    Auto Color does a really good job of general color correction, but it sometimes overcompensates. If it's not perfect, then you can go further and fine-tune it using an adjustment layer-something like Color Balance or Selective Color-to control precisely the hue in your image.

Auto Contrast: Bringing Out Detail Without Changing Colors

Unlike Auto Tone, which affects both the tonal range and color, Auto Contrast adjusts the contrast without affecting color, which makes it perfect for photos where color should not change. This may be very handy if you're shooting black-and-white or if the color tone is intentional.

The following explains using Auto Contrast:

- Open your image and go to **Image > Auto Contrast**, or **Alt + Shift + Ctrl + L** for Windows or **Option + Shift + Command + L** for Mac.

The way Auto Contrast works is that it remaps the darkest and lightest pixels without color hue or saturation changes. A common result is a clearer, crisper image that possesses better contrast in details. Since it does nothing to alter color information, Auto Contrast can sometimes be a 'safer' option if your image has already reached color balance yet lacks depth.

Auto Contrast provides a way out for photographers and designers working with vintage photos or images that need to retain their original color while enhancing the depth and clarity of such images.

When and Why to Use Automated Adjustments

The best scenarios where you should use automated adjustments include:

- **Quick Edits**: If you're on a tight deadline or want something quick, these instant improve tools will help you arrive at the best result in a very short time.

- **Balanced Foundations:** These act as a foundation on which you can easily make the other necessary adjustments.

- **Beginner-Friendly Corrections**: Most color grading applications come with intuitive correction tools; hence, even for a beginning editor, professional-looking adjustments may be made without requiring in-depth knowledge of manual correction tools.

However, automated adjustments are not a one-size-fits-all. They don't represent the best for every image, especially those with complex lighting or ones where precise color matching needs to be done. In such cases, manual adjustments in Levels, Curves, Hue/Saturation, and Color Balance can provide more custom results.

Customizing Automated Adjustments

Despite the term **"auto,"** there's some customization that needs to be done in Photoshop for the automated adjustments. To change how Auto Tone, Auto Color, and Auto Contrast behave, you have to pop into the Image Adjustments preferences. This allows a user to set custom clipping values, meaning you can dictate how Photoshop goes about treating the darkest and brightest areas. The lower the clipping percentage is, the softer the adjustment will be. Higher clipping values make much stronger changes that can be helpful in high-contrast images.

Using Histograms to Guide Adjustments

What is a Histogram?

The histogram in Photoshop is a graphical representation showing the distribution of the brightness of the pixels in an image. The scale runs from black (0) on the left to white (255) on the right. The left side of the histogram shows the shadows, the middle represents the midtones, and the right side displays the highlights. Taller regions reflect a larger number of pixels within that value of brightness, while the lower ones reflect fewer pixels. By looking at this chart, you will understand if your image is under- or overexposed, or whether it falls within the balance and take steps for adjustment where needed.

Why Use a Histogram?

Sometimes, what appears in a visual can be deceiving; our perception of brightness and contrast is influenced by settings on the monitor, ambient light, and even personal biases. Histograms display a non-subjective view of an image's tone and help the user to see where any potential problem areas may lie without immediately being visible. In that way, you can create specific enhancements to bring detail into shadows, contain highlights, or maintain even exposure across an image. By working with the use of a histogram, you will be able to create images that look similar across various screens and under different lighting conditions.

Opening Histograms within Photoshop 2025

Histograms in Photoshop 2025 can be viewed in real-time as you make adjustments. Under the Window menu, select Histogram to open the histogram panel. You'll see the various channels represented that are RGB and each Red, Green, and Blue channel that gives very detailed information about the color distribution. For example, an RGB histogram plots overall brightness, while separate color channel histograms help identify potential color imbalances.

The histogram in Photoshop is dynamic, and refreshing as you make adjustments to show you right away what changes are affecting the tonal range. By keeping an eye on the histogram, whether adjusting exposure, contrast, or color balance, you can keep a balanced image.

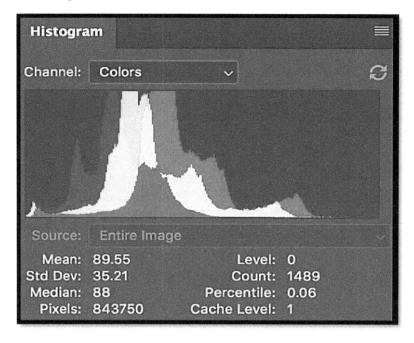

Interpreting the Histogram

A histogram will give you an immediate sense of the quality of the exposure of your image. Here are some common patterns and what they suggest:

- **Left-Heavy (Underexposed):** If most data clings to the left, your image can be too dark, and might not have detail in the shadows.
- **Right-Heavy (Overexposed):** Where there is heavy data on the right, the image may be too bright, the highlights will blow out, and not possess detail.
- **Centered (Balanced Exposure):** When it is even across the histogram, an image is well exposed, and the details are retained in the shadows, midtones, and highlights.
- **Peaks and Valleys (Contrast):** Distinct peaks tend to show high contrast, while valleys may indicate flatter areas with low contrast.

The foregoing will help you be aware of local areas that need adjustment.

Using Adjustment Layers to Modify Histograms

You are going to use adjustment layers. These will allow you to work on the tones and color of the image without actually touching the underlying image. Let's explore a few important adjustment layers and how they can affect the histogram:

Levels Adjustment

The Levels tool is the ultimate for micro-adjusting exposure by independently adjusting shadows, midtones, and highlights. Inside the Levels panel you'll find a histogram and three sliders:

- **Shadow Slider (Left):** Moving this slider inward will darken the shadows and shift the histogram left.
- **Midtone Slider (Middle):** Tugging on this will change the midtones and shift the histogram accordingly.

- **Highlight Slider (Right):** Tugging on this slider cuts the highlights and shifts the histogram right.

Levels adjustment to provide more contrast or correct minor exposure issues. Histograms are useful monitoring for clipping, indicating where a loss of detail has occurred.

Curves Adjustment

The Curves adjustment layer allows for finer control of tonal adjustments. You can drag points along the curve to brighten or darken specific tonal ranges. Of course, you can add many different points on that curve and manipulate separate areas of the shadows, midtones, and highlights.

- **Lifting Shadows:** For example, you may want to lift the shadows by pulling the lower end of the curve upwards to add brightness to the shadow areas without affecting midtones and highlights if your histogram indicates too much dark tonal range.
- **Boosting Highlights**: If your picture lacks light values, pull the top end of the curve to raise bright highlights.
- **Create Contrast**: If you need to create more contrast in your photograph, just draw a gentle "**S**" shaped curve, and it will darken the shadows while lightening the highlights.

Like Curves, it is very powerful but sensitive; always keep an eye on the histogram to avoid over-adjusting.

Adjusting Image Brightness/Contrast

This tool helps carry out quick exposure adjustments, though it is not as finely tuned as Levels and Curves. An increase in brightness moves the histogram to the right, and adjusting contrast stretches or compresses it. This adjustment should be used sparingly because sometimes unheeded applications of this adjustment can result in unwanted effects.

Exposure Adjustment

Where the image has more critical issues in exposure, the Exposure adjustment layer provides more specific control over Exposure, Offset, and Gamma correction.

- **Exposure**: The overall brightness of the scene is adjusted. This shift increases towards the right and decreases by pushing towards the left.
- **Offset**: The midtones are shifted, which makes for finer adjustments that do not affect the highlights or shadows as badly as exposure.
- **Gamma Correction:** This adjusts the brightness of the image by shifting the midtones to refine the exposure and avoid clipping highlights and shadows.

Balancing Color Using Histograms

Color histograms in Photoshop 2025 are used to reveal individual channel information to enable color correction. For example, if the blue channel is skewed to the highlights, the image will appear too cool. A rebalancing of the color by bending the blue curve down in highlights or up in shadows may be required. To correct a color cast the same way, or bring an image warmth, adjust a red or green channel.

CHAPTER TEN

MASKING TECHNIQUES

Understanding Layer Masks: Basics of Masking and Transparency Control

What are Layer Masks?

Succinctly put, a layer mask is a grayscale image that controls the transparency of a layer. You can conceptualize masks as attachments to layers through which you can show or hide selective parts of that layer without being able to delete the pixels. This opens up a world of creative experimentation without actually touching your original image.

Masking works by using the values of black, white, and gray:

- **White**: The white areas painted on a mask are full, allowing the full view of the underlying layer.
- **Black**: The black areas painted on a mask are completely transparent, concealing those parts of the layer.
- **Gray**: Gray areas painted in a mask produce partial transparency depending on how dark or light the gray is.

This grey scale control is an excellent way to merge images, create seamless composites, or make adjustments with refinement.

Creating a Layer Mask in Photoshop 2025

Begin to apply the use of layer masks in a photo editing project by following these steps:

1. **Select the Layer:** Within the Layers panel, highlight the layer that will obtain a mask.

2. **Add a Mask:** At the bottom of the Layers panel, the "**Add Layer Mask**" button takes the form of a rectangle with a circle in it. This adds a layer mask to a layer.

3. **Editing the Mask:** When you create or select a layer mask thumbnail in the Layers panel, you can start painting on it with either a black or white brush to mask out parts of your layer, depending on the color of your brush.

Photoshop will display the mask as a thumbnail along with your layer in the Layers panel. Clicking this thumbnail selects the mask so you can edit it.

Editing the Layer Mask

With new brush tools and real-time mask previews, editing layer masks is easier and more precise than ever in Photoshop 2025.

1. **Choose a Brush:** Press the hotkey for the brush tool (B) or click the icon to the brush tool and then make sure that the mask is selected.

2. **Choose Black or White**: Overpaint the layer black to mask it, white to reveal, and gray for partial transparency.

3. **Adjusting Brush Settings**: To further give you more options for getting the right feather and density with your mask, Photoshop also allows you to set the brush size, hardness, and opacity. Lower opacity allows subtle transitions within the image, while a harder brush edge provides sharper contrasts between hidden and visible areas.

You can toggle between black and white super quickly by hitting **X** on your keyboard.

Working with Gradient Masks

Gradients are a great way to create smooth transitions between visible and hidden areas on a mask. To apply a gradient:

1. **Select the Gradient Tool:** Choose the **Gradient tool** (hot key G) and select the layer mask.

2. **Apply the Gradient**: Click and drag across the layer mask to apply a gradient that allows the layer to fade out or into the underlying layer. For example, a black-to-white gradient allows the layer to feather smoothly and subtly its way into the background for a fade effect.

Advanced Masking Techniques

1. **Refine Edge and Select Subject**

    Select Subject and Refine Edge, powered by AI in Photoshop 2025, make it easier to create detailed masks, especially around complex edges such as hair or fur.

    *   Click the **Select Subject tool**; this automatically detects objects in the image using AI. Here, you can immediately select your subject.

    *   Go to **Select > Select and Mask**, and enter a refinement workspace for edge refinement - making adjustments for transparency and controlling how smooth the mask is.

2. **Using Clipping Masks for Control**

    Clipping masks allow you to create toggled visibility depending on another layer's contents. When you apply a clipping mask, the layer's visibility is out sourced to the layer beneath it.

    *   Position the layer you want to mask above the layer you want to clip to.

    *   Right-click the top layer and choose **Create Clipping Mask**. The top layer will be visible only where the bottom layer has content.

3. **Blending Multiple Layer Masks**

    To implement more than one mask in Photoshop, you have to group layers and apply masks to those groups. This is very beneficial when you work with complex projects where you can blend and mask many layers simultaneously as one from which you might select anything. According to the project demand, masks are used in the real world for many purposes and can be effectively exploited in layer editing.

1.   Select many layers, right-click, and select **Group**.

2.   Add a mask to the group. This will be done by selecting the group and clicking Add Layer Mask.

3.   Edit group mask like any other mask.

Common Use Cases for Layer Masks

1.   **Composing and Blending Images**: Layer masks play an important role in enabling different photos to be merged into one composition. You can reveal the parts of each layer to seamlessly integrate backgrounds, add foreground elements, or add textures without obvious edges.

2.   **Selective Adjustments**: Every adjustment layer, when applied adds a mask by default, be it Brightness/Contrast or even Hue/Saturation. Such a mask allows for selective adjustments whereby one enhances portions of an image without the inclusion of an entire photo.

3.   **Creative Effects and Double Exposures:** Masks are good for achieving artistic effects, like double exposures or surreal, multi-layered compositions. You can mask parts of your images that are different and change their transparency to creatively layer your visuals.

Using Clipping Masks: Linking Layers for Targeted Effects

Understanding Clipping Masks in Photoshop

In Photoshop, a clipping mask is a layer that is clipped into the boundaries of the layer below it. Applying a clipping mask will confine the top layer's contents to those from the visible pixels of the immediate top layer and create a sort of "**masking**.". This gives great flexibility in ensuring that an adjustment impacts only part of your design, and it enables detailed edits to be possible without affecting the balance of the rest of the composition.

Practically speaking, a clipping mask can include a color fill layer, texture, adjustment layer, or even a duplicate of the original image-all constrained by the shape or transparency of the layer below.

For example, you want to edit a portrait and adjust the brightness and contrast of a subject's face without touching the background. Applying a clipping mask will ensure your adjustment layer affects only the face layer, leaving the background intact.

How to Set Up a Clipping Mask in Adobe Photoshop 2025

Setting up a clipping mask is relatively easy in Photoshop 2025. Here's how you do it:

1. **Add Your Base Layer**

    Start by opening your image or creating a new layer in your Photoshop document that will serve as your base layer for the clipping mask - this layer provides the visible area to which other layers are to be clipped.

2. **Create the Targeted Adjustment or Effect Layer**

    Follow with the layer that you want to clip to the base layer. The clipped layer can be a texture, color fill, gradient, or adjustment layer, like Levels, Curves, or Hue/Saturation. For example, you can add a Brightness/Contrast adjustment layer over the face layer if the adjustment of brightness is an edit about the subject's face.

3. **Apply the Clipping Mask**

    In essence, there are two ways to create a clipping mask in Photoshop: There are two ways of clipping one layer on top of another. First, right-click on the layer to clip and select **"Create Clipping Mask"** from the context menu. Alternatively, clicking in between two layers within the Layers panel while holding **Alt** (Windows) or **Option** (Mac), will initiate a clip when you see the icon for a clipping mask-a small square with an arrow pointing to its bottom.

4. **Adjust the Masked Layer as Needed**

    Once clipped, any modifications to the top layer are restricted to visible pixels of the base layer. You may want to adjust its opacity or blending modes or even layer effects to achieve the effect you want. For example, you can obtain some cool typography effects by applying various blending modes on a texture layer that is clipped onto a text layer.

5. **Repeat for Multiple Layers**

    Clipping masks are not limited to one layer. You can overlay multiple clipped layers over one base layer, achieving complicated, multi-layered effects in just one area of the image, without affecting the other areas.

Practical Applications of Clipping Masks

Clipping masks have loads of creative uses in Photoshop. A few of the common applications and their techniques are as follows:

1. **Selective Adjustments**

    With clipping masks, you can adjust the selected parts of your image. In portrait retouching, this can be used to confine adjustments, such as brightness or color correction, into a selected facial feature for a polished look without affecting the whole image.

2. **Texture Overlays**

    Add textures to selected elements to give more life and interest to your work. Using a grunge texture on a particular text layer, for example, requires overlaying the texture layer on top of the text layer, allowing you to apply a clipping mask so the texture doesn't bleed out from the edges of the text. Experiment with layer blending modes, like Overlay or Multiply, for a perfect merge between the texture and underlying layer.

3. **Custom Typography Effects**

    Well, clipping masks are amazing and can give cool typography. You can clip an image, gradient, or texture to a text layer; it would fill the text with a certain effect and leave the areas outside of the text as it is. It is very helpful and can be used in logo designing, social media graphics, and advertisements where you need catchy text.

4. **Non-Destructive Editing with Adjustment Layers**

    Since adjustment layers work with clipping masks, they can permit non-destructive editing. By this, we mean that you can apply effects without permanently destroying the original image layer. For example, a Hue/Saturation adjustment layer clipped to one layer allows you to change colors in one area and leave other layers as they are. Since such a combination can be reverted at any time, it is suitable for ongoing projects.

5. **Layered Composite Effects**

    Clipping masks can be in control when it comes to showing and blending each element in composite photography, where multiple images become combined into one artwork. You can clip shadows or highlights to certain objects in the composite for a much more realistic scene, as you can be in full control of the lighting and shadowing.

Tips and Tricks for Working with Clipping Masks

- **Use Shortcuts to Save Time:** To create a clipping mask, hold down the **Alt** key (Windows) or **Option** key (Mac), and click between layers to create a quick clipping mask. This will in turn save a lot of time working on a project that has multiple clipped layers.

- **Combine Clipping Masks with Layer Masks:** Take it a step further if needed, and hit a layer mask on the clipped layer. This will allow you to mask or reveal the clipped layer, hence giving you full flexibility.

- **Play with Blending Modes and Opacity**: Blending modes and opacity adjustments can make very radical changes in the appearance of your clipping mask effects. Overlay, Soft Light, and Multiply modes work wonders to achieve subtle and striking effects.

Mask Refinement: Edge Detection, Feathering, and Adjusting Density

Correct masking is an important part of almost any image editing work in Adobe Photoshop 2025, whether it involves compositing or making selective adjustments. Powerful refinement options let the masks in Photoshop 2025 seamlessly blend into the surrounding elements to give a realistic professional look.

Edge Detection

Edge detection is a premium tool that refines edges based on the selection or mask boundaries. It's great in areas that are just a little too complicated to work on manually, like hair, fur, or other complicated edges.

How Edge Detection Works

Edge detection in Photoshop works by setting an area in which Photoshop should look for edges using a Radius setting. You'll find the tool within the Select and Mask workspace that's accessed via the **Select > Select and Mask** once a selection has been made. Once in this workspace, you can click to enable Smart Radius, which automatically changes the radius of edge detection based on the complexity of the edges within the selected area.

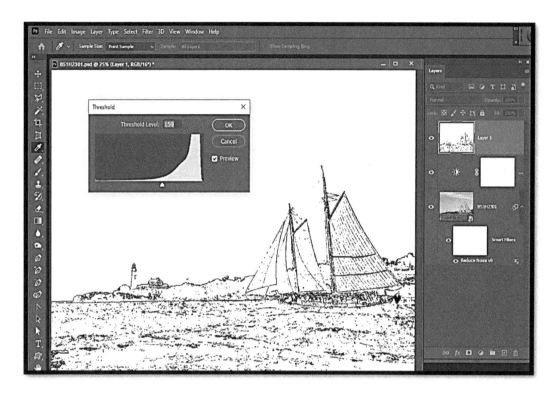

Using Edge Detection

1. **Select Your Subject**: Make a rough selection using any selection tool including the Quick Selection or Object Selection tool. Refine it in the Select and Mask workspace.

2. **Adjust Radius**: Move the Radius slider to set a value for how far the item from the edge of the selection Photoshop should look for bleed. A higher radius setting will give good results when a subject has soft, fine edges - which in fact may include hair - whereas subjects with sharper, more defined edges can do quite nicely with lower radius settings.

3. **Enable Smart Radius**: Put a check in the Smart Radius option to auto-adjust the radius by Photoshop where the selection edge changes in the level of complication. This will particularly be useful in subjects that have both soft and hard edges.

4. **Use the Refine Edge Brush Tool:** Overpaint areas manually with the Refine Edge Brush Tool. It is more of a selector where Photoshop needs to apply its efforts in edge detection to remove unwanted backgrounds and refine the selection edge.

Tips for Edge Detection

- **Zoom In:** You will need to enlarge the image to review and fine-tune the minute details. The detection works best when you are closely looking at the edges of your subject.

- **Use High Radius Sparingly**: This may result in accidentally introducing unwanted background elements. Balance it and avoid over-expanding a selection.

Feathering

Feathering is a way of softening the edges of a mask for smooth transitions between masked areas and the backgrounds. An example would be where feathering in composite works well; this approach becomes helpful in blending images.

How Feathering Works

Feathering essentially works by blurring the edges of a mask, something you can do quite easily if you're working in the Select and Mask workspace with a basic slider. The more feathering you apply, the softer the transition of the edge becomes. However, once you over-feather the image, important details around the edges tend to get lost, so it needs to be applied judiciously.

How to Feather a Mask

1. **Create Your Selection:** First of all, you'll want to make a selection and open it in the Select and Mask workspace.

2. **Adjust the Feather Slide:** Tap the **Feather slider** to soften the edge. Immediately, you will notice how the edges began to blur and blend into the background much more elegantly.

3. **Refine the Amount**: Observe the preview for the feathering to be just about right in ensuring that the transition remains smooth yet sharp.

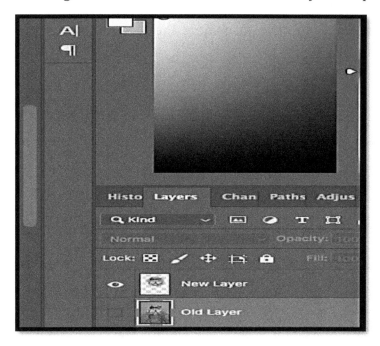

Feathering Tips

*   **Feather in Small Steps:** Smaller steps often work better since many subjects have at least sharp edges. Too much feathering tends to make edges unnatural.

*   **Combine with Edge Detection**: This works in conjunction with edge detection quite well, allowing edge detection to pick up the fine lines, feathering smoothes out.

Density Adjustments

With density adjustments, you will have complete control over the opacity of a mask and send some areas into complete transparency or partially. This is likely useful if you need to reveal some subtle background details while maintaining defined edges in your subject.

How Density Adjustments Work

The Density slider will change the mask's opacity to let you **"fade"** parts of the masked area. Since this is a non-destructive effect, at any time you can return to it and do readjustments without affecting the original mask. In practice, density adjustments often work out well to produce partially transparent masks, helpful in layer blending and soft compositing.

Steps to Adjust Mask Density

1. **Create a Mask**: Apply a layer mask to your desired layer.
2. **Open the Properties Panel:** With the mask selected, go to the Properties Panel, where you can adjust the Density slider.
3. **Adjust the Density Slider**: This will be moved to the left to lower the density. It's a process that makes the mask less opaque, which in turn will allow further blending of the edges or partial transparency in some areas.

Tips for Adjusting Density

- **Real-time Preview:** As changes in density are not as evident, it is nice to have a real-time preview of the adjustment for mask transparency that best suits the image.

- **Combine with Other Tools**: Bracketing the density adjustments with feathering and edge detection allows even further refinement in transparency.

Practical Applications of Mask Refinement Techniques

To illustrate in view how these tools interact with each other, consider a typical editing scenario: the isolation of a person from a background containing trees. Apply edge detection with a medium radius to help the tool differentiate between the subject and complicated backgrounds, capturing stray hairs. Feathering can then soften the edges of this mask to ensure a natural look against the new background. Lastly, slight adjustments in density will allow parts of the tree line to bleed through for a well-integrated composite image.

Mask Refinement Tips

- **View in Multiple Modes**: When making refinements in the workspace of Select and Mask, switch among different viewing modes (like Onion Skin or Overlay) to get a clear idea of what each modification will do to your selection.

- **Experiment with Brush Size and Hardness:** In the case of a tool like the Refine Edge Brush, this will let you reach into smaller, more detailed areas simply by adjusting the brush size and hardness.

- **Use Layer Masks for Non-Destructive Editing**: Making edits with layer masks versus selecting directly allows one to go back and refine the edit at any time.

Creating Complex Composites with Masks: Masking for Multi-Layer Composites

Understanding Masks in Photoshop

Masks are critical to control the visibility of specific parts of an image, layer, or adjustment. A mask in Photoshop is essentially a grayscale image associated with a layer. The areas that you paint black on this mask will be concealed, while the white areas on it will be visible. Gray gives partial transparency, allowing you to create smooth transitions between layers. You can mask what part of each layer is visible to make complex composites with precision.

Adobe Photoshop 2025 introduces more intuitive masking, advanced options for Select Subject and Refine Edge, and AI-based masking. Such upgrades will make it faster to isolate intricate objects by making mask composites easier and more precise.

Step 1: Preparing Your Layers

First things first: organizing your images into layers is how you build a multi-layer composite. Each image or element in your composite should be on a separate layer for individual adjustments.

1. **Import Your Images**: Have each image open in Photoshop that you plan to use, and position them within your project canvas.

2. **Label Each Layer:** Name your layers based on content or position in the scene, such as **"Foreground Tree," "Background Sky," or "Subject,"** because complex compositions are easier to keep track of that way.

3. **Position and Resize Layers**: Determine the order in which the layers should appear: the foreground layer is to go to the top and the background to the bottom. Now resize and reposition each to create a rough composition of the basic layout.

Step 2: Basic Layer Masking

We will start with basic masking for the seamless transitions between layers.

1. **Adding a Mask**: After selecting the layer that you want to edit, click the **"Add Layer Mask"** icon at the bottom of the Layers panel; doing this will add a mask thumbnail attached to your selected layer.

2. **Hide and Reveal Parts of the Layer**: On mask, with a soft black brush, paint on areas to be hidden. This will initiate the feathering of the edge of the selected layer with the lower layers.

3. **Refine Mask with Brush Tool**: Start to create a subtle fade by gradually changing the opacity or using different brushes altogether to gain textured transitions.

Masks are especially useful when blending skies, water, and natural landscapes-natural features that usually require subtle transitions.

Step 3: Advanced Masking with Select Subject and Refine Edge

For more complicated selections, the updated Select Subject and Refine Edge in Photoshop 2025 can make your life so much easier.

1. **Use Select Subject:** Under the menu bar, select **Select > Subject**; by default, Photoshop uses AI to automatically detect a selection for the main subject of the image. Refine this selection if necessary, using the Lasso or Quick Selection tool.

2. **Refine the Edges**: Once the subject is selected, click on **Select** and **Mask**. Use the Refine Edge Brush to capture fine details such as hair or leaves. Then move the radius slider to increase the sensitivity of the edges, and play with options such as "**Smooth**" or "**Feather**" to soften transitions.

3. **Apply the Mask**: Once you're happy, mask the selection to create a mask. This works well for subjects with a lot of details on the edges, which have to blend naturally into the background.

Step 4: Adding Natural Shadows and Highlights

Adding lighting and creating shadows adds more realism to your composites. Masks allow you to add or adjust the shadows and highlights on specific layers.

1. **Add Shadow Layers:** Duplicate the layer, and move that layer to where the shadow needs to be. Fill it with black, reduce the opacity, and Gaussian Blur for softer shadows.

2. **Mask the Shadow:** Add a mask to this shadow layer, and with a soft black brush, paint away what you don't want or give refinement to the shape of the shadow. In subtle shading, let the brush's opacity be low and just build up the gradual tones.

3. **Add Layer Styles to Enhance**: Adding an Inner Shadow and Inner Glow with layer styles will give it that subtle effect of 3D, thus making the illumination of an individual element more realistic.

Step 5: Color Matching and Blending

Color grading is important to ensure everything matches the scene. Even if every layer has been masked out perfectly, incongruous colors pull the realism right out from under the composite.

1. **Use Adjustment Layers:** Hue/Saturation, Color Balance, or Curves Adjustment Layers will fix color discrepancies between layers. To get the most out of these adjustments, clip them to the layers they should affect.

2. **Mask Adjustment Layers**: By adding masks to the different adjustment layers, you can color-correct specific parts of the shot. For instance, you might adjust the blue tones in the sky but not affect your foreground subject.

3. **Match Lighting and Color**: Subtle adjustments to warmth, brightness, and saturation unify the elements together to create one cohesive composite.

Step 6: Fine-Tuning with Smart Filters and Masking Techniques

Smart Filters, along with masking, make for non-destructive editing and provide flexibility. Why? Because of the following reasons:

1. **Apply Smart Filters**: Convert your layers to Smart Objects so that the filters applied are non-destructive. Use filters like Blur, Noise, Sharpen, etc., to match the textures and levels of focus.

2. **Mask the Filters:** Every Smart Filter applied has a mask applied therewith. For example, you can apply a filter to an entire layer and then mask out portions where you want areas to remain sharp or blurred to extend the depth of field.

3. **Apply Blend Modes:** Apply a blend mode to masked layers to adjust how each element will interact with the other. The Overlay, Multiply, and Screen modes can even change the light and texture interaction amongst these multiple layers.

Final Touches and Layer Organization

Once all elements have been successfully merged, revisit your masks and soften any rough edges: **"Clean up each mask to make the transitions super smooth."** Then, group related layers together and name them so it may be easier to navigate back to the parts of interest. A well-organized file is the key to easily revisiting or adjusting your composite.

Quick Mask Mode: Temporary Masking for Precise Selections

What is Quick Mask Mode?

Quick Mask Mode enables you to edit your selections as a grayscale mask rather than with traditional selection lines like **"marching ants."** When you enable Quick Mask, Photoshop represents your selection by covering the non-selected areas with a red, semi-transparent overlay. The overlay is there for visual indication so one may easily see where exactly your selection begins and ends for more precision.

Unlike permanent masks, Quick Mask Mode is temporary. Its main function is perfecting a selection before adjustment and changes one does in this mode do not affect the image directly; instead, they are applied to the selection's boundary. Once you are satisfied with the refined selection, you can then toggle back to Standard Mode and apply your desired adjustment, filter, or effect to the selected area.

Why Use Quick Mask Mode?

There are several advantages of Quick Mask Mode:

1. **Precision**: You get a good overview of what you're selecting, whether it is a detailed shape or has delicate edges.
2. **Flexibility**: Other selection tools cannot be modified by brush or gradient and edits happen very linearly.

3.   **Non-Destructive Editing**: The result is that Quick Mask Mode allows for non-destructive edits as it lives on a temporary layer where you can experiment freely.

For designers, photographers, and digital artists, this mode relieves them from much effort and provides great selection detail with the least amount of effort expelled; thus, becoming ideal for projects that require accuracy.

Times to Apply Quick Mask Mode

Quick Mask Mode can be applied in work scenarios where selections need detailed refinement. This may involve:

- Choosing between complex edges of hair, feathers, or grass
- Grouping subjects that have irregular or soft outlines
- Developing gradients or soft transitions within a selection
- Making complex selections that overlap areas of similar color or tone

    It has been a great companion to the other selection tools in Photoshop, such as the Lasso Tool, Magic Wand, and Select and Mask, and can afford you greater fineness in selection areas before committing to edits.

How to Use Quick Mask Mode in Photoshop 2025

Step 1: Make an Initial Selection

First, perform a rough selection by using one of the several selection tools in Photoshop; it may be the Lasso Tool, Magic Wand Tool, or Quick Selection Tool. Though your selection needs not be perfect, it should outline the general area to be refined in Quick Mask Mode.

Step 2: Activate Quick Mask Mode

With your initial selection in place, press the **Q** key on the keyboard or select the icon at the bottom of the toolbar to engage Quick Mask Mode. Quick Mask Mode activates, overlaying a red tint on the parts that are not selected. The parts of your image that you have selected will remain visible without an overlay to enable the user to see the boundary of their selection.

Step 3: Refining the Selection Using Brushes

In Quick Mask Mode, you are allowed to add to or subtract from your selection using Photoshop's Brush Tool:

- **Black Brush**: You will paint with black to add to the mask - remove the areas from the selection.

- **White Brush:** You will paint with white to remove from the mask - adding areas to the selection.

That way, by adjusting the hardness and opacity of the brush, one can achieve soft edges or feathered areas to allow for a subtler transition between images. This is quite useful, especially when selections contain soft or feathered edges.

Step 4: Use Gradient Tools for Soft Transitions

If your selection requires a soft fade, or gradient the Gradient Tool in Quick Mask Mode can help you create subtle transitions. For instance, if you are selecting on a horizon or adding a shadow the Gradient Tool allows you to soften that edge with a feathering effect.

Step 5: Adjust Selection Density with Opacity

Quick Mask Mode in Photoshop 2025 also enables features such as changing the mask opacity for better viewability. The reason why one would lower the overlay opacity is so that minute details are visible when refining selection, especially in lighter images.

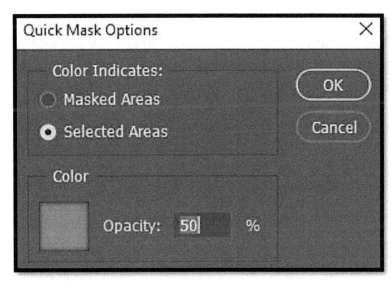

Step 6: Exit Quick Mask Mode

Once you have made the desired adjustments to your selection, strike the **Q** key again to exit Quick Mask Mode. The refined mask will be converted back into a standard selection, complete with marching ants, in Photoshop so additional refinements can be made to the image by adding an effect, color correction, or removing of background.

192

Tips for Using Quick Mask Mode Effectively

1. **Duplicate a Layer for Complicated Edits**: If it's a complicated selection, duplicate the image layer and work in Quick Mask Mode in the duplicate layer for an added layer of security in case of reversals.

2. **Save Your Selections**: Once you have masked a selection and are out of Quick Mask Mode, simply go to **Select > Save Selection** - it will save your selection as an alpha channel. This means you can use it at any time without having to draw your selection all over again.

3. **Feel Free to Change Your Brush Settings**: Particularly, change the brush size, hardness, and opacity. With soft brushes, you will get soft, subtle fades, while with hard brushes, you can draw sharp edges accurately.

4. **Utilize Refine Edge for Extra Detailing**: If you need more refinement than you feel you can accomplish in Quick Mask Mode, use Select and Mask to access other refining options including feathering, smoothing, and adjusting contrast.

CHAPTER ELEVEN

COLOR BALANCE, HUE/SATURATION, AND SELECTIVE COLOR

Color Balance for Temperature Adjustments

Understanding Color Temperature and White Balance

Color temperature - the warmth or coolness of an image - measured in Kelvin (K). Images shot using a low Kelvin value will appear much cooler, more blue in tint, while an image captured with a higher Kelvin value will be much warmer, more yellow or orange in tint. White balance, closely related to color temperature, refers to making colors appear more in their natural hue by compensating for the light source of the image. For instance, indoor photos taken using tungsten lighting might turn out too warm, while those taken outdoors on cloudy days get too cool. Proper color temperature adjustment makes the image retain the proper color representation without looking blue or yellowish unnecessarily.

Color Balance: Its Role in Temperature Adjustments

Color Balance in Photoshop enables the user to locally shift colors in an image through direct manipulation of the red, green, and blue channels. These shifts alter the temperature without directly affecting the master saturation or brightness, making it a great tool for refined adjustments. Refined controls in the 2025 update to Photoshop further extend user control in manipulating color temperature within the Color Balance adjustment layer.

Accessing the Color Balance Tool

To start using Color Balance for temperature adjustments, follow these steps:

1. **Open your image**: Activate your image in Photoshop with which you have to work.

2. **Create a Color Balance Adjustment Layer**: At the lower section of the Layers panel, click the icon "**Adjustment Layer**" and select **Color Balance**. This will open the Color Balance dialogue box. Editing with an adjustment layer allows non-destructive editing.

3. **Adjust Midtones, Shadows, and Highlights**: Once the Color Balance panel opens, you will have the option to adjust color balance within the midtones, shadows, and highlights of the picture. The segmentation is very useful because sometimes different parts of the image may benefit from different temperatures.

Adjusting Color Temperature with Color Balance

When adjusting color temperature in Color Balance, you'll typically focus on increasing or decreasing the blue and yellow tones. Here's a breakdown of each option and how it affects temperature:

- **Midtones**: This is the starting point for most temperature adjustments, as it affects the overall color without overly impacting shadows or highlights. Adjusting the midtones is helpful for general warmth or coolness adjustments.
    - To make the image warmer, move the slider towards red and yellow.
    - To cool down the image, move the slider towards blue and cyan.

- **Shadows**: Use this to control the temperature in the darker areas of the image. This can be particularly helpful if the shadows are too cool or warm compared to the rest of the image.
    - For a warmer shadow tone, increase the red and yellow sliders.
    - For cooler shadows, increase the blue and cyan sliders.

- **Highlights**: This affects the brightest areas of the image. Adjusting the temperature of highlights can help balance the image when bright areas are skewed towards blue or yellow.

- Warmer highlights: Increase red and yellow.
- Cooler highlights: Increase blue and cyan.

You can make a better balancing of temperature by adjusting each range separately. For example, you may add warmth to midtones while maintaining highlights a little cooler to get an even, natural look.

New Features in Photoshop 2025 for Color Balance

Adobe Photoshop 2025 has extended the Color Balance tool with several new features that enhance user control over temperature adjustments:

1. **Enhanced Slider Sensitivity**: In Color Balance, sliders are more sensitive for fine tunings; thus, the user will be able to make micro-adjustments without jumping to large steps in color shift. It will be easier this way to get to the ideal color temperature without over-editing.

2. **Color Wheel Integration**: The Color Balance tool now includes an optional color wheel for better visualization and intuitive manipulation of color shifts. It will provide temperature gradients as a visual reference for warm and cool tones on the wheel.

3. **Split-Toning Option**: This new feature allows the maker to apply different temperature adjustments to both the highlights and shadows simultaneously, which is a trendy effect in film-like photography. This split-toning control will be more effective in mood-driven images where you want cooler shadows and warmer highlights.

Practical Temperature Adjustment Tips

1. **Use a Reference Image**: If possible, use a reference image with the correct temperature and color tone to base the adjustments. This helps most when one is working on product photos or portraits where the color has to be very accurate.

2. **Check-in Full Screen:** Temperature adjustments may look different for screen size and lighting. Make sure to check the temperature of your shot in full-screen mode so that it looks natural.

3. **Combine with Other Adjustments:** Use Color Balance in conjunction with other adjustments like Levels, Curves, or the Camera Raw filter to make holistic alterations for the correction of temperature. In this way, you can take further steps toward refinement of contrast, exposure, and saturation to complement your temperature adjustment.

4. **Zoom In and Out**: When correcting color temperature, also consider viewing the entire picture along with its cropped portions. Often skin tones in portraits or green foliage in landscapes may need just a little more care to keep colors natural and consistent.

Best Practices for Realistic Color Temperature

- **Shun Overcorrection**: It is often so easy to push colors too far, to the extent that your picture doesn't look natural. Most natural results are derived from subtle adjustments.

- **Pay Attention to Lighting Conditions**: If the shot was taken in the golden hour of daylight or special lighting conditions, retain the color temperature. Adjust only enough to enhance and not overwrite the image's intrinsic warmth or coolness.

- **Use the History Panel**: The history panel available in Photoshop allows you to step back through your adjustments. This is helpful when you want to compare the edited image from various steps to identify the most natural temperature setting.

Adjusting Hue, Saturation, and Lightness

Understanding Hue, Saturation, and Lightness

Before looking into adjustments, it is important to understand what each component represents. These are:

- **Hue**: It refers to the color per se, on a color wheel, measured in degrees from 0 to 360. Since hue adjustment in Photoshop revolves around color along this color wheel, you can replace, shift, or enhance colors.

- **Saturation**: This deals with the intensity of color. When less saturated, it results in a grayer appearance, which tends to be more subtle; increased saturation, on the other hand, can make the color more vivid and draw attention.

- **Lightness**: Used to adjust the brightness or darkness level of a color, this dictates how bright or dark a color will appear.

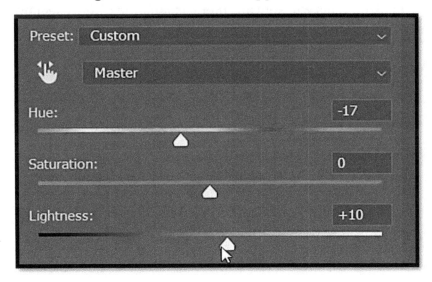

Each of these adjustments may be done independently or in concert with others, offering full freedom to achieve the desired look.

Step 1: Creating the Hue/Saturation Adjustment Layer

1. Create Hue/Saturation Adjustment Layer: Open your image in Photoshop. Click the **Adjustment Layer icon on the Layers panel** (the half-filled circle) and select **Hue/Saturation** from the pulldown menu. This will create a nondestructive adjustment layer that will keep you experimenting without touching the original image.

2. **Open the Properties Panel:** When you create the Hue/Saturation layer, by default, Photoshop opens the Properties panel. Within this Properties panel, there are three major sliders, namely hue, saturation, and lightness.

Step 2: Use the Master Adjustment

By default, within the Properties panel, the option of Master is preselected. This takes over the image, making all colors change in the image at the same time. This proves pretty helpful when one needs to adjust the whole mood and atmosphere of an image.

1. **Adjusting Hue:** This will spin all colors around the color wheel by moving the Hue control left or right. A rightward shift in the slider will take reds into oranges, blues into purples, and so on. Try numerous color combinations until you find one that adds to your image. Be wary of large shifts as these will distort natural colors.

2. **Adjust Saturation:** Saturation affects the general increase or decrease in the colors of a frame. This will be useful if your picture tends to appear too dull or too bright. Moving the slider to the right enhances color vibrancy while moving it to the left produces a washed-out or desaturated look.

3. **Adjust Lightness:** This slider, to lighten or darken the image in general, has to be moved accordingly. The right goes brighter, and to the left goes darker. Useful when there is a need to emphasize other areas of the image and/or to tone down the colors if they are too bright.

Step 3: Adjusting Individual Color Ranges

You can also work with discrete color ranges rather than applying effects over the entire image. This is done via the following steps:

1. **Select Color Range:** Starting with the Properties panel, click the dropdown menu next to Master. In this menu, you will see a list of options regarding color ranges, including Reds, Yellows, Greens, Cyans, Blues, and Magentas. Click to select any one of these options that target that color range.

2. **Refined Range**: Once you have selected a color, Photoshop automatically selects the range down at the bottom of the Properties panel. Refine what part of that color range you want to affect with the sliders. This of course comes in handy if there is any color in a selected range that you do not want affected. Say, for instance, you want to select just that shade of red and not affect similar colors.

3. **Adjusting Hue, Saturation, and Lightness of Selected Colors:** Now, move the Hue, Saturation, and Lightness sliders as described above, but be aware that your changes will affect only the color range that you have selected. For example, if you have chosen Blues and move the hue slider, only blues will shift in color, while other colors remain unaffected.

Step 4: Using the On-Image Adjustment Tool

Adobe Photoshop 2025 includes an On-Image Adjustment Tool, which offers intuitive, interactive control over hue and saturation directly on the image.

1. **Choose the On-Image Adjustment Tool**: In the Properties panel of a Hue/Saturation layer, click the hand icon that represents this tool.

2. **Adjusting Colors on the Image**: Click and drag directly on a specific color in your image, and instantly Photoshop will have selected that color range and increased or decreased the hue, saturation, or lightness based on the action taken. Horizontal dragging modifies hue, while vertical does saturation. This

is a great tool for subtle adjustments for those not familiar with traditional methods of color selection.

Step 5: Resetting and Preserving Changes

Sometimes the changes can be over-complicated, or you just want to return to default.

1. **Reset Changes**: This requires just one click from the reset icon, a circular arrow at the bottom of the Properties panel. You will be returned to the original position of all sliders.

2. **Save Changes**: If you like a combination, then save the adjustment as a preset by clicking on the gear icon in the Properties panel and selecting **Save Preset**. This will help you to easily apply the same HSL setting to other images in the future.

Advanced Tips for Hue, Saturation, and Lightness Adjustments

- **Masking with Adjustment**: By default, the Hue/Saturation layer will affect the entire image. If you want to make adjustments over some areas, use the mask. Select any adjustment layer mask thumbnail and, using the brush tool, paint areas of the adjustment that you want to hide or reveal.

- **Working in LAB Color Mode**: If you want even more subtlety, try converting your image to LAB color mode. In LAB, colors are split apart more than in RGB, and you have much better access to luminance independent of color.

- **Layer Blending Modes:** Experiment with blending modes on the adjustment layer to achieve unique effects. For added contrast and intensity, modes like Soft Light and Overlay will work in combination with hue/saturation adjustments.

Using Selective Color for Targeted Edits

What distinguishes Selective Color is the fact that one can perform exact changes within a specific range of colors, like reds, yellows, blues, and greens, together with neutrals (grays), whites, and blacks. It is useful and important in the following perspectives:

1. **Enhancing Certain Elements:** You will be able to edit only the colors of the sky or even a piece of clothing without having all the other elements in your photo change.

2. **Smoothening of Skin Texture:** Changes in red and yellow hues work wonders for skin tone enhancement in portrait photography

3. **Creating Dramatic Effects:** One of the awesome features of Selective Color is that you can change the entire mood of your picture by simply changing a couple of colors while other color characteristics remain intact.

Access the Selective Color Tool

To open Selective Color in Photoshop, you would go to the **Layers panel** and click on that half-black, half-white circle icon at the bottom to select a new adjustment layer. Then, under the dropdown, you'll find Selective Color. Immediately, you'll open up a new non-destructive layer and your adjustments will be made on a new layer, not directly on your original image.

Basic Elements of the Selective Color Interface

When you open up Selective Color, notice:

*   **Color Channels:** A drop-down providing color range options to select from, that will range from Reds, Yellows, Greens, Cyans, Blues, and Magentas to Whites, Neutrals, and Blacks.

*   **Sliders:** There are Cyan, Magenta, Yellow, and Black sliders for each color channel. Each slider affects only the selected color channel and does not interact with the other color channels.

*   **Methods Options:** Two options are available (**Relative** and **Absolute**). The Relative method changes according to the source color values in an image and,

therefore, produces more subtle adjustments. Absolute mode effects are more dramatic, changing the chosen color universally throughout the image.

How to Use Selective Color

1. **Choose Color to Adjust**

    First, you should select to choose the color you want to adjust. If you're manipulating blues in a sky, for example, select "**Blues**" from the drop-down.

2. **Move Sliders to Achieve the Desired Effect**

    Each color channel is represented by the Cyan, Magenta, Yellow, and Black sliders. These work in the following manner.

    *   **Cyan Slider:** Move to the right and add cyan while removing red in that color range.

    *   **Magenta Slider:** Move to the right add magenta and remove green.

    *   **Yellow Slider**: Move to the right add yellow and remove blue.

    *   **Black Slider:** The lightness and darkness within the color range are controlled with this slider; to get much deeper, saturated tones, the slider is moved to the right, or it lightens left.

    To achieve an even more dramatic sunset in a landscape for example, select "**Reds**" and then move the Yellow and Magenta sliders to the right, which would push the temperature of the sky and bump up reds and oranges without affecting the rest of the shot.

3. **Use Relative and Absolute for Finer Control**

    *   **Relative**: This will give a more subtle edit to realism by only changing partial color matching the selected color channel and blending it with the surrounding colors.

    *   **Absolute**: This is used for bold edits in which you want more apparent changes; hence, this mode will change every pixel within that color range to your set slider settings for a more apparent result.

You might want to play with these two modes to get the best balance for your image if you're working with portraits where skin tone is something you want to be careful with.

4. **Layer Masking for Extra Precision**

   The Selective Color adjustment layer also contains a layer mask. If you want the color adjustment to appear in specific places on the image, you must paint over the mask with black over areas of your image that you'd like to conceal the adjustment. This will come in handy quite often when you have images that require only certain areas to change color, such as enhancing a dress or flower in a busy scene.

Practical Applications of Selective Color

Enhancing Landscape Photography

In landscape photography, colors such as blues, greens, and yellows tend to need enhancement. Selective Color will allow you to:

- Increase the blue in the sky without affecting other elements of the shot.
- Add life to foliage by working in the Greens channel with an added amount of Yellow and Black for depth.
- Work Neutrals or Blacks for added depth in shadow areas, thus giving your image a far more dynamic range in contrast.

Refining Skin Tones in Portraits

Selective Colors can subtly adjust skin tones in portraits by working within the Reds and Yellows.

- To do this, lower the Cyan in the red channel to reduce unwanted red tint, or adjust the Magenta and Yellow to bring warmth or coolness into the skin without over-saturating it.

Tips for optimum usage of Selective Color

- **Use Non-Destructive Workflow**: Always work with adjustment layers so that edits are flexible and can be easily reverted.

- **Combine with Other Tools**: The Selective Color tool is normally at its best when used with the other color correction tools, such as Hue/ Saturation, for an overall balanced result.

- **Be Mindful of Over-Editing**: It is very easy to overdo it with this tool, especially in Absolute mode. Regularly turn your adjustment layer on and off to check your adjustments are staying realistic.

- **Try Blending Modes**: See what creative effects you get by changing the blending mode for the Selective Color adjustment layer to Overlay or Soft Light, for example.

Applying LUTs for Quick Color Grading

What is a LUT?

A LUT is essentially a color transformation that is predefined but can alter colors and tones in an image. These have gained huge popularity in video editing but have also grown in the world of photography and digital art due to how fast and consistent color-grade images are. This saves a lot of time since you're just applying a preset color scheme or mood, from which you can do fine-tuning for your particular project.

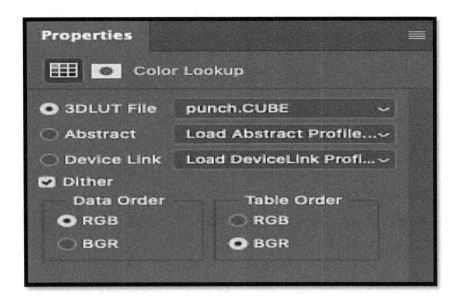

In Photoshop, LUTs are available through adjustment layers that offer the ability to edit non-destructively. That is, you can add or remove LUTs without making permanent changes to the original image. You can try out a range of different looks without having to start over.

Why Use LUTs in Photoshop 2025?

Photoshop 2025 enhances the color grading features, making the application of LUTs and their management a little quicker and more intuitive. It also introduces additional library options to select from, including support to import custom LUTs, covering a wide range of styles and color grading needs. Updates have also seen improved rendering speed, which will now let users see the effect of a LUT much faster and is a great timesaver for big projects or high-resolution images.

Applying LUTs in Photoshop 2025

1. **Open Your Image in Photoshop**

   To begin with, open your image in Photoshop. Choose one that you think would look great with a color grade. Anything can have LUTs applied to it, but generally, the most spectacular scenes are high-contrast dramatic ones.

2. **Create a New Color Lookup Adjustment Layer**

   - To start, in the Layers panel, click on the "**Adjustment Layer**" icon (a half-black, half-white circle).

   - Select "**Color Lookup**" from the pulldown menu: This will open a Color Lookup adjustment layer on top of your image layer, so whatever LUT you load will be non-destructive.

3. **Access 3D LUT Preset**

   Once the Properties panel opens for the Color Lookup layer, you'll notice that there are three different options to load a LUT:

   - **3DLUT File:** Import a proprietary 3D LUT file. While Photoshop 2025 defaults include an updated list of presets, you can import external LUT files in the most common formats, like.CUBE or .3DL.

   - **Abstract and Device Link**: Less common for photography but useful nonetheless for specific looks.

   To start, click on the dropdown menu next to "**3DLUT File**" and take a look at some of the presets that are already in the application. The "**FoggyNight,**" "**TealOrangePlusContrast**," and "**Crisp_Warm**" options give you some pretty popular cinematic feels. Click on one to have Photoshop apply directly to your image immediately.

4. **Adjust LUT Intensity (Optional)**

   Photoshops always apply LUTs at full strength by default. If you want to make a more subtle adjustment, you can click on and lower the opacity for the Color Lookup adjustment layer inside the Layers panel. You can also often get a balanced look by lowering opacity to 50% to 70%, but this won't overpower the original image.

5. **Adjust Further with Additional Adjustment Layers**

   In cases where the LUT overdoes it with your image, adding more adjustment layers such as Curves, Levels, and Brightness/Contrast may be necessary. You can add the adjustments above or below your Color Lookup layer to help complement certain aspects of the LUT. For example, if a particular LUT completely darkens the image, having a Brightness/Contrast layer above will help recover some lost detail.

6. **Experiment with Blending Modes**

   Other ways to customize the impact of a LUT include using the Color Lookup adjustment layer blending mode. In the Layers panel, its blending mode is set to options like **"Overlay," "Soft Light,"** or **"Color"** to show how they impact the appearance. Each blending mode interacts differently with an image, and sometimes this experimentation produces surprising results.

7. **Exporting Custom LUTs**

   Well, within Photoshop 2025, you can also save your customized color adjustments as LUTs. Once you have fine-tuned the adjustments, go to **File > Export > Color Lookup Tables**. This will let you save your grading as a new LUT file that you can reuse in future projects or even within video editing software. This feature is especially useful if you want to maintain a consistent look across multiple images or within a video project.

Tips for Effective LUT Use in Photoshop 2025

- **Use the LUTs Starting Points**: You should not view applying LUT as the last step in color grading. They are better used as the beginning of setting a tone in your image capture. Further adjustments can be made to customize the feel for every image.

- **Match LUTs to Your Subject Matter**: Some LUTs are more meant for specific subjects. For example, warmer LUTs tend to work with portraits and nature scenes well, while cool or high-contrast LUTs complement urban and night shots well.

- **Combine Multiple LUT:** While you cannot layer or stack LUTs on a single Color Lookup layer in Photoshop 2025, you can do multiple Color Lookup layers and adjust the opacity of these to combine disparate LUT effects. This may result in a look that is multi-layered and complex.

Working with Gradient Maps

What is a Gradient Map?

A gradient map applies a gradient across the tonal range of an image. Instead of mapping colors based on the colors that already exist in an image, Photoshop uses the luminance values (from dark to light) to apply color from a gradient you choose. Dark areas in the image receive colors from the left side of the gradient, midtones are mapped to colors in the middle, and light areas receive colors from the right.

With new tools and even better processing, Photoshop 2025 has gotten a whole lot smoother and way more versatile when it comes to working with gradient maps. Here's how you can exploit this tool to the fullest.

Step 1: Opening the Gradient Map Adjustment Layer

1. Open your image in Adobe Photoshop 2025.
2. At the bottom of the Layers panel, click the **Adjustment Layer icon**. A pop-up menu will appear where you will choose **Gradient Map**.
3. This will open a new Gradient Map adjustment layer on top of your image, and you will instantly notice it change because of the default gradient that Photoshop puts on. Editing with an adjustment layer and not directly is advantageous since one can do non-destructive editing.

Step 2: Choosing and Customizing a Gradient

Once you have added the Gradient Map layer, now it is time to edit your gradient. By default, Photoshop 2025 pops the Properties panel open when you add a gradient map, giving you quick access to options regarding the gradient itself.

1. Click the gradient bar within the Properties panel. Opening the Gradient Editor presents an opportunity to either select a preset gradient or create a new, custom gradient.

2. The Color Stops, Opacity, and Blending Options in the Gradient Editor in Photoshop 2025 are improved, making constructing a gradient to fit the vision quite easily.

Creating a Custom Gradient

To create a custom gradient:

*   Click any of the several color stops located below the gradient bar. This opens the color picker where any color can be selected.

*   You can also add color stops by simply clicking directly below the gradient bar or remove stops by dragging them off of it.

*   Move each color stop to ultimately change the color blending and transitions across the image. Of course, Photoshop 2025 features real-time previews, making experimentation much easier.

Gradient Types and Presets

By default, Photoshop 2025 offers a long list of preset gradients, from which you can select everything from warm sepia tones to high-contrast neon colors, which will be an amazing starting point or allow you to achieve certain effects even faster.

*   In photo editing and color grading, you will more likely want to work with very subtle gradients transitioning between shades of one color, for example, from blue to green or from brown to beige.

- In creative or artistic projects, bold gradients like rainbow or sunset can add a brilliant touch and an innovative look to your image.

Step 3: Adjusting Blending Mode and Opacity

After one chooses the gradient, some experimentation with the blending mode could yield a variety of different effects.

1. In the Layer panel, under the Gradient Map layer, click on the **Blending Mode** drop-down menu.

2. The blending modes, such as Overlay, Soft Light, and Multiply, will greatly impact how the gradient interacts with the underlying image.

   - **Overlay** and **Soft Light** work well for subtle coloring in a fashion that does not overpower details in an image.

   - **Multiply** will darken the image, while **Screen** can lighten it; this is useful if you want to lighten shadows or add depth to highlights.

Also, bring the opacity of the Gradient Map layer forward for subtle changes in intensity. Lowering the opacity will soften the effect to a more natural one, while 100% keeps the gradient fully opaque.

Step 4: Refining with Masks

Masks enable you to indicate exactly where the gradient map is visible on your image, thus allowing one to have several kinds of effects on one's image.

1. With the Gradient Map layer selected, click the **Layer Mask icon** in the Layers panel.

2. Now select the mask and paint black - softly - over areas you want to hide with the Brush tool. Alternatively, you can paint with white to reveal, or gray for partial effects.

What makes gradient maps versatile, though is layer masks. So, for example, you could apply a gradient map to give a sky a warm tone in a landscape photo without affecting the foreground.

Advanced Gradient Map Techniques

Using Multiple Gradient Maps

For more complex work, you can use multiple Gradient Maps each with their blending mode and mask applied. Building up multiple layers of Gradient Maps on top of one another can create complex yet subtle color effects.

Gradients with Selections

You can also use selections and apply the gradients to just a portion of the image. For example, select the subject using **Select** and **Mask**, then add a **Gradient Map**. The ability to allow only the background or foreground to be adjusted will make a subject pop or create surreal color combinations.

Gradient Maps Adding Texture

To summarize everything, the Gradient Map along with overlaying textures in Photoshop 2025 can give it that gritty, worn, or even painted look. Just apply a gradient map and then add an image of texture over it, changing its mode to multiply or overlay. Then adjust the opacity until the effect looks seamless.

Tips for Gradient Maps in Photoshop 2025

1. **Experiment Freely**: A gradient map opens a whole world of endless possibilities. Get out of your comfort zone and try unusual colors, blending modes, and combinations without being too concerned.

2. **Use Presets for Inspiration**: The presets in Photoshop 2025 range from retro to very modern. Use the preset as a starting point and edit it to fit your aesthetic taste.

3. **Combine with Adjustment Layers:** Gradient maps work well when used in conjunction with other adjustment layers, such as Curves or Color Balance, to offer increased control over contrast and tone.

CHAPTER TWELVE

THE HEALING BRUSH AND RETOUCHING TOOLS

Healing Brush, Spot Healing, and Patch Tool: Removing Imperfections and Blemishes

Adobe Photoshop 2025 remains the first choice of both professionals and hobbyists involved in photo retouching and image editing. From a set of tools that cater to editing, the Healing Brush, Spot Healing Brush, and Patch Tool excel in the light of their ability to remove imperfections and blemishes so easily.

The Healing Brush Tool

The Healing Brush is one of the powerful tools in Photoshop that corrects blemishes and imperfections while maintaining original texture, lighting, and shading.

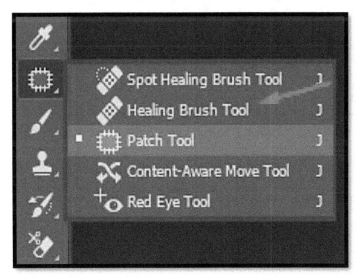

How It Works

The Healing Brush tool enables the sampling of pixels from any part of the image that usually contains a clean area, then blends them with the targeted area where one tries to remove a blemish or unwanted detail. This is helpful in portrait editing for maintaining natural skin tones and textures.

Step-by-Step Guide

1. **Select the Healing Brush Tool**: It can be toggled by pressing **J** on the keyboard or selected from the toolbar.

2. **Click to Select Sample Area**: Press the **Alt key** for Windows or the **Option key** on Mac; then, click a portion of the picture that is clear and unmarked. This will serve as your reference area.

3. **Adjust the Brush Setting:** Set the size of your brush slightly larger than the blemish you want to remove. You can adjust the hardness depending on the detail in the area you are working on. Softer edges will help in blending skin, while areas that have texture can probably do with harder edges.

4. **Paint Over the Imperfection**: Click and drag across the blemished area. Photoshop will automatically replace this section with the pixelated image sampled earlier and blend it seamlessly in with the rest of the skin area.

Tips for Best Results

- Select a sample area that has the same lighting and texture as the target area to ensure that the tone will naturally set in.

- Work on small portions to ensure control over the process of blending, more so if skin tones are concerned.

- For minor correction when there is only a little blending required, it is advisable to have a low opacity setting.

The Spot Healing Brush Tool

The Spot Healing Brush replaces a lot of the quick fixes. Unlike the Healing Brush, which always requires you to sample an area by first hitting **ALT**, the Spot Healing Brush automatically samples from surrounding areas, making it quicker for minor imperfections. With Photoshop's AI-driven technology in 2025, this tool has also become a bit 'smarter' now, as it seamlessly adapts itself to various textures and lighting conditions.

How It Works

It deploys the use of Content-Aware Fill technology in analyzing surrounding pixels for a perfect blend in the elimination of unwanted elements. Ideal for removing minor blemishes, dust spots, or even minor scratches without having to manually select a source.

Step-by-Step Guide

1. **Select the Spot Healing Brush Tool**: This tool can be accessed by either going into the Healing Brush menu or by using **J** via the hotkey.

2. **Adjust the Brush Size:** The brush should be slightly larger than the imperfection you wish to remove.

3. **Adjust the Blending Mode**: From the options bar, you can choose from among several modes. Usually, Content-Aware will work; Proximity Match works great for nearby, similar textures.

4. **Click or Drag Over the Imperfection**: For smaller imperfections, one click will do the trick; drag across larger blemishes.

Tips for Best Results

- Drag with short controlled strokes to minimize distortion, especially in high-textured areas.

- Retouch on a duplicate layer with the Spot Healing Brush, so that you can lower the opacity or even mask parts of the retouch if needed.

- Avoid using this tool near edges, as it may blur the edges of high-contrast areas.

The Patch Tool

The Patch Tool is more flexible to use in larger and more complicated areas. It lets you define an area that you want to repair and then **"patch"** this with a sample from another area. The Patch Tool is really useful for larger blemishes, distracting details, or even unwanted objects within an image.

How It Works

In the Patch Tool, you outline manually the area that you would want to replace and then drag over a cleaner portion of the image. Automatically, Photoshop will blend the textures, shadings, and tones, and it is a very great tool for major corrections.

Step-by-Step Guide

1. **Choose the Patch Tool**: Find this tool in the toolbar under the Healing Tools section or just press **J**.

2. **Define the Area to Patch**: Draw around the imperfection by clicking and dragging to make a selection of the area you want to remove.

3. **Drag to a Clean Area:** Once the area is selected, click inside of the selection and drag it to a clean area you'd like to use as the source. It will preview the result as you move the selection.

4. **Adjust Patch Tool Settings**: In the options bar, make sure Content-Aware is enabled, and then refine Structure-a slider that controls how much of the original texture is preserved-and Color-a slider that governs color blending to better match source and target areas.

Tips for Best Results

- For areas with fine details, use higher values for Structure to maintain detail integrity.

- Apply a lesser color setting if you notice color mismatches after applying the patch.

- For detailed areas, such as near edges, you can always use the Clone Stamp to smoothly feather the edges later.

Advanced Retouching Techniques: Content-Aware Fill for Complex Edits

Understanding Content-Aware Fill in Photoshop 2025

Content-Aware Fill uses Photoshop's AI framework, Adobe Sensei, to intelligently fill a selection based on neighboring textures, colors, and patterns. In Photoshop 2025, Content-Aware Fill has been optimized to do a better job of recognizing and mimicking complex patterns, lighting, and fine details of things such as hair, foliage, and detailed textures. The new algorithms allow users to perform more complex edits while requiring fewer additional touches.

Setting Up for Content-Aware Fill Success

The moment you plunge into a complicated Content-Aware Fill edit, you want to prepare your workspace and take the next steps to ensure that your results are optimized.

- **Work on a Duplicate Layer**: Start by duplicating your background layer so that the original image is preserved. Work on a separate layer so that edits are non-destructive.
- **Select the Target Area Precisely:** It is done with the Lasso Tool, Quick Selection Tool, or the Object Selection Tool. If the effect requires finer control, choose **Lasso Tool** and zoom into the area for a perfect demarcation of what needs to be changed or replaced.
- **Feather the Selection**: As the hard edges are not wanted, feather the selection by about a few pixels. Go to **Select > Modify > Feather** and adjust the feather radius according to the complication of the background.

Using Content-Aware Fill for Complex Backgrounds

While working on a complex background, say some textured walls, water, or foliage, Content-Aware Fill can be a great help. To handle such refined edits, Photoshop 2025 brings in more detailed controls:

- **Enable Content-Aware Fill**: Once the selection has been created, go to **Edit > Content-Aware Fill** to open the **Content-Aware Fill** workspace, which will give a live preview of the results.

- **Edit the Sampling Area**: This is the area that Photoshop will use to base the fill in the selection. It will automatically generate a sampling area, but on a complex background, it often pays to fine-tune it. Use the Sampling Brush Tool to add or remove areas of the sampling area. This allows you to exclude areas of specific patterns or colors that might break up the fill.

- **Adjust Fill Settings:** New color adaptation settings in Photoshop 2025 can help fine-tune the fill for detailed backgrounds. Experimenting with color adaptation settings such as **"None," "Default," "High**," and "**Very High**" should be done to find out which best merges the fill into the surrounding area. "**Rotation Adaptation**" can be useful to align the textures when filling areas of directional patterns, such as wood grain or water ripples.

Advanced Techniques for Fine Details

For images that feature fine details, like hair or fur, or even minute details in the background, Content-Aware Fill becomes an application that's a little bit more of an art than a science.

- **Partial Selections and Iterative Fills**: Sometimes when an image presents complex edges-a hair bank or foliage. It's advisable to select less at a time and go for multiple selections. By doing this, you give Photoshop a chance to scrutinize the details in-depth and fill the gap as authentically as possible.

Iteratively applying Content-Aware Fill in smaller sections helps to keep continuity in complex textures.

- **Merging with Clone Stamp Tool**: Content-Aware Fill might, after being used, still leave some minor inconsistencies. Immediately switch to the Clone Stamp Tool by using the S shortcut key to allow the blending of any awkward transitions that may have occurred between the filled area and surrounding texture. Change the size and opacity of the brush for feathered edges and smooth those edges out in highly detailed areas.

- **Refining with Healing Brushes:** This will iron out any apparent seams. For example, the Healing Brush and the Spot Healing Brush allow you to iron out the seams that are still visible. If you're editing a section with intricate textures such as bricks or pebbles, then small imperfections in texture continuity can be effectively repaired using the Healing Brush Tool.

Working with Reflections and Shadows

When removing or replacing objects that cast shadows or are mirrored through reflection, a few additional considerations come into play:

- **Mirror Selections for Reflections**: If you are working on reflections on water or glass, just mirror the part of the image by using **Transform > Flip Horizontal** or Vertical before Content-Aware Fill to maintain the realism of your reflection without you manually redoing it.

- **Manually Re-create Shadows:** After you remove an object, there are instances wherein you need to re-create some of the shadows just to maintain continuity in depth and light. To subtly shade shadowing, use the Brush Tool with a soft, low-opacity brush along with layer blending modes like "**Multiply**." Aside from those, you can duplicate a layer of similar objects, or you can use a selection from the original object before it was removed to create a shadow.

Advanced Workflow Efficiency in Using Content-Aware Fill

There are several shortcuts and tricks within Photoshop 2025 that can make using Content-Aware Fill much quicker. To save a selection for reuse:

- **Save Selection for Reuse:** If you're performing multiple fills on a similar area, go to **Select > Save Selection** to avoid reselecting the area each time.

- **Using the History Panel:** Keep an eye on the History panel for quick access to previous stages of your edit. If a fill doesn't work out as expected, revert to an earlier stage and adjust the sampling or fill settings.

- **Try Generative Fill (Beta):** New in Photoshop 2025, Generative Fill (Beta) uses AI to fill entire sections of an image based on textual prompts. Not quite there yet, it does show promise when working together with Content-Aware Fill for larger background replacements or creative compositions.

Troubleshooting Common Issues

Complex fills do not always work as expected the first time. The following lists some common issues and solutions:

- **Inconsistent Textures**: When filling a region, sometimes the filled area exhibits mismatched textures. Try going back and clicking on the sampling area to ensure there is only the inclusion of similar textures.

- **Unnatural Patterns**: If it seems like Photoshop is filling an area with some pattern that isn't like anything in nature, try adjusting the Rotation Adaptation setting and making smaller selections.

- **Color Inconsistencies**: If the colors don't match up, try adjusting the Color Adaptation settings or use the Clone Stamp Tool to fine-tune the area.

Clone Stamp Tool: Manual Cloning for Precise Corrections

Understanding Basic Clone Stamp Tool Principles

The clone stamp simply copies the pixels from one location of an image to another. Now, that sounds uncomplicated, yet for the simple reason that this tool is very versatile, from minor touching up to extensive alterations, various types of corrections can be carried out, and it's extremely useful when you must have complete control over the source of the pixels and the area you are editing.

To access the Clone Stamp Tool:

1. Open Adobe Photoshop 2025 and open any image you want to work on.
2. Go to the left toolbar and click on the **Stamp** icon or use "**S**" on your keyboard as a shortcut to choose it.

The moment you do that, you will notice from the top toolbar settings for brush size, hardness, opacity, and flow. These can make a huge difference in your results, and you should know how each works.

Setting Up Your Clone Source for Precision

With the Clone Stamp Tool, you select a source area spot you want to clone from a target area where you will paste those pixels. You define the source by hitting "**Alt**" (or "**Option**" on Mac), clicking on the area you want to replicate, and then moving to the area you want to correct and start painting over it.

Another new feature in Photoshop 2025 is the Live Clone Preview. It gives, in real-time, what cloned pixels would be like in the target area. This is going to go a long way, especially when matching up textures or patterns because it allows one to very definitely see exactly how the cloned pixels will integrate into the target area before committing to it.

Tips for Choosing the Right Source Area

1. **Select Similar Textures and Colors**: Try to select source material in a similar texture and color to the one you are working on; this will give a natural result.

2. **Use Multiple Source Points**: When working on a large area, do not clone from one source point because it results in patterns of repetition. Instead, pick up new sources as you move along across the target area.

3. **Use Source Overlays**: Source overlays were introduced into Photoshop 2025, which helps you to view a ghostly preview of your source pixels lying over the target area. This overlay is necessary for placing it with the correct adjustment over its opacity.

Adjusting Brush Settings for Control

The Clone Stamp Tool allows you to make fine adjustments in your correction to perfectly match the surrounding area.

- **Brush Size**: For areas of detail, like edges and contours, use a smaller brush size, while for larger and smoother surfaces, increase it.

- **Hardness**: Basically, this sets the sharpness of your brush edges. A low hardness gives a soft merge, which is good for skin retouching or subtle transitions. Higher hardness is great for hard edges and well-defined textures.

- **Opacity and Flow:** While decreasing opacity makes the effect lighter, you can then build up cloned pixels gradually. Also, the amount of flow controls at what speed the brush applies the color. Start with a lesser opacity to build up until your correction starts looking natural for precision correction.

Using Clone Sources for Complex Edits

The Clone Source Panel in Photoshop 2025 is indispensable when performing edits that require more than one source point, such as object removal and the recreation of backgrounds. To open this panel in Photoshop, follow the menu path **Window > Clone Source**.

Here you have the following options in this panel:

- **Set Up to Five Different Source Points**: This will let you switch sources fast without having to reselect the source manually.

- **Rotating Scaling Clones:** Change the angle or size of the cloned area to match perspective, which is helpful when cloning objects that need to be at an angle that adheres to perspective and lines or shapes in the image.

- **Offset Clones**: Fine-tune the position of the clone source for complex patterns or aligned textures.

    These features will ease the pain when working with more complex tasks, such as reconstructing partial background areas or creating uniform textures.

Refining the Edit with Layer Masking

One of the great ways to edit non-destructively is by working with a Layer Mask. Go back to your cloned edits, and create a new layer by selecting **Layer > New > Layer**. From here forward, make use of the Clone Stamp Tool on this layer and not directly on your image.

A Layer Mask will allow you to:

- **Show or Mask the Clone Area:** If a region doesn't blend in, then with the masking-off option available you will be able to edit what the cloned pixels show.

- **Refine the Edges**: A soft brush on the mask will give you a feathered edge so that these cloned areas will better blend into the original pixels.

Avoiding Repetition with Texture Variations

One problem with the Clone Stamp Tool is that it tends to repeat itself, especially in areas of a particular pattern or texture. To eliminate these repeats, do the following:

- **Switch Sources Often**: Occasionally switch your source point. This will provide more texture variation in the cloned area.

- **Adjust the Clone Position**: Light shifts in this direction or that will prevent repeating patterns from taking hold and result in cloned areas that appear organic.

- **Use Multiple Layers:** Create cloned areas in different layers to enable easy adjustments and blending afterward.

Practical Application of Clone Stamp Tool

The Clone Stamp Tool finds wide applications in various scenarios in real-life applications, such as:

- **Erasing Unwanted Objects**: It can be only a hair, a speck of dust, or an entire object. Clone Stamp Tool helps get rid of distractions seamlessly.

- **Retouching of Skin and Details**: Retouch the skin by cloning similar tones of skin coming from the nearby area to create a natural look. Set lower opacity for smooth blending, which plays a very vital role in portrait photographs.

- **Correcting Background and Texture**: Duplicate pieces of the sky, wall, or any other background to repair any damaged section or fill up the gap after cropping.

Final Touches and Adjustments

Once the cloning is done, zoom out to check the overall composition for repeated patterns or unmatched textures. Make slight adjustments with the Healing Brush Tool as needed, which may turn out to be better at blending cloned areas, particularly around the edges.

Correcting Skin Tone and Texture: Techniques for Portrait Retouching

1. **Preparing Your Image**

Before delving into the retouch, make some simple enhancements to get a better base for your image. First, open up your portrait in Camera Raw (or Lightroom) and adjust the White Balance. White balance is essential because it will determine overall skin tone, so seek a neutral, true-to-life temperature and tint that best describes the subject's natural coloring.

Next, you will want to **Exposure, Contrast,** and **Highlight** to bring out detail in the face. Just remember to make light adjustments so as not to overexpose or lose detail. Once your basic edits are complete, open your image in Photoshop 2025 to start skin retouching.

2. **Addressing Skin Tone with Color Correction**

Skin tone correction is important in portrait retouching since it gives the portrait a natural even look. The Hue/Saturation adjustment layer can be powerful in this regard. Create a Hue/ Saturation layer, and through its drop-down menu, narrow your focus only to reds and yellows, since these are the key colors that affect skin tone.

Use the Hue slider to the left to decrease unwanted redness or sallowness from the skin. If the tone is a bit pale, you slightly increase the Saturation to bring life back to the face. For even finer detail control, use the Selective Color Adjustment layer: in this layer select Reds and then adjust Cyan, Magenta, Yellow, and Black sliders to your desired tone.

For more complex skin tones or irregular textures, a layer mask is more useful with Curves. Add a new Curves adjustment layer, click the hand icon to sample areas of skin, then adjust to lighten darker areas or reduce highlights.

3. **Removing Blemishes and Irregularities Using Spot Healing Brush and Healing Brush**

The minor blemishes, acne, and stray hairs in the picture can be treated using the Photoshop Spot Healing Brush and Healing Brush tools. Open a new layer for the retouching so that the original layer remains intact. For the small blemishes, the "**Content-Aware**" mode will automatically sample surrounding pixels with the Spot Healing Brush to fill them in seamlessly.

With larger areas or more complex corrections, proceed with the Healing Brush Tool. In this one, you sample skin manually in an area by **Alt-click**, and overpainting on the imperfection gives much better control. Remember to always sample new areas of skin to maintain consistency in tone and texture.

4. **Smoothing Skin Texture Using Frequency Separation**

   Frequency Separation is a powerful technique that allows you to separate skin texture from color and have full control. First, duplicate your image twice: name the first duplicate "**Low Frequency**"-it will contain color and tone-and the second one "**High Frequency**," which will contain fine details.

   - In the Low-Frequency layer, you are going to apply a Gaussian Blur to blur the details and keep only the color.

   - Now go to the **Image > Apply Image** using the settings shown below. Maintain the Layer as Low Frequency, Blending as Subtract, Scale as 2, and Offset as 128.

   Set the blending mode for the High-Frequency layer to Linear Light now. Now with the Lasso Tool selected start picking out problem areas on the low-frequency layer and apply light blur Gaussian blur, for example, to smooth skin tones without affecting the texture above.

5. **Refining Skin Texture with Dodge and Burn**

   Dodge and Burn is a technique that will selectively lighten or darken areas of the skin to accentuate natural contours and balance uneven tone. Make a new layer and set its mode to Soft Light or Overlay, then fill with 50% gray. First, dodge the darker areas of the skin and burn overly highlighted areas with a low-opacity brush of 5-10%. The Dodge and Burn can also be used on the cheekbones, jawline, and other natural contours to sculpt the face and add depth and dimension.

Another way is the Dodging and Burning with a Curves Adjustment Layer. You have two Curve layers, one for dodging and another for burning, and mask out each effect to apply it only where it's necessary. This gives more control over the tonal adjustments.

6. **Refining Pores and Texture with the Skin Smoothing Filter**

In Photoshop 2025, Skin Smoothing gets its filter within Adobe's Neural Filters. The feature, truly powered by artificial intelligence, performs magic by smoothing rough skin while preserving pores and fine details. Then select **Filter > Neural Filters > Skin Smoothing**. Move the Blur and Smoothness sliders to your taste, but do make sure you are careful to avoid over-smoothing.

The Skin Smoothing filter does save one a lot of time, but it's best utilized in moderation. Subtle adjustments here go a long way in enhancing natural texture without making the skin look "**plastic**."

7. **Final Color Grading and Sharpening**

Once your retouching is done, it's time to add a cohesive color grade that ties together the general tone of the portrait. Add a Color Lookup Adjustment Layer and try some presets for a soft, professional look, such as "**Fuji**" or "**Kodak**" film emulations. If the effect feels too strong, adjust the layer opacity.

As a finishing touch, give your image a slight sharpening to emphasize the details. Convert your image to a Smart Object and then apply the Unsharp Mask (**Filter > Sharpen > Unsharp Mask**). Set the Amount to about 50-80%, Radius 1.0, and Threshold to taste.

Frequency Separation: Advanced Technique for Professional Skin Retouching

Frequency separation has become an important tool for photographers, retouchers, and digital artists who have to achieve skin perfection while maintaining texture and detail. One of the most current techniques in high-end beauty and portrait retouching is frequency separation, where, traditionally, one can divide an image into two layers-one holds the texture, another captures color and tone. By separating these layers to edit individually, you will be able to smoothen skin, remove blemishes, and balance out the tone without compromising important details.

Understanding Frequency Separation Layers

The frequency separation works by dividing an image into two primary components:

1. **Low Frequency Layer:** This layer contains color, tone, and shading of the object but with no texture. While editing this layer, you can work on skin tone adjustment and make it even remove color irregularities, thus making it smooth without changing any inherent skin details.

2. **High Frequency Layer:** Everything that is fine details such as skin texture, hair, and pores, resides on this layer. You will find that changes you make on this layer affect only the textures and therefore enable refinement in these areas without disturbing color.

   Frequency separation enables skin refinements that retain an organic feel, which your clients and your viewing audience have come to expect from a professional image.

Creating Frequency Separation in Photoshop 2025

1. **Duplicate the Background Layer:**
   - Open your image in Photoshop 2025.

229

- Duplicate the background layer by hitting **Ctrl + J** for Windows or **Cmd + J** for Mac twice.
- Label the first duplicate "**Low Frequency**" and the second "**High Frequency**" for ease of recognition.

2. **Adding a Gaussian Blur to Low Frequency Layer:**
   - First, click on the eye icon of the High Frequency layer to turn it off.
   - Now, select the **Low Frequency** layer, and go to **Filter > Blur > Gaussian Blur**.
   - Adjust the blur radius to a point where you lose the fine details but still can see the general shapes and tones. Usually, an 8-10 pixel radius does the work, but depending on your image resolution, it may be different.

3. **Extract the High Frequency Layer:**
   - Turn the visibility of the High Frequency layer back on and select it.
   - Navigate to **Image > Apply Image**.
   - Change the Layer to "**Low Frequency,**" mode. Subtract, Scale 2 Offset 128. This will leave the texture on the High Frequency layer.
   - Change the Blending mode for the High Frequency layer to Linear Light and immediately the image should return to its original appearance.

Now you have two layers, together they recreate the original image. But as they're separated into color and texture, you can retouch each independently.

Retouching with Frequency Separation

Smoothing Skin Tone on the Low Frequency Layer

1. **Select the Low Frequency layer and use the Lasso Tool (L):**
   - Set the feather radius to around 20-30 pixels for a soft selection edge.
   - Make a selection over the area you wish to smooth, such as the cheeks or forehead.

2. **Apply a Gaussian Blur:**
   - o   With the area selected, go to **Filter > Blur > Gaussian Blur**.
   - o   Adjust the blur radius to smooth out the skin tone without losing the overall shape of the face. The value will depend on the image's resolution but generally stays around 10-20 pixels.
   - o   Repeat this process on other areas of the face that require tone smoothing.

Refining Texture on the High Frequency Layer

1. **Use the Healing Brush or Clone Stamp Tool:**
   - o   Select the **High Frequency** layer and choose the **Healing Brush Tool (J)** or **Clone Stamp Tool (S).**
   - o   Set the brush to "**Current Layer**" only.
   - o   Carefully paint over blemishes, spots, or fine lines on the High Frequency layer. This will maintain the natural skin texture while removing unwanted imperfections.

2. **Focus on Precision:**
   - o   Keep your brush size small for detailed corrections, targeting only the areas where texture needs adjustment. Avoid heavy-handed retouching, as this can create an unnatural, overly smooth look.

Advanced Tips for Professional Results

1. **Blend Gradually:**
   - o   Instead of applying extreme adjustments all at once, make gradual changes. Subtlety is key to maintaining a natural look, especially for professional beauty retouching.

Utilize Photoshop 2025's Neural Filters:

- Photoshop 2025 introduces AI-powered Neural Filters that can assist in retouching. While Neural Filters won't replace manual frequency separation, they can complement it.
- Try using the Skin Smoothing filter for an additional layer of refinement on the Low Frequency layer. Adjust the slider conservatively to avoid an artificial result.

2. **Use Layer Masks:**
   - If you find that frequency separation affects areas beyond the face, use a layer mask to apply the effect only where needed.
   - Create a layer mask on either the Low or High Frequency layer and paint with a soft black brush to hide unwanted adjustments.

3. **Dodge and Burn for Additional Dimension:**
   - After completing frequency separation, you may want to add depth and dimension with Dodge and Burn.
   - Create a new layer set to Soft Light or Overlay mode, and use a low-opacity brush to lighten (dodge) or darken (burn) specific areas, enhancing the contours of the face.

Common Mistakes to Avoid

1. **Over-Blurring:** Over-application of Gaussian Blur on the Low Frequency layer may result in an unnatural, plastic-like look. Always check different values of blur and adjust according to the skin type and resolution.

2. **Ignore Color Shifts**: Frequency separation can sometimes present color as uneven in some areas, the under eyes or around the mouth can be quite evident. If required balance the color with the Brush Tool set to Color blend mode in the Low Frequency layer.

3. **Over-Texture Removal**: In case you remove too much texture in the High Frequency layer, that skin turns out to be unnatural and flat. Always balance edits and leave some natural imperfections so they look real.

CHAPTER THIRTEEN

FILTERS AND EFFECTS

Introduction to Photoshop Filters

What are Photoshop Filters?

In Photoshop, filters are pre-set effects that can be applied to an image layer or a selection. They allow users to make rapid visual transformations, ranging from subtle refinements to bold artistic effects. Filters can be applied to create blurs, sharpen images, give textures, and even distort shapes. The foremost advantage they provide to users is that they can achieve complex visual results with just a click or a few adjustments, thereby being time-savers regarding creative projects.

Photoshop filters have been found quite useful in several design contexts:

1. **Photo Editing:** Filters help photographers enhance their photos by adjusting for sharpness, brightness, contrast, and so on.

2. **Digital Art and Illustration**: Filters give artistic highlights such as brush strokes, texture, and surreal effects, which make your digital paintings or designs look more vibrant.

3. **Graphic Design**: Filters give depth and dimension to text and other graphic elements, allowing the designs to look more dynamic, such as posters and banners.

Types of Photoshop Filters

Below are different categories of filters in Adobe Photoshop 2025, together with the functions of each:

1. **Blur Filters:** These are used to soften images whereby they reduce the details that are contained in photos. This class of filters works best for background effects, depth of field simulations, and noise reduction. The most common blur filters include Gaussian Blur, Lens Blur, and Motion Blur.

2. **Sharpen Filters**: These filters sharpen to accentuate edges and details; thus, they are very helpful for photographers who desire clear and focused shots. Filters like the Unsharp Mask and Smart Sharpen provide users with control over the amount of sharpness applied.

3. **Distort Filters:** These filters are used to change the shape and form of an object in an image. Many of them, such as Liquify and Pinch, are in great demand for use in graphic designing and surreal art projects to achieve different kinds of visual effects.

4. **Noise Filters**: Noise filters add or remove noise in a picture, which adds either a retro feel or cleans up digital artifacts within the image. Commonly used to either Add Noise or Reduce Noise for an artistic or corrective function.

5. **Stylize Filters**: These filters, falling under the category of Stylize, really give the image an artistic effect, making it look very different. For instance, the filter Emboss gives it a 3D effect, while Oil Paint gives it the appearance of an oil painting. In digital painting, stylized filters can be used quite frequently to give texture and dimension.

6. **Render Filters:** Unlike other filters, the render filters create effects from scratch instead of modifying existing image details. Examples are Clouds and Lens Flare-the former builds a pattern, while the latter builds a light effect.

7. **Filter Gallery:** A special section where multiple artistic filters can be browsed and applied together for easy experimentation with a variety of combinations. This gallery provides options like Sketch, Artistic, and Texture filters.

Applying Filters in Photoshop 2025

Adobe Photoshop 2025 has made applying filters much easier, and the process is more straightforward. There are two major ways to apply filters on images:

1. **Direct Application**: The direct use of a filter from the Filter menu will automatically affect the active layer. Further modification can be easily done through the property that pops up.

2. **Smart Filters**: Once you apply a filter on your Smart Object, that filter becomes a smart filter because it's a non-destructive method of editing; you can come later and adjust the filter settings or even switch to another one. You can put a Gaussian Blur on your Smart Object, for example, and later increase the intensity or change the blur effect.

Adobe Photoshop 2025 also introduces dynamic filter stacking, which allows a feature to layer several filters onto one Smart Object and change the order of the filters to achieve complex effects. This feature is quite useful in creating depth within images, as each filter may interact with other filters for subtle results.

New Filters Features in Photoshop 2025

Photoshop 2025 has introduced several new exciting features with the filter system:

1. **AI-Powered Adaptive Filters**: New Artificial Intelligence-powered filters, such as Adaptive Portrait and Adaptive Landscape will analyze your image and automatically apply an appropriate effect based on content and style. For example, Adaptive Portrait would be able to automatically identify faces, soften skin, enhance eyes, and adjust lighting to make it look professional without requiring manual adjustments.

2. **Enhanced Neural Filters**: Since its introduction, Neural Filters have been one of the coolest features in Photoshop. With these brand-new, AI-powered filters, you will be able to change the mood of a picture, change facial expressions, and even change backgrounds with ease. Improved controls for Neural Filters such as Depth Blur, and Colorize, and added options like Style Transfer that lets you apply famous art styles to your images are included in version 2025.

3. **Live Preview and Real-Time Adjustment**: Photoshop 2025 gives a live preview of filters. The effect will be viewed right away instead of having to wait for rendering. This enhancement is useful mainly for computationally intensive filters such as Lens Blur and Smart Sharpen, saving you time in showing results directly.

4. **Customizable Filter Presets**: For those users who consistently apply the same filter settings, Photoshop 2025 can save any filter preset. The capability for customization enables you to save adjustments for future use, hence the consistency of projects and speedy application of effects.

Tips for Effective Filter Use

Where filters can indeed be very powerful, judicious application forms the basis of professionalism in results:

- **Start with a Smart Object**: Get into the habit of converting your layer to a Smart Object before you apply the filtering. This is a method through which you will enable yourself to go back and modify or delete the filter at any stage.

- **Layer Multiple Filters**: More complicated effects can be achieved by layering filters. A light Gaussian Blur, for example, followed by a Sharpen filter can achieve focus on details in key elements while softening everything else.

- **Use Mask for Precision**: Layer masks work by applying filters in selected areas so the effect focuses on where one wants it to be. This gives full control to achieve the desired look.

Smart Filters: Non-Destructive Application of Filters on Smart Objects

Smart Objects are layers that maintain an image's original properties and allow edits to be applied in a non-destructive manner. Once the image layer is converted into a Smart Object, Photoshop encapsulates the layer, maintaining the original details and pixel quality of the layer inside. You can scale this encapsulated layer, warp it, and manipulate it several times without degrading its quality.

Smart Filters are special filters applied to a Smart Object, enabling editing and modification of filters as many times as desired without destroying the original. Unlike the **'normal'** filters which affect the actual pixels on a layer, Smart Filters are applied as editable effects that can be adjusted anytime, masked, and ordered.

The benefit of Smart Filters in Photoshop 2025

1. **Non-Destructive Workflow**: Classic filters work right in the picture and change the pixels, while Smart Filters keep their filter adjustments separate from the content of the layer, meaning the source data of an image does not change.

2.   **Flexible Editing**: It is easy to readjust filter settings at any time, set the order in which multiple filters are applied, and adjust blend modes and masks for each filter. This flexibility is key to complex projects that call for numerous iterations or revisions.

3.   **High Quality and Scalability**: Since the filter is applied to a Smart Object, all transformations such as resizing do not affect the quality of the image.

4.   **Increased Efficiency:** For its efficiency, Photoshop 2025 allows smoother previews; now you can view changes in real-time without having to wait for the software to render the whole filter.

How to Apply Smart Filters in Photoshop 2025

Step 1: Convert Your Layer to a Smart Object

To start working with Smart Filters, convert the layer to a Smart Object:

*   Right-click on the layer in the Layers panel.

*   Select **Convert to Smart Object**, and you will see that a little icon now appears on the layer's thumbnail. The icon indicates that it is a Smart Object. Or, from the top menu go to **Layer > Smart Objects > Convert to Smart Object**.

Step 2: Apply a Smart Filter

Once your layer is a Smart Object, you can apply any filter as a Smart Filter:

1.   Go up to the **Filter** menu and select any filter; **Gaussian Blur, Sharpen, Noise, and Camera Raw.**

2.   In the dialog box that opens, refine the filter settings. When you're satisfied click **OK**.

You will now see that, after adding the filter, a new Smart Filters sub-layer is added in the Layers panel below your layer. That sub-layer simply represents that filter applied on your Smart Object. You can modify or change that one as required.

Step 3: Refining the Smart Filter Settings

You can always double-click the Smart Filter name in the Layers panel to reopen its settings and change these. And this is very handy if you later decide that a blur needs to be stronger, or you want to change the settings of a Camera Raw filter.

Step 4: Working with the Filter Mask

One of the strong suits of Smart Filters is the Filter Mask that comes with each filter applied. The Filter Mask allows you to specify where the filter is applied over the layer by using some painting:

- **White** reveals the filter, applying it fully in that area.
- **Black** hides the filter, making it invisible in that area.

To refine the Filter Mask, select the mask and then, with the Brush Tool, paint over areas where you want to change the visibility of the filter. This mask is very useful in applying a filter selectively, which finds a lot of applications in portrait editing where one would want to blur the background without touching the subject.

Step 5: Editing Smart Filter Blending Options

Smart Filters in Photoshop 2025 have editable Blending Options. To proceed, do the following steps in continuation of the previous ones:

- Double-click the **Blending Options** icon next to the name of the Smart Filter.
- A Blending Options dialogue box opens where one can edit the Blend Mode and Opacity of the smart filter.

Blending modes can be applied with Smart Filters to apply the filter in a range of combinations with the underlying image. For example, applying a Gaussian Blur filter set to Soft Light will produce a dreamy, soft-focus effect.

Organizing Multiple Smart Filters

With Photoshop 2025, you can now add more than one filter to a single Smart Object and reorder them to prioritize one effect over another. Since each filter will affect the output of another, applying filters in a different order could affect how the final image looks. To do so, click and drag on a filter name in the Layers panel.

Practical Applications of Smart Filters

Smart Filters are useful in a wide range of editing scenarios. Here are a few practical examples:

1. **Portrait Retouching**: Nondestructively smoothening skin with filters like Surface Blur or Noise Reduction. Masking particular areas allows you to keep other areas sharp and defined.

2. **Landscape Editing**: Enhance dynamic range and color in landscape photography by applying Camera Raw or HDR Toning as a Smart Filter.

3. **Creative Effects**: Apply the Distort and Sharpen filters among others, for special stylizing effects, remembering that these are easily modifiable or maskable results.

Common Filters Used in Photography: Blur, Sharpen, Noise Reduction

1. **Blur Filters**

    One of the important tools used for creating depth, drawing attention, or adding an artistic touch to a photograph, blur filters come in more than one type in Photoshop 2025, along with their respective uses. These include:

    *   **Gaussian Blur**

        The Gaussian Blur filter represents the classic way of softening an image to make it appear smooth and dreamy. It very often serves for noise and detail reduction, skin tone smoothing, and the softening of generally harsh edges. By adjusting the radius, users control the intensity of the blur-the higher the value, the more blur visible.

Note: You can apply the Gaussian Blur to a duplicated layer and then adjust its opacity or add a mask for selective softening. Very handy in portrait photography, this allows you to blur your background to make your subject stand out.

- **Motion Blur**

The Motion Blur filter is great for simulating movement, perfect for action photography. This adds a streaking effect to the viewer for some perception of velocity or movement. This can be used sparingly to help a viewer focus on certain parts of an image.

Tip: Try to match the direction of the motion in the photo by using the angle setting. If your subject is moving diagonally, it looks better if the angle setting follows the direction of motion.

- **Lens Blur**

The filter simulates the shallow depth of field of a camera, which in turn gives an attractive bokeh effect. This is great for putting the focus on anything within your image, allowing everything else out of focus, which can emphasize the subject.

The trick here is to duplicate the layer on which you want to apply the Lens Blur, and using a layer mask, apply the blur only in parts of the image to be able to keep the background blurred and your subject in focus. This will allow you to achieve a very professional portrait effect and make your subjects stand out.

- **Field, Iris, and Tilt-Shift Blur**

Advanced blur effects can be achieved through Photoshop's Blur Gallery for greater control by the user. Field Blur smoothly transitions the image from sharp to blurry, Iris Blur allows the user to simulate a shallow depth of field, and the Tilt-Shift Blur will create the appearance of a miniature.

Tip: The Blur Gallery provides some very creative ways to create depth in an image. These are particularly great to be used in landscape photography, where you want to bring focus onto part of the image.

2. **Sharpen Filters**

Sharpen filters enhance the clarity and definition of an image, making it perfect for images that come out a bit soft or that lack detail. Care must be taken when sharpening, however, because oversharpening can tend to create unnatural pictures.

*   **Smart Sharpen**

    Smart Sharpen in Photoshop 2025 is one of the most commanding tools for a photographer to selectively sharpen images. This also comprises methods for noise reduction while sharpening, which maintains the look in a balanced manner. Amount, radius, and reduced noise can be controlled within the same filter-a real all-in-one sharpening tool.

    As this can sometimes create halos or harsh edges, this is often more effective using a lower radius setting. Place the filter on a duplicated layer and adjust the layer opacity to refine the effect.

*   **Unsharp Mask**

    With its confusing name, Unsharp Mask is a sharpening filter. This filter increases detail by increasing contrast between adjacent pixels. Such a filter works best on photos where subtler sharpening is needed without changing the overall look.

    Tip: Use a low amount/radius and increase it, so you don't have too much grainy effect on the image. Unsharp Mask works fantastic for print images, as it adds detail that may not be as visible on screens but will pop on paper.

- **High Pass Sharpening**

    High Pass Sharpening is one sure way to emphasize fine details within an image, especially for those photos that involve architecture or landscapes. This filter works by isolating the edges in the image, thereby allowing users to sharpen those edges without affecting the rest of the image.

    Tip: Apply High Pass Filter on a duplicated layer, then change the blending mode of the layer to Overlay or Soft Light and adjust its opacity. This will provide a less apparent effect of sharpening, yet you can combine it with other sharpening options to get a balanced result.

Noise Reduction Filters

Where noise can be major, especially in low light, visible grainy or pixelated textures can show up in an image. Noise reduction features are powerful in Photoshop 2025, therefore making clean, polished photos even out of the high ISO shots possible.

- **Reduced Noise**

    The **'Reduce Noise'** filter in Photoshop addresses a few major noise issues, including luminance and color noise, which are common problems in high-ISO shots. This filter lets you sharpen your advanced noise reduction settings for detail, color, and sharpness.

    Tip: Be careful not to over-smooth the image. Generally, a balance of noise reduction and preserving details will be the better approach. Start with a low value for noise reduction and increase the value incrementally as needed.

- **Camera Raw Noise Reduction**

  Camera Raw allows Photoshop users to have advanced noise reduction, utilizing sliders that adjust luminance, color noise, and recovery of detail for further advanced noise reduction. This utility is ideal in the case of raw photographs when the photographer needs more granular refinement of noise reduction without losing the details of the image.

  Tip: For minimal noise, one should use a combination of the luminance and color sliders. In addition to that, detail and contrast sliders can be used to retain clarity in an image while bringing down the noise. It is also a great tool for portrait and low-light photography.

Balancing Filters for Optimal Results

Since all of these filters enhance an image in one way or another, real professionalism comes with how well one combines them. Start by removing noise; sharpening should thereafter be applied wherever the details need emphasis. Introduce blur to selected portions in the background if one wants to take the focus off some objects in a picture. Non-destructive editing in Adobe Photoshop 2025 can be done by applying these effects on separate layers for increased flexibility and control.

Creative Effects with Distort, Render, and Stylize Filters: Effects for Digital Art

1. **Distort Filters: Warping and Reshaping Reality**

   The filters for distorting in Photoshop offer a variety of tools to manipulate image geometry. Ideal to construct some surrealist, otherworldly effects by changing proportions, lines, and textures. This is now more refined in its 2025 version with smooth rendering and in real-time, both of which digital artists find important to get out from under the burden of realistic depiction.

Some of the most popular Distort filters include:

- **Ripple**: Creates wavy, ripple-like distortions across an image. This is great if one wants to give the impression of something reflected in water or even to apply a heat wave effect, as it adds a dynamic and fluid quality to the piece. Playing with various scales and amounts can turn quite a still scene into a vibrant, pulsating composition.

- **Twirl**: Spins the pixels around any chosen point in a vortex. Twirl is often used to bring a swirling energy into an image. It works best in abstract art and fantasy scenes. By changing the angle and size of the twirl, it can be applied from a relatively soft spiral to a big, sweeping turn of force.

- **Spherize**: Deforms the selected area as if it were a projection on a sphere. This effect is fantastic to give pictures a three-dimensional effect so that they seem like bubbles, domes, or ellipsoidal shapes. Digital artists can use Spherize to obtain simulated glass globes, crystal balls, or even planet-like elements in a cosmic scene.

- **Wave**: This filter creates the most elaborate wave patterns across an image by shifting the pixels along multiple sine waves. By having control over the wavelength, amplitude, and number of wave generators, Wave can effectively capture the texture of water, intense glitch effects, or simply add an organic feel to compositions.

Creative Applications of Distort Filters

Digital artists love the flexibility and freedom offered by the distort filters. The Ripple or Wave can take a landscape image and morph it into a surreally dreamlike image, while portrait artists will subtly reshape features to achieve an ethereal or otherworldly effect. The distorted filters with layer masks and gradient maps result in layered compositions where only portions are distorted. Adding depth and dimension, this effect is usually evident.

2. **Render Filters: Building Unique Environments and Textures**

Render filters create the fancies of light, clouds, fibers, and other environmental effects that are good for setting moods and placing realistic or fantasy backgrounds on an image. Enhancements have made this category within Adobe Photoshop 2025 even better, with new AI-driven adjustments that offer even more realism.

Key Render Filters:

- **Clouds and Difference Clouds**: Creates cloud-like textures with foreground and background colors. The Clouds filter is ideal for the rapid creation of atmospheric effects that can be layered or combined to achieve several sky or texture effects. Difference Clouds create more contrast and can be used in fiery and stormy skies or a marble-like effect.

- **Lens Flare**: Light burst effect imitating the lens flare coming from a camera. This filter can add a focal point in lighting to enhance the realism in the scene for direct sources of light or stylize an image in a cinematic fashion. There are multiple flare types, and by allowing them to be customized, the digital artist can adapt these to scenes with different brightness levels and moods.

- **Fibers**: This filter creates textures resembling cloth, wood grain, or brushed metal which is a rapid means for the artist to add fine textures. Adjusting fiber strength and variance can lead to more control over the coarseness or the smoothness of the texture, which may be useful in backgrounds or the creation of fabric-like textures on digital clothes.

- **Lighting Effects:** The most powerful of Render filters, the feature presents light sources that can be modified by intensity, angle, and color. Lighting Effects are necessary to give depth, draw viewer focus, or emulate real-life lighting in fantasy and portrait artworks.

Creative Applications of Render Filters

Render filters can create everything from surreal textures to ethereal backboards or enhance the realism of a scene. Together, Clouds and Lighting Effects can produce haunting skies or dramatic light settings for digital artists. Fibers, if applied on background layers, can simulate canvas texture and thereby give a very organic feel to digital paintings. Creative applications with Render filters increase further when done in combination with blend modes.

3. **Stylize Filters: Adding Artistic Touches and Unique Patterns**

   Stylized filters add the final, defining touches that often transform everyday pictures into dramatic works of digital art. The stylized filters accentuate edges, amplify textures, and otherwise perform a kind of artistic magic that changes images into compelling works of art.

   Key Stylize Filters:

   - **Oil Paint**: Probably the most used Stylize filter, Oil Paint smooths and swirls pixels to create a painterly effect. The Brush, Cleanliness, and Shine controls let the artist get just the right look, from giving portraits an old-master feel to making landscapes impressionistic.

   - **Emboss**: This filter changes the texture of an image so that the object appears to be raised or etched. The result in an emboss filter gives a three-dimensional, tactile feel to the image. This will be effective with some abstract compositions, typography, and also in adding depth with the textures of a pattern or surface in design.

- **Find Edges**: This filter outlines the edges in a 'sketchy' manner. It may be very helpful for artists when they have to mix line art with digital painting, or simply as an initial step in a chain of filters that enhance the image in a textured three-dimensional way.

- **Diffuse**: That imparts softness or directional blurring to the image, very good for dreamy blended backgrounds. Diffuse is a technique in which digital artists soften the details of a scene, or it may be used to simulate a fog effect in a landscape work.

Creative Applications of Stylize Filters

Stylized filters represent a broad range of tools for the digital artist wishing to add that handcrafted feel. The Oil Paint filter allows the artist to apply a consistent, painterly feel to a digital canvas, while embossing can give elements like stone or metal grit and reality. To attain this look with more layers, artists can merge several of the Stylize filters and add layer masks to select where the effects are applied, giving a composition depth.

Using Camera Raw as a Filter for Enhanced Editing

What is Camera Raw?

Adobe Camera Raw, also called ACR, was originally written to work with raw files. A raw file is essentially an uncompromised image that contains all the data that was captured by the camera's sensor. When you use Camera Raw, it allows for non-destructive editing, as all edits to your image are made without actually touching any data of the original file. But since it's also a filter within the application, one can use it to apply Camera Raw adjustments directly onto any layer of any source file, be those JPEGs, TIFFs, or whatever format.

Why Use Camera Raw as a Filter?

Opening Camera Raw as a filter in Photoshop enables sophisticated editing, normally used in the processing of raw files, to be applied to non-raw files. This flexibility goes so far as to provide further, more precise adjustments of exposure, contrast, color correction, and enhancements of detail. The benefits of Camera Raw as a filter in Camera Raw include the following:

1. **Non-Destructive Editing**: Using Camera Raw as a Smart Filter on a Smart Object layer allows for non-destructive editing adjustments in Camera Raw, you can return to Camera Raw settings at any time and make adjustments without penalty on the original image quality.

2. **Improved Color and Tone Adjustments**: The Camera Raw filter has a variety of tone and color adjustment tools, which are more powerful compared to the standard Photoshop Adjustments panel.

3. **Enhance Details**: Camera Raw provides advanced sharpening, noise reduction, and clarity adjustments that can be made without damaging the image quality in general.

4. **Selective Adjustments:** The Adjustment Brush, Graduated Filter, and Radial Filter can be utilized for local adjustments. Unlike global adjustments, with Camera Raw, you can target parts of the image.

5. **Improved Workflow**: Camera Raw as a filter will keep you in Photoshop and allow you to make superior adjustments to enhance your editing workflow.

How to Apply Camera Raw as a Filter

To apply Camera Raw as a filter, follow these steps:

1. **Convert Layer to Smart Object**: Convert your image layer to a Smart Object by right-clicking the layer in the Layers panel and choosing "**Convert to Smart Object**." This ensures that when you apply filters, they can be non-destructive. You will be able to revise them if needed.

2. **Open Camera Raw**: First of all, ensure that a layer is selected, then activate the Camera Raw Filter by going to **Filter > Camera Raw Filter**. The Camera Raw opens, showing a variety of sliders and options for edits.

3. **Adjust in Camera Raw:**
   - **Basic Panel:** The basic panel here forms the main control points: exposure, contrast, highlights, shadows, whites, and blacks. These enable you to adjust the tonal range in your image.
   - **Adjust Color:** With the HSL/Color panel, you can adjust the hue, saturation, and luminance of individual colors in your image. You'll find that quite helpful when you want color correction or need a certain mood or tone in your photo.
   - **Detail Panel**: Sharpen your image and apply noise reduction. In the Photoshop 2025 version, the detail sliders are enhanced to give you fine-tuned control over texture and noise reduction.

4. **Use Local Adjustments to Perform Targeted Edits**:
   - **Adjustment Brush**: You can make adjustments with the Adjustment Brush by simply painting over selected areas of an image. You will be able to alter the exposure, contrast, and more on selected areas. This makes it great for selectively enhancing areas of an image.
   - **Graduated Filter and Radial Filter**: You can apply these features to make adjustments with a gradient effect. It is ideal for enhancing skies, driving interest in a place, or even vignettes.

5. **Retouch with Curves and Color Grading:**
   - The Curves tool will let you make refined adjustments to the contrast in your image. In Curves, you'll have major control over the highlights, midtones, and shadows.

- Color Grading panel-formerly called split toning allows you to add color tones into the shadows, midtones, and highlights that add mood to an image.

6. **Adjust Optics and Geometry**: This allows you to correct lens distortions and perspective problems that might be part of the picture. Camera Raw in Photoshop 2025 also updated several tools that provide fine control over the adjustment of perspective, which helps you easily correct lines that come out distorted in architectural or landscape pictures.

Finishing and Saving Your Edits

After you have made your edits, click **OK** to apply the Camera Raw filter to your Smart Object layer in Photoshop. You will be returned to the main workspace in Photoshop, with the Camera Raw filter represented under the layer as a Smart Filter. If later you want to change any of the Camera Raw settings for the filter, you can simply double-click the filter in the Layers panel to reopen the Camera Raw workspace.

CHAPTER FOURTEEN

GRADIENT AND COLOR FILL ADJUSTMENTS

Working with Gradients: Linear, Radial, and Custom Gradients

Creating Gradient Overlays and Backgrounds

Gradients in Photoshop refer to all subtle transitions between two or more colors. These can be used for background purposes, overlays, and creating slight depth feelings within the picture. There are many ways one can customize gradients using Photoshop 2025. Let's have a brief introduction to getting started with the new gradient editor and real-time preview options available:

1. **Create a New Document:** Open Photoshop and create a new document. Decide on the size of the canvas that suits your needs and resolution for whatever work you're doing. By design, for a website background, for instance, you will need to start with 1920x1080 pixels at 72 DPI.

2. **Access the Gradient Tool:** Select the **Gradient Tool** from the toolbar, or press **G** on your keyboard. The Gradient Tool in Photoshop 2025 contains more intuitive options to apply and edit the gradients directly on the canvas.

3. **Select a Gradient Type:**

Photoshop has five major gradient types:

- **Linear**: These colors blend in a straight line.
- **Radial**: Colors radiate outward from a center point.
- **Angle**: This creates a gradient in a sweep around a center point.
- **Reflected**: Mirrored gradient on both sides of the starting point
- **Diamond**: Gradient in diamond shape from the center

Each type of gradient type creates different visual effects and hence can be given a trial to fit your design requirements.

Creating a Gradient Overlay

Gradient overlay is a great way to achieve subtle or bold colored effects over text, shapes, or images. Here is how to implement a gradient overlay in Photoshop 2025;

1. **Select Your Layer**: Choose the layer on which you want to apply the gradient overlay. It could be a text layer, shape, or image.

2. **Launch the Layer Style Panel:** Open the Layer style panel from **Layer > Layer Style > Gradient Overlay**. This is where all your options will be for altering how your gradient overlay looks and feels.

3. **Choose Your Gradient and Blend Mode**: Click the gradient box in the Gradient Overlay panel to open the Gradient Editor. Although Photoshop 2025 has a Gradient Library that contains preset gradients, you can create your custom gradient. Now choose a blend mode - Multiply or Overlay for example - to allow you to see the gradient on top of the layer underneath it. You can achieve soft transitions to vibrant contrasts with the different blending modes.

4. **Adjust Opacity and Scale:** Move the slider over Opacity to adjust the transparency of the gradient, and Scale to increase or decrease the effect of the gradient across your layer. You can lower the opacity to 50-75% for a softer and less obvious overlay.

5. **Adjust the Gradient:** Play with the Angle slider to set the direction in which your gradient falls. This option will be grayed out for you if you have chosen a radial or diamond gradient. If you'd like, now drag the gradient overlay onto the canvas and release it in the perfect position.

Designing a Gradient Background

Creating a gradient background can be even easier yet just as effective. Here's how you create gorgeous backgrounds with gradients:

1. **Select a Background Layer**: In a new document, create or select a background layer. If your background layer is locked, double-click to unlock it and rename it if you like.

2. **Get the Gradient Tool and Put on Your Gradient**: With the Gradient Tool selected, choose your kind of gradient and your colors. Click and drag across your canvas. Dragging it from different directions, for instance, top to bottom or corner to corner, changes the way it appears.

3. **Editing Your Gradient Colors:** Click the gradient preview bar along the top options bar to open the Gradient Editor. Inside it you'll be able to manipulate color stops, each a representation of one of the colors in your gradient. To set up a color stop click under the gradient bar and to remove any stop drag it off from the bar. Drag the position of the stop to smoothly transition into another stop, or to create an abrupt break between colors.

4. **Save Your Gradient:** If you've created a personalized gradient that you'd like to reuse, Photoshop 2025 does allow you to save gradients. Just click on the New button in the Gradient Editor and it's saved in your gradient library for projects to come.

Using Gradient Maps for Advanced Effects

The Gradient Map in Photoshop 2025 is an advanced feature wherein a gradient is applied based on the image's tonal values, especially to create a certain surreal effect or colored tone of a photograph. Here's how you do this:

1. **Add a Gradient Map Adjustment Layer**: Open your image and head to **Layer > New Adjustment Layer > Gradient Map**. Instantly, this will apply a gradient that is based on the shadows, midtones, and highlights of the image.

2. **Adjust the Gradient Map**: Double-click the gradient in the properties panel to open up the Gradient Editor. The left side represents shadows, the middle midtones, right side the highlights. Manipulate colors within a range from

extreme to toning your color. For example, you can make your shadows cool-toned, while your highlights are warm-toned, which gives you this movie-type feel instantly.

Working with Solid and Pattern Fill Layers

Understanding Fill Layers in Photoshop

Fill layers in Photoshop differ from the regular raster layers in the fact that they are non-destructive and allow editing without destroying the underlying image. In other words, you can modify and adjust settings and experiment with combinations without actually applying permanent changes to your layer. Another good thing about fill layers is that they respond to layer masks, blending modes, and changes in opacity, which gives you huge possibilities for flexing and manipulating your design elements.

How to Access

To add a Solid Color or Pattern Fill Layer, follow the steps below:

1. **Access the Layers Panel**: Ensure that your Layers panel is opened. If it isn't open, you can open one via **Window > Layers**.
2. **Click the Adjustment Layer Icon**: At the bottom of the Layers panel, you will notice an icon of a circle (half-filled) showing adjustment layers. Click on it.
3. **Choose Fill Layer Type**: In the menu select one of the two options: **Solid Color** or **Pattern**, whichever corresponds to what you want to create as a fill layer.

Working with Solid Color Fill Layers

In this type of fill layer, you will use a single color over your project. Here is how you can create and edit a Solid Color Fill Layer:

1. **Create a Solid Color Fill Layer**: After the adjustment layer icon has been clicked and Solid Color selected, a color picker will be opened in Photoshop, where any color can be chosen. Once you have selected your color, click **OK**.

2. **Change the Color**: To change the color of the Solid Color Fill Layer, you need only double-click the color thumbnail in the Layers Panel, which will reopen this color picker so that you can choose another hue and shade for your desired effect.

3. **Using Blending Modes**: Blending modes let you modify how the solid color fill layer interacts with the layers below. You can adjust the blending mode by clicking on the drop-down at the top of the Layers Panel. Multiply or Overlay mode is one of the most common for a Solid Color layer. That will instantly bring some life and depth to your design.

4. **Opacity Adjustment**: Adjust the intensity of the fill layer in the Layers panel by adjusting its layer opacity. The lower the Opacity, the more the layer allows some of the underlying image to show through, thus giving a subtler effect.

5. **Adding Masks to Refine Effects:** To do this, so that the layer Solid Color is visible only in some places of your image, you will need to attach a layer mask. Having the Solid Color Fill Layer selected, click the icon of the Layer Mask at the bottom of the Layers Panel. Now take the brush and paint black in places where you want the color to be hidden. Such an option will allow you to point exactly where the fill should be visible.

Creative uses of solid color fill layers are limitless. For example, here are some:

-   **Color Correcting Backgrounds**: This will let you color balance a background without touching the rest of your image so it can match your subject.

-   **Adding Mood Overlays:** This comprises using dark colors with the blending mode Overlay or Multiply to create moody images with vignetted effects.

-   **Creating Monochromatic Effects**: Add a color wash over your image by adding a Solid Color layer in combination with low opacity. It's one of the quickest ways to add some style to your project.

Working with Pattern Fill Layers

Pattern Fill Layers work much like any other fill layer but allow you to apply pre-defined patterns or custom textures to your project. This is a great option for backgrounds, textures, or even custom overlays.

1. **Create a Pattern Fill Layer:** After selecting **Pattern** from the adjustment layer menu, by default, Photoshop will open the Pattern Fill dialogue window. You can see a default pattern, which you can change just by clicking the grayed pattern preview area.

2. **Select and Scale Patterns:**

- You can select the patterns and scale them by clicking the pattern thumbnail in the Pattern Fill dialogue window. You will see a default set of different patterns preset in Photoshop, or you can load your custom pattern.

- Scale the pattern to fit your project. The downscaling of the scale gives you a more detailed pattern, whereas upside scaling makes it the opposite and gives you a large-sized pattern with prominence. Move the Scale slider for an appropriate pattern fitting in your design.

3. **Adjust Blending Modes and Opacity**: Like the **Solid Color Fill** Layers, you can also change the mode and opacity of a Pattern Fill Layer to see how it interacts with the underlying layers. Nice with modes like Soft Light, Overlay, or Multiply.

4. **Adding Masks for Custom Patterns**: Apply a layer mask to the layer to which you want to apply a pattern, if you only want the pattern on part of your design. This is extremely useful if you want the pattern to involve only a background or other discrete objects.

Creative Applications of Pattern Fill Layers

Pattern Fill Layers have loads of creative potential. Here are some ideas to get you going:

- **Create Textured Backgrounds:** Patterns add a little extra to a flat background. Subtle textures like linen or paper add a more refined aesthetic.

- **Add Patterns to Specific Elements:** Layer masks enable you to add patterns on selected elements only. As an example, you can add texture to the text layer for that worn and grungy feeling.

- **Overlay Patterns for Artistic Effects**: If you wish to experiment, use geometric or abstract patterns in low opacity to give your image that trendy, artistic feel.

Applying Gradient to Change Layer Styles in Photoshop

Layer styles are a great way to apply cool effects to your layers without touching the layer itself. You can apply shadows, glows, bevels, gradients, and more to a layer without destroying it. Layer styles are non-destructive, meaning that you can go back at any time and change or delete them without affecting the original layer. To apply layer styles, right-click on a layer and select **"Blending Options"** or click the icon at the bottom of the Layers panel. The opening panel, Layer Style, will show you the different effects available to apply, such as gradients.

The Role of Gradients in Layer Styles

Gradients in layer styles are something flexible. That will give you the ability to transition colors across an object by simulating light, shadow, or even depth. You can easily create metallic effects with gradients by adding realistic shadows and highlights, or add colorful transitions to your designs. Advanced gradient features introduced in Photoshop 2025 make fine-tuning the look and feel of these effects easier than ever.

Applying a Gradient Overlay

The Gradient Overlay is probably one of the most popular layer styles. Here's how to apply it:

1. **Layer Selection**: Choose the layer you want to put a gradient overlay on.
2. **Open Layer Style**: Click on the menu option **Layer > Layer Style > Gradient Overlay**. This opens the Layer Style panel with the options for Gradient Overlay.

3. **Choose a Gradient**: Click the gradient preview to open the Gradient Editor. New preset gradients and extended gradient libraries in Adobe Photoshop 2025 offer you a huge selection to choose from.

4. **Edit Gradient**: You can edit the colors inside Gradient Editor and change the gradient's style, which could be Linear, Radial, Angle, Reflected, or Diamond, and change scale and angle.

Fine-Tuning the Gradient Settings

Gradients are highly customizable in Photoshop 2025. Basic options that one might want to understand in a gradient setting include:

- **Blend Mode**: Choose any of the several blend modes, such as Normal, Multiply, Overlay, and Screen, to determine how the gradient interacts with your underlying layer colors. Experiment with different modes until you achieve the effect you like.

- **Opacity**: The opacity value of the gradient. Lower opacity means that more of the underlying layer will appear through, which is super useful for subtle effects.

- **Reverse**: On/Off toggle for flipping the direction of the gradient. Super helpful when you want to quickly change where the lighter and darker colors land on your design.

- **Angle**: Choose the angle of the gradient. A linear gradient of 0º will run from left to right, while one at 90º will run from bottom to top. Rotation of the angle will give you various light effects.

- **Scale**: Size of the gradient. The bigger the scale is, the more stretched the gradient will appear; the smaller the scale, the more compact or vivid the colors will be.

Creating and Saving Custom Gradients

This is a great way to personalize your design and create your gradients within the Gradient Editor. To do so, follow these steps:

1. **Launch the Gradient Editor**: Click on the gradient within the Gradient Overlay panel to open the Gradient Editor.

2. **Adjust Color Stops:** To edit color stops, click on them. To add color stops, click anywhere along the bar.

3. **Change Color Opacity**: Click on the color stop and adjust the slider for Opacity to create either a smooth transition or a hard break in color.

4. **Saving the Gradient:** When you are satisfied with the gradient, click "**New**" to save it in the Preset section so you can reuse your newly created custom gradients anytime in upcoming projects.

Combining Gradients with Other Layer Styles

You can combine gradients with other layer styles for that dynamic look. Some of the effects you can create by mixing gradients with other styles include:

- **Gradient with Drop Shadow**: By default, adding a gradient overlay gives you a smooth color transition effect. Adding a drop shadow including an angle along with adjusting the opacity to complement the direction of the gradient can be done.

- **Gradient with Bevel & Emboss:** This will give a 3D effect for metallic and textual effects by the usage of Bevel & Emboss along with a gradient overlay. It gives a fine impression of light on the different surfaces.

- **Gradient with Inner Glow or Outer Glow**: Adding a glow will subtly simulate the lighting. Choose colors that complement the gradient or those that would give an excellent contrast to add even more intensity.

CHAPTER FIFTEEN

USING TYPOGRAPHY AND TEXT EFFECTS

Working with Text Layers: Adding, Editing, and Formatting Text

Text is one of the commanding aspects of design. Adobe Photoshop 2025 has a great set of tools that are beneficial in adding, editing, and formatting text for any creative project. Whether it is designing posters, websites, and advertisements, or adding simple captions to an image, the methodology behind working with the text layers will greatly help and enhance your designs.

Adding Text

Adding text in Photoshop is relatively easy. To do so, follow the steps below:

1. **Select the Text Tool:** The Text Tool can be accessed from the toolbar located on the left side of your screen. It includes a "**T**" icon. It is also available from your keyboard via **T**.

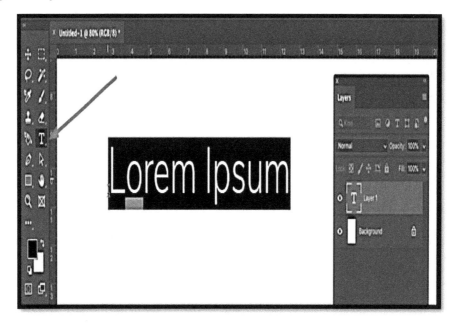

2. **Choose Horizontal or Vertical Text:** Photoshop has two types of text directions, namely horizontal and vertical. You can select whichever suits your design.

3. **Create a Text Box**: Just click anywhere on the canvas to immediately begin typing into a free-form text layer, or click and drag to create a text box. This is ideal to use when you want to contain longer bodies of text in a specific area so that you can better control the alignment and spacing.

4. **Enter Text**: Begin typing in the box you have just created, or in a free-form area. Note that each entry automatically opens a text layer in the layers panel in Photoshop, which can be accessed separately for manipulation.

Editing Text

After having placed text, you can relatively easily edit its contents, appearance, and position of the:

-   **Enable the Text Layer**: Select the text layer to be edited from the Layers panel.

-   **Use the Text Tool:** Clicking on text with the Text Tool will activate the text edit mode. You can directly add, delete, or change text.

-   **Moving Text without Editing**: For moving text across the screen without opening the text edit option, you would want to use the Move Tool under the shortcut **V**. Then drag it across to the position you want it on the canvas.

-   **Layer Management:** You can protect, hide, or group text layers right within the Layers panel for a clean workspace when you are working on a document with many texts. You can access the Duplicate Layer and Rasterize Layer options when you right-click on the text layer to turn your text into a pixel-based image.

Formatting Text

The formatting options in Photoshop 2025 range from font type to size, color, and other styling variables. Proceed with the following steps for availing such features in Photoshop:

- **Font Selection**: One of the best things that you could do is select a font from the ones already installed on your computer or make use of Adobe Fonts, which can be availed within the Character Panel of Photoshop. The best part is that Adobe Fonts have a host of fonts that you can enable and immediately start using inside Photoshop.

- **Font Size and Weight:** You can also use the Character Panel to change the size of the font and its weight, such as bold or italic, to begin developing emphasis or order of importance in your design.

- **Color Adjustments**: Change the color of the text by selecting the text layer and clicking the **Color Picker** in the toolbar or Character Panel. Choose your desired color. Photoshop 2025 also supports gradient overlays for text available under the Layer Style options.

- **Text Alignment and Justification**: Align left, center, or right, or use full justification for paragraph text. Alignment tools in text boxes provide balanced layouts, which have been very helpful, particularly where multi-column designs are involved.

- **Advanced Text Styling Options:** Photoshop 2025 added new advanced features of the Warp Text option for detailed text distortions. To access the Warp Text option, select the text layer, then choose **Edit > Transform > Warp**.

Adding Text Effects with Layer Styles

Text becomes much more exciting when layer styles are added to the text to give it depth and dimension. To apply styles to text:

- **Add Layer Effects:** Highlight your text layer and then head to **Layer > Layer Style** to pop open a box of different effects that include Drop Shadow, Outer Glow, and Bevel & Emboss, among others.

- **Customize Layer Effects:** Most of the effects have variable parameters. For instance, Drop Shadow offers opacity, angle, distance, and size. You can get really very subtle or quite dramatic just by playing with those settings, depending on what you want to do.

- **Save and Reapply Styles:** Photoshop 2025 gives the facility to save the style of layers as a preset. If you are using consistent text styles across many designs, saving the style helps you apply it fast across projects.

Working with Paragraph and Character Panels

The character and paragraph panels in Photoshop give you specific control over the typography. Here is how you can work with these two effectively:

- **Character Panel:** This panel will be used for specifying font, size, kerning (the space between letters), leading or spacing between lines, and tracking the spacing between words. By adjusting all these properties, you will be able to refine the appearance of the text to make it more readable and visually appealing.

- **Paragraph Panel:** Align, indent, and set spacing options for paragraph text. The paragraph panel is useful when you're designing magazine layouts, book covers, or anything else that has over one line or column of text.

- **OpenType Features:** If you are working with an OpenType font, the Character Panel allows you to access stylistic alternates, ligatures, and other typographic features. OpenType features make typing more flexible and elegant, especially when using decorative or handwritten fonts.

Saving and Exporting Text Layers

Once your text design is complete:

- **Exporting**: Exporting in Photoshop 2025 There are several ways of exporting in Photoshop 2025. To export, use the menu: select **File > Export > Export As**; save the design in a format, such as PNG, JPEG, or PSD. Save the file as a PSD if it contains editable text to keep the layers so that opening and editing are straightforward.

- **Flattening Text Layers:** While sending the file, you may not want the text to be editable; that's when you merge or rasterize text layers. Merging sends the text to combine with other design elements. Rasterizing turns your text into a static image layer for good.

Text Transformation and Warping: Creating Dynamic Text Shapes

Adobe Photoshop 2025 has several powerful features for text transformation and warping, which can help designers make visually attractive text effects that bring character into their work.

Step 1: Setting Up Your Canvas

Initially set up the canvas before transforming or warping any text.

1. Open Adobe Photoshop and open a new document. Choose appropriate dimensions according to your needs. For example, for social media, you could use 1080x1080 pixels, but you might want something like 1920x1080 for a presentation slide.

2. Using the toolbar on the left, select the **Text Tool (T)** and click anywhere on the canvas to begin typing your text.

3. Change your font, size, and color through the options on the top menu. Make your text large enough to see the before and after of your effects.

When you have your text in place you can begin to transform and warp it.

Step 2: Basic Transformations

Photoshop offers a range of options to transform text from simple resizing and rotating to distortion of the text:

1. On the Layers panel, highlight the text layer.
2. Go to **Edit > Free Transform** or press **Ctrl+T** for Windows or **Command+T** for Mac. You'll see a bounding box around the text.
3. The corner handles rescale your text; if you hold down the **Shift key**, the aspect ratio will be maintained. If you don't hold Shift, it will stretch the text.
4. To rotate the text, click on it outside of the bounding box and drag it to whatever angle you like.
5. To make a perspective, right-click inside the transform box and click on **Perspective**. Now, one of the corner handles can be dragged to produce an angular transformation, which will introduce a bit of depth into the text.

   These default transformations are good to change the size and orientation of your text. For more interesting effects, though, the warping tools in Photoshop are quite convenient.

Step 3: Apply the Text Warp

Warp Text allows you to bend and shape your text in some very interesting ways:

1. Select your text layer and go to **Edit > Transform > Warp**.
2. A mesh will be cast over your text, and a top menu will pop up displaying Arc, Bulge, Fish, Flag, Wave, etc.
3. In the drop-down menu select a style to warp. You can further refine things in the **Bend, Horizontal Distortion,** and **Vertical Distortion sliders**. Feel free to play with different values, observing how the text responds.

For example, the Arc warp will warp text into a semi-circular shape, while the Wave warp gives an undulation, which is very good for dynamic designs. You can adjust the sliders to modify the intensity of the warp, from very subtle to very dramatic.

Step 4: Advanced Warp Adjustments

If you want to make your warp even more unique, Photoshop provides further manual adjustments:

1. In Warp mode, drag individual points of the grid to perform distortions on the image as desired, stretching or compressing parts.

2. To drag a point independently of the others, hold down **Alt** on Windows, or **Option** on Mac, while dragging, and do asymmetrical warps.

    Manual warping is going to give you even finer control of your text shape, which is great for those one-of-a-kind projects that need you to make just the right adjustments. You can push and pull points in any direction, giving you creative license to mold and shape that text just the way you want it.

Step 5: Creating Custom Paths for Text

Consider using custom paths for truly dynamic text shapes:

1. Using the Pen Tool, draw a path on the canvas to form your desired line or shape that you want the text to follow.

2. Follow with the Text Tool by dragging it near your path until you see a bent line pop up next to the text cursor.

3. Click the path with your cursor to initiate typing along the path.

4. You can also adjust the start and end points using the **Path Selection Tool** by dragging the text along the path.

    This is one of the great ways to make text circular, wavy lines, or any other shape you come up with. It has a lot of applications in design, where text must fit in with other elements, such as logos or complicated layouts.

Step 6: Combining Multiple Warp Effects

You might notice that in more complex compositions you will want to combine multiple warp effects:

1. First, lay on a warp or transformation as explained above.

2. When you have the first effect to your satisfaction, right-click the text layer and choose **Rasterize Type**. This will convert the text into a pixel-based layer and let you perform further effects.

3. Use the **Edit > Transform menu** and give it a second warp or transformation. Such layering of effects can yield complex and striking visual effects since one is no longer constrained to a single style of warp. For example, you might wave warp first, then perspective warp it to suggest motion and distance.

Step 7: Final Adjustments and Enhancements

Once you have warped, here is where you want to consider making those last few touches to enhance your overall design:

- **Add a Drop Shadow:** To create depth, allowing your text to pop off of the background, go to **Layer > Layer Style > Drop Shadow**.

- **Add a Gradient Overlay**: Click **Layer > Layer Style > Gradient Overlay** and press to apply the gradient effect for adding colors that transition nicely with the warped shape.

- **Add Texture or Patterns**: If you want a bit more texture, add a pattern overlay or mask a texture layer onto your text.

Layer Styles for Text Effects: Drop Shadows, Strokes, and Glows

Text effects can make or break any design, allowing it to either pop, blend, or even convey mood and tone. Adobe Photoshop 2025 has great tools for text effects mainly through Layer Styles. Three of the most used styles applied to text are the Drop Shadows, Strokes, and Glows.

Drop Shadows

Drop shadow adds depth to text by creating a perception that text has been lifted off the background onto which it drops a shadow. It's versatile for the creation of everything from subtle depths to more dramatic 3D effects.

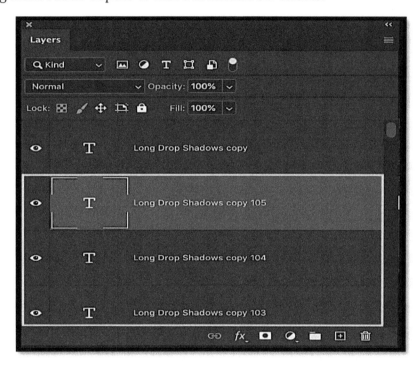

Adding a Drop Shadow:

1. Select your text layer.

2. Click the "**fx**" icon at the bottom of the Layers panel, and select **Drop Shadow**.

3. In the Layer Style dialog, you'll see a range of controls to make many different kinds of shadows.

Key Settings for Drop Shadows:

- **Blend Mode**: Controls how the shadow will blend with the background. "**Multiply**" is a good default for naturalistic shadows.

- **Color**: This should be a color that makes your text easier to read. Black and dark grey are typical, but colored shadows can be a cool effect.

- **Opacity**: Sets the transparency of the shadow. The lower the opacity, the softer and subtler it will be; higher opacity gives a full darker shadow.

- **Angle**: This sets the direction of the shadow. The default is usually about 120°, which simulates light coming from above left, but you can change that according to your design's lighting.

- **Distance**: This is how far the shadow is away from the text. Use this to help you decide how high or low the text is supposed to sit in the background.

- **Spread**: This increases the width of the shadow. The higher the spread, the harsher the shadow will feel and the softer it will be at lower values.

- **Size**: This controls how much blur is applied to the edges of the shadow. The larger the value, the softer the shadow will be; the smaller the value, the crisper the shadow will be.

How to Effectively Apply Drop Shadows:
- Work with distance and size to make them look more realistic.
- With dramatic effects, use larger-size, higher-opacity settings with low spread.
- Set the angle from the overall light source in your design for cohesion.

Stroke

The stroke layer style adds an outline to your text and can make it more readable against busy backgrounds. Strokes can be done in various sizes, colors, and positions to give both subtle and bold outlines.

How to Add a Stroke:
1. Select the text layer on which you want to add the stroke.
2. Navigate to the **fx** menu and choose the **Stroke option**.

Stroke Key Settings:

1. **Size**: Sets how thick the outline of the text would be. Thinner strokes can be 1-3px to provide slight emphasis, while thicker ones can go way higher depending on taste.

2. **Position**: The three types of settings here are as follows:
   ○ **Inside**: A situation where the stroke is within the text boundaries, making the words a bit more readable and defined.
   ○ **Center**: This makes the stroke half inside, and half outside the text edges.
   ○ **Outside**: It puts the stroke around the outside of the text; best used when needing a strong, graphic outline.

3. **Blend Mode**: Enables the stroke to blend with the background. The default "**Normal**" is usually applied, but you can try modes such as "**Overlay**" for more subtle results.

4. **Opacity**: Changes the stroke's transparency.

5. **Color**: Use a hue that will complement or provide contrast with your text and background. For instance, white or black strokes will give you bold borders, while soft colors can draw attention to your text without overwhelming it.

Working with Stroke

- Use an Outside position with a bold color to make text pop against busy or textured backgrounds.

- Try dual strokes by duplicating the text layer and adding a smaller stroke on the top layer in another color.

- For cohesive designs, make the stroke color the same color as other elements in your design palette.

Glow Effects (Outer and Inner Glow)

The glow effect adds a soft, luminescent halo either around or inside the text to produce either an ethereal or spotlight effect. In Photoshop, there exist two types of glow effects: the Outer Glow and the Inner Glow.

Adding Glow Effects:

1. Highlight your text layer.
2. Click the **fx icon** and from the dropdown select either Outer or Inner Glow.

Key Glow Effect Settings:

1. **Blend Mode:** "**Screen**" is often used to achieve a glowing effect with light. Other choices, such as "**Overlay**" or "**Soft Light**," can provide various light effects.

2. **Opacity**: Makes it visible according to choice. If the opacity is higher, then the brightness is low, and if low, then the brightness is soft.

3. **Noise**: This option gives a glowing texture. The more the noise the lesser the smoothness; this gives it a grainy look.

4. **Color**: Pick a color that goes well with your text and the design. Commonly, white or a light color has a good effect, but colored glow gives personality.

5. **Technique**:
   - **Softer**: Gives a diffused, rather natural, soft glow.
   - **Precise**: Sharpens the edges for a clearer effect.

6. **Spread and Size:**
   - **Spread**: Controls the thickness of the edge of the glow. A high value for spread gives a thicker glow around the border.
   - **Size**: Controls the overall spread of the glow. The larger the size is, the softer and wider it will be; the smaller the size gets, the more the glow becomes confined to the text.

Glow Effects Tips

- Outer Glow can be used for neon text effects if a bright color is set and the size and opacity are increased.

- For a soft subtle glow, set a small size and low opacity for a soft radius around the text.

- Add Inner Glow and Outer Glow to the same text layer to give a layered, even more immersive effect. Makes for fantastical, otherworldly, or dreamy designs.

Combining Layer Styles for Advanced Text Effects

Combining Drop Shadows, Strokes, and Glows will make powerful, striking text effects. Some ideas for the combination of these styles include the following:

- **Outline and Shadow:** Outline your text using a bold Outside Stroke, then give it a soft Drop Shadow for depth.

- **Outer Glow with Drop Shadow**: Apply an Outer Glow to create a neon-like effect; then, an added Drop Shadow gives it an even better feeling of depth.

- **Dual Strokes and Glow**: Duplicate the text layer; apply a thick Outside Stroke on the bottom layer and a finer Inside Stroke on the top layer. Further, add an Outer Glow to get an Outstanding glowing outline.

Creating Selections from Text

Selections from the text in Adobe Photoshop 2025 open an entirely new dimension of creative possibilities. From creating complex masks to filling letters with textures or imagery, making text selections is one of the most powerful tools for designers and digital artists.

Setting Up Your Document

Start by opening Adobe Photoshop 2025 and creating a new document. Set the dimensions depending on what the project calls for. For example, if you are making a poster, you could make it 11 x 17 inches at 300 pixels per inch. If this is for web use, you can get away with much lower resolutions, such as 72 DPI.

Next, choose your background color, which can be a blank or a particular color that you may think will best fit your design. Click on **File > New** and create your dimensions in the New Document dialog box.

Add and Format Your Text

Select the **Type Tool [T]** from your left side toolbar. Click on the canvas and type what you want; in this example, let's use "**Create**."

Choose the font, size, and color from the top menu bar. Alternatively, you can open the Character panel by going to **Window > Character**. This opens up a selection of fonts for you to choose one that suits your style and gives you the ability to change the size: A bold, thick font is best for selections because it gives you a strong, defined area to work with.

Once you have chosen your font, and have typed the text, now you'll want to size and position by choosing the **Move Tool (V)** and dragging your text into place. You're now ready to create a selection from this text.

Converting Text to a Selection

With your Type layer active in the Layers panel, right-click on the text layer and click **Convert to Smart Object**. This will allow us to maintain the quality of the text while being able to work with the text in various ways. Now well create a selection from the text.

Selecting from the text layer:

1.   Press and hold down the **Ctrl** key when using Mac, use **Command**, and click on the thumbnail of the text layer in your Layers panel. In doing this, you will

select a range or shape of your text, and each letter will now be highlighted as a marquee outline.

2. You now have a **"marching ants"** selection outline around each letter, indicating to you that you have selected something.

Otherwise, to keep the text editable, you can skip converting it into a Smart Object and click directly on it with the Magic Wand Tool (W). This will work best for simpler fonts and shapes.

Using the Selection

Now that you have actively selected your text, it's time to do something with the selection. The possibilities include:

- **Creating Masks:** With your text selected, you can create a mask on any layer. For example, add a new image layer above your text selection, and with the image layer active, click the **Add Layer Mask** button at the bottom of the Layers panel. This will mask the image layer to the shape of your text (a nice effect with the image coming through within your text).

- **Color Filling**: Having an active selection, create a new layer, choose any color through the Color Picker, and fill the selection with your desired color using either the Paint Bucket Tool or **Edit > Fill**. This might be one way to achieve vibrant typography or custom-colored text effects.

- **Adding Textures**: Another thing you could do with your selection is fill the text with texture or patterns. For this, you will need to make a new layer with your desired texture, move that over the text selection, and add a Clipping Mask by right-clicking the texture layer and choosing **Create Clipping Mask**. This will clip the texture to the shape of the text and will add more visual interest and depth to your typography.

Refining the Selection

Sometimes, once you have made your selection, you would have to make minor adjustments for perfect selections. Well, in Photoshop, there is a set of tools that allows you to refine the edges of your selection to perfection, especially if it contains delicate fonts.

With the selection active choose **Select > Select and Mask**. The Select and Mask workspace opens, allowing you to refine the edges, adjust feathering, and smooth or shift the edges. In this panel, you can:

- **Smooth** the selection for round, soft-edged selections.
- **Feather** the selection to add a soft transition blending the edges of the text with the background.
- **Shift Edge** allows you to nudge up or down the size of the selection a smidgeon to help perfect the fit of the selection.

  Once you are satisfied with the refinement, click **OK** to apply them.

Saving and Exporting Your Text Selection

If you will reuse this text selection, save it as an alpha channel by going to **Select > Save Selection** and naming the selection for future reference. This will create a channel mask in your Channels panel, which can be used at any time to reinstate the selection.

To save the entire project, go to **File > Save As** and select the Photoshop PSD format to retain all layers and edits. If you want to export it as a flattened image, go to **File > Export > Export As** and select a format like JPEG or PNG.

Adding Dimension and Lighting for Impact

Setting the Foundation with Layers and Smart Objects

First of all, before proceeding with the lighting effects, it is necessary to prepare our layers in such a way that gives us flexibility throughout the design process. Being key elements, turning them into Smart Objects allows you to work non-destructively, apply filters, or change properties in a layer without losing quality. Imagine having several objects or figures in your image; making each one a Smart Object lets you alter changes in light, scaling, or rotation at any point in time.

Smart Objects also allow for the new Live Gradient and Shadow Layers in Photoshop, brought in by Photoshop 2025. They let you see in real-time and make adjustments to gradients and shadows so that you know exactly how changes affect the depth of the composition.

Using the 3D Lighting Effects Tool

With Photoshop 2025, the tool of 3D Lighting Effects has been extended further to give great and realistic lighting with the creation of depth. It now offers more control over the intensity, spread, and angle of light for more realistic shadows and highlights. In using this tool, follow the following steps:

- **3D Lighting Effects:** Access the **3D Lighting Effects** via the **'Filter'** menu, selecting the object or layer you want to work on.
- **Light Source Positioning:** Drag the light source location within the workspace. A position high up produces very dramatic overheads, while a low position gives a variety of evening or spotlight effects.
- **Shadow Adjustment**: Change the opacity, blur, and angle of the shadow. In Photoshop 2025, the adjustment of shadows is more intuitive since it has added functionality for real-time preview.

- **Add Multiple Light Sources**: Additional functionalities now available within Photoshop can help you add multiple sources of light on a single layer and achieve the complex results needed to make your images mimic either a natural or even studio environment.

  The ability to have these features within one platform introduces an added feeling of realism and precision, invaluable when working with images requiring professionalism.

Layer Styles: Adding Inner and Outer Shadows

Layer styles are one of the basic ways to create dimension in Photoshop, and Adobe has opened up some new possibilities for 2025. Adding an Inner Shadow and an Outer Shadow effect can give depth to a flat object by making it appear to hover above or be sunken below the background.

- **Inner Shadow**: Highlight first the layer in which you want these changes to be made. Again, go into the Layer Style dialog box and click on "**Inner Shadow**." From here, you'll be able to change the angle, distance, size, and opacity. This gives the impression of a shadow inside your object and works great on providing inset objects to appear as if they have depth within themselves.
- **Outer Shadow**: A shadow is referred to as Outer Shadow when an element needs to be jumping off the background. Outer Shadows applied for the first time a feature called "**Highlight Overlay**," which allows you to create soft or diffused shadows in Photoshop 2025.

Photoshop 2025 also adds Dynamic Shadows that update according to the position of the object within the workspace. If you move an element, the shadow itself automatically recalculates the direction and length, making it easier to experiment with composition while maintaining consistent lighting effects.

Adding Dimension with Gradient Maps

Gradient maps add a dimension of depth by allowing you to remap the brightness values of an image via color. You can simulate lighting effects with a Gradient Map, similar to color temperature changes that allow the image to feel even more realistic.

- **Applying Gradient Maps**: Move back to the layer that you would like to adjust, click on **'Image'**, then down to **'Adjustments'**, and select **'Gradient Map'**. From here, you can select a preset or manually create your own based on the colors of your preference and the conditions of lighting.

- **Blending Modes**: The Gradient Maps especially work wonderfully with the blending mode **'Overlay'** or **'Soft Light'** in Photoshop 2025. You will be able to play along with the blending mode and opacity of the Gradient Map layer to get a subtle light effect that brings warmth or coolness to your image, hence enhancing dimension.

- **Layer Masks**: Use Layer Masks so that the gradient can be applied selectively, exaggerating the areas where light normally hits while the transition from light to shadow is soft and subtle.

Gradient Maps come into their element with portraits, landscapes, and product shots because you can introduce realistic lighting without relying on layer adjustment in complicated ways.

CHAPTER SIXTEEN

PEN TOOL, PATHS, AND ADVANCED SELECTION TOOLS

Using the Pen Tool for Precision Selections: Paths, Curves, and Anchor Points

Understanding the Basics of the Pen Tool

The Pen Tool works by laying down paths, which are essentially an outline or form that you can turn into a selection, a mask, or a vector image area. Unlike either of the brush or marquee tools, the Pen Tool allows complete accuracy regarding the point and curve locations on your path. You'll find the Pen Tool in the toolbar-or you can use the **"P"** key shortcut to select the tool and begin creating points and paths on your canvas.

Paths are, in effect, lines or forms made up of points, known as anchor points, and the segments between these points. Thus, they are vector-based, and resolution-independent, which means they don't lose any quality when they're scaled up. While creating a selection with the Pen Tool, you aren't getting stopped or restricted by the pixel limitations of a bitmap; instead, you're working with a clean, scalable outline.

Anchor Points and Segments

A very important concept in working with the Pen Tool is the anchor point. As you click on your canvas, you will create an anchor point that starts a new path segment. Every new click of the mouse will create another anchor point and Photoshop draws line segments between each of them. The two main types of anchor points are:

- **Corner Points:** These are created upon a click without dragging. It gives you straight segments, hence perfectly suited for geometric shapes or selections having sharp angles.

- **Smooth Points**: These are created upon a click and drag to build curves. You can make adjustments to the curvature as well as to the direction of your path by pulling the direction handles out, which then produces flowing lines that are smooth.

Control of the Pen Tool is all about mastering how to work with these two types of points. You will trace even the most intricate shapes quite accurately by switching from straight segments to curves and vice versa.

Creating Curves with Direction Handles

Now, curves are where the real power of the Pen Tool lies. After having clicked to set your initial anchor point, from there forward you should click and drag on where the next anchor point will be. As you drag, Photoshop creates direction handles from that anchor point. These direction handles define the shape of that curve, essentially setting the direction and steepness of the curve from that particular anchor point.

- **Editing Curves**: Sometimes you may not get the perfect curve in a single attempt; you can edit it afterward. Choose the **Direct Selection Tool** by pressing "**A**" and click on any anchor point to move it. You can also click on the direction handles after selecting the anchor point, which allows you to have more precision in the direction and shape of the curve.

- **Shorten and Lengthen Handles:** The shorter a handle is, the subtler the curve it can produce; the longer the handle, the more exaggerated the curve. If you carefully position each handle with just the right length and angle, nearly any curvature you could want is possible, and you will be able to do some pretty great detail work when creating paths.

Working with Path Options: Creating, Editing, and Saving Paths

Once you have created a path, you will notice that it has appeared in the Paths panel - which you can open via **Window > Paths**. You have in this panel options to save, edit, and transform paths into selections. A few important options that you'll find useful:

- **Creating a New Path:** When a new path is created, automatically Photoshop christens that path as the "**Work Path**." It is temporary. Of course, if you want it to be permanent, you can double-click on the Work Path and give it some other name. This way, you will save your path and avoid the chances of its accidental deletion.

- **Editing** Paths: You can go back and make changes to your path by selecting the Direct **Selection Tool (A)** and moving anchor points or changing handles.

- **Convert Paths to Selections**: To convert any path to a selection, once the path is complete, right-click on it, and click on "**Make Selection**." This converts your path into a selection that you can use for masking, cutting, or refining your design.

Adding and Removing Anchor Points

With the Pen Tool, at any point along your path, you can add or delete anchor points, if for some reason you seem to think that a segment should be given more or less precision, or that that part of your path is over-specified or not simplified enough.

- **Add Anchor Points**: This is done through the Add Anchor Point Tool nestled in the Pen Tool; click on any segment where you feel the need to add more control.

- **Delete Anchor Points**: The Delete Anchor Point Tool can be used to remove any extra points. This will often simplify and clean up your path.

Advanced Techniques: Working with Curved Paths and Complex Shapes

Complex shapes often involve the need to work with both straight and curved segments, especially when working with organic shapes such as faces or other natural shapes.

- **Create Symmetrical Shapes**: In objects where there is symmetry, the middle of the object can be gained through guides or rulers. Go via **View > Rulers** and create paths on one side. To get a symmetrical object, duplicate and mirror horizontally by going to **Object > Transform > Reflect.**

- **Combine Paths:** If you have multiple segments, you can combine them into a single path. Just click on the end of one of the paths using the Pen Tool to start a new path segment from it - or with the Path Selection Tool choose multiple paths and combine those.

Path Creation and Editing: Manipulating Paths and Shapes

Understanding Paths and Shapes in Photoshop

A path in Photoshop is essentially a vector outline that can define the edges of an object or act as a guide for applying effects. Paths are resolution-independent, meaning they can be scaled up or down without any loss of quality. Paths can be used to create selections, masks, and even strokes, giving users great flexibility in design.

Photoshop 2025 provides two primary tools for working with paths and shapes:

- **Pen Tool:** Used for drawing custom paths with anchor points and Bezier curves.

- **Shape Tools:** Allow for the creation of basic shapes (rectangle, ellipse, polygon, line, and custom shapes) that can be manipulated and edited.

Creating Paths Using the Pen Tool

The **Pen Tool** is central to path creation in Photoshop. It allows for the drawing of paths with great precision by placing anchor points and adjusting their curves.

- **Using the Pen Tool:** To start a path, select the **Pen Tool (P)** from the toolbar. Click to create an anchor point, and click again to add a second point, connecting them with a line. Drag the mouse while creating a point to introduce curves.

- **Bezier Curves and Handles:** When you drag while placing an anchor point, Photoshop creates Bezier handles, which control the curvature of the path. Adjusting these handles will allow you to create smooth curves and intricate shapes. **Alt-click** (Option-click on Mac) on an anchor point to adjust individual Bezier handles without affecting the adjacent curve.

Editing Paths with the Direct Selection Tool

Editing paths in Photoshop 2025 have been made even more intuitive. The **Direct Selection Tool** (A) allows you to select and modify anchor points and path segments.

- **Selecting and Moving Anchor Points:** Click on an anchor point with the Direct Selection Tool to activate it. You can then move it to adjust the shape. To select multiple points, hold down the **Shift** key while clicking each point.

- **Adjusting Curves:** Use the Direct Selection Tool to drag the Bezier handles connected to each anchor point. For fine adjustments, use the arrow keys to nudge points precisely.

Creating Shapes with Shape Tools

Photoshop's Shape Tools provide an easy way to create basic shapes quickly. These shapes are vector-based, making them scalable and perfect for use in graphic design.

- **Rectangle Tool:** Ideal for creating rectangular and square shapes. Click and drag to form the shape, or click once on the canvas to enter exact dimensions.

- **Ellipse Tool:** Used for circles and ovals, this tool functions similarly to the Rectangle Tool.

- **Polygon and Line Tools:** The Polygon Tool lets you specify the number of sides, allowing for the creation of triangles, pentagons, hexagons, etc. The Line Tool creates straight lines of any length and thickness.
- **Custom Shape Tool:** Photoshop 2025 offers an expanded library of custom shapes and lets users save and reuse shapes for complex designs.

Combining Paths and Shapes

Photoshop 2025 allows users to combine multiple shapes or paths into one. This is particularly useful for creating complex shapes out of simpler components.

- **Combining Shapes:** With multiple shapes selected, use the options in the **Path Operations** dropdown (found in the Options Bar) to unite, subtract, intersect, or exclude overlapping areas. This allows for the easy creation of unique shapes without manually drawing each segment.
- **Path Interactions:** To combine a path with a shape, select the shape and use the Pen Tool to add to or modify the existing path. This flexibility lets you blend vector shapes with hand-drawn paths.

Converting Paths to Selections and Masks

Paths are often used to create precise selections. Once you've created a path, it can be converted into a selection, which can be used for masking or editing specific parts of an image.

- **Creating a Selection from a Path:** With the path selected, go to **Window > Paths** and select the path. Click the **Load Path as a Selection** button at the bottom of the Paths panel. This will turn the path into a selection that you can edit, mask, or fill.
- **Creating Masks with Paths:** To create a mask from a path, select the layer you want to mask, then choose your path and click the **Add Layer Mask** button in the Layers panel. Photoshop will use the path's outline to create the mask.

Transforming Paths and Shapes

Photoshop 2025's Transform options let you resize, rotate, distort, or warp paths and shapes. This can be done using **Free Transform (Ctrl+T** on Windows or **Command+T** on Mac).

- **Free Transform Options:** With the path or shape selected, activate Free Transform. You can then scale, rotate, or skew the path as needed. Hold down Shift to constrain proportions while scaling.

- **Warping Paths:** Photoshop 2025 has introduced enhanced warping capabilities for paths. Go to **Edit > Transform > Warp** to bend and reshape paths using a grid overlay.

Stroking and Filling Paths and Shapes

Paths and shapes in Photoshop can be filled with color or patterned strokes to add a finishing touch to your designs.

- **Applying a Stroke:** Select the path or shape, and go to **Edit > Stroke Path**. Choose the brush or pencil tool to define the width and color of the stroke.

- **Filling with Color or Gradient:** Choose the **Paint Bucket Tool** or **Gradient Tool** to fill the area within a closed path. You can also set fill and stroke properties in the **Properties** panel for shapes, choosing solid colors, gradients, or patterns.

Saving Paths for Future Use

Finally, you may want to save paths for future editing or re-use. In the Paths panel, double-click the path to save it. Named paths will be stored in the file even if you close Photoshop, allowing you to come back and edit or reuse them.

Refine Edge, Quick Mask, and Object Selection

Working with Channels for Selections

Understanding Channels in Photoshop

Before diving into making selections, it's important to understand what channels are. The channels in Photoshop reflect the colors in grayscale format. Thus, each color model may have its channels, depending on the color composition of the image. For example, an RGB image will have three channels—Red, Green, and Blue—whereas a CMYK image will have four channels: Cyan, Magenta, Yellow, and Black. In practice, each channel is a gray-scale representation of one color component in the image, and greater brightness corresponds to greater intensity of that color.

Along with the color channels, Photoshop has an option Alpha Channel. The alpha channels are gray-scale representations that carry transparency information. They are very convenient for creating and saving selections.

Accessing and Navigating Channels

1. **Open the Channels Panel**: To work with channels, first select the Channels panel by going to **Window > Channels**. This panel shows you a listing of each color channel, along with any alpha channels that you have created.

2. **Displaying Individual Channels**: To see an individual channel (Red) click on it. It allows you to see if there is a good range of contrast between your subject and background. The more contrast you have between your subject and background in the channels, the easier it is to make a selection.

3. **Channel Contrast:** The higher the contrast of a channel, the easier it will be to differentiate between the subject and the background which is essentially what a selection is all about. For example, if the image that one is working with contains a blue-toned subject, then the Blue channel might show the subject with more detail in comparison with the rest of the channels.

Selections Using Channels

1. **Identify the Best Channel for Selection**: Choose the best channel by opening each channel and looking to see which one provides the greatest contrast between the subject and the background. This will be the base for your selection.

2. **Duplicate that Channel**: Now that the best channel is selected, right-click on it and choose **Duplicate Channel**. Since you are working on a duplicate of the original channel, your original color information will not be affected.

3. **Contrast Adjustment of Copied Channel:** Go to **Image > Adjustments > Levels or Curves**. The increased contrast will further remove the subject from the background by darkening the greys that represent the background and lightening the greys that represent the subject.

4. **Refined Masking**: Refine with a Brush or Dodging and Burning areas that perhaps are still merging into the backgrounds. For instance, with a white brush, one can solidify the edges of a subject or, with a black brush, get rid of the backgrounds.

5. **Load Channel as a Selection:** Once you have refined the mask, load it as a selection. In the Channels panel, hold **Ctrl/Cmd** and click on the channel thumbnail. This will cause Photoshop to make a selection based on the white of the alpha channel that represents the subject.

Refining the Selection

Using Select and Mask

1. **Open the Select and Mask Workspace**: After you've created your selection, go to **Select > Select and Mask** and begin fine-tuning this selection. This is the workspace where all of your edge refinement tools will be shown, which becomes extremely significant when a subject has a lot of hair or fur.

2. **Edge Detection**: Spend some time working on the edge refinement with the Refine Edge Brush Tool, particularly around areas where the delicate shading of the background merges into the subject.

3. **Refine Edge:** Smoothen, feather, adjust contrast and shift edge with sliders to refine your mask. Feathering blurs the edges of a selection, whereas contrast will sharpen it. Shift Edge is used to contract or expand the selection slightly.

4. **Decontaminate Colors:** If color from the background spills onto the subject, then run the Decontaminate Colors option to fix it. This happens particularly when you are dealing with a complex background.

5. **Output Settings:** After refining the selection, set your output settings. You might want Selection, Layer Mask, and New Layer with Layer Mask among others depending on your editing needs.

Saving and Reusing Selections with Alpha Channels

1. **Save Selection to Alpha Channel:** Once you have your selection, to save it for later use, go to **Select > Save Selection** and click **New**. This will save your selection as an alpha channel in the Channels panel.

2. **Load Saved Selections**: To revisit your selection at any time, under Select, choose **Load Selection** and select the saved alpha channel from the pull-down menu. This way you can make reusable and editable complex selections during all stages of your process.

Advanced Techniques: Combining Channels for Complex Selections

Sometimes it is necessary to combine the channels since one channel may not yield the best possible selection.

1. **Merge Channels:** Select at least two channels that carry information useful for the selection. Copy each one and, in a new document, create layers by pasting.

2. **Use Blending Modes**: Each layer should have blending modes applied to see what works best for your selection. For example, Multiply or Overlay mode may help you accentuate the details by making a composite from grayscale contrasts in each channel.

3. **Flatten and Reapply**: Flatten the document, import it back into the original file as an alpha channel, then load it back as a selection.

CHAPTER SEVENTEEN

EXPORTING AND SAVING FILES

Exporting for Web and Print: Choosing File Types and Optimizing Quality

Understanding Export Needs: Web vs. Print

Before getting into the specifics of file types and settings, let's take a moment to clarify the main differences between web and print outputs:

- **Web**: Web images should load up fast, for which most often the file size is required to be smaller. Screen resolution is usually 72-150 PPI. Also, color spaces should be sRGB because it is a color space standard for online uses.

- **Print**: Printing demands high-resolution images, usually above 300 PPI for a sharp and full-of-details final product. The color space that works for printing is CMYK, which is best for printers and their ink.

Each of these mediums also has different file types that work better than others, depending on the complexity and purpose of the image.

Choosing the Right File Types

In Adobe Photoshop, several file types can be used, but when it comes to web and print, the following are some of the most relevant ones:

For the Web

1. **JPEG (JPG):** Ideal for photographs, complex images with subtle gradients. JPEG files can be easily compressed to balance quality and file size. That makes them excellent for websites.
   - **Pros**: Small file size, highly compatible.
   - **Cons**: Compression could drop the quality, especially in multiple saves.

2. **PNG**: Best for images of transparent backgrounds, graphics, and simple images. PNGs are lossless, meaning that they will not lose quality when saved.
   - **Pros**: Lossless quality, supports transparency.
   - **Cons**: Much bigger as compared to JPEG; hence, it slows down the loading of web pages.
3. **GIF**: This format is used mainly for animations or pretty simple graphics that have fewer colors. GIFs have an 8-bit color depth and are much more restricted in their detail.
   - **Pros**: Small in size, support animation.
   - **Cons**: Limited color range, low detail.
4. **SVG**: a vector format good to go for logos, icons, and graphics that need to be scalable without any loss of quality. For responsive designs, SVGs have been popular.
   - **Pros**: Scalable without quality loss, editable in code.
   - **Cons**: Limited to vector graphics, not suitable for photographs.

For Print

1. **TIFF (TIF):** A preferred format for high-quality images in print. TIFF files are typically uncompressed, preserving all details and quality.
   - **Pros**: Lossless quality, high resolution.
   - **Cons**: Large file size, slower processing.
2. **PDF**: A versatile format that can maintain vector information, making it perfect for documents with text and graphics.
   - **Pros**: High quality for vector and text elements, compatible with many print workflows.
   - **Cons**: May require particular export settings for image-heavy designs.
3. **EPS**: This format is used frequently for vector images and logos. These file types can be used in a great number of print and graphic applications.

- **Pros**: Maintains quality for vectors, highly compatible.
- **Cons**: Very limited use outside of vector graphics and print.

Apart from choosing the right file type, there comes a need to put the right export setting to optimize your image quality.

Optimizing Export Settings

Photoshop 2025 has refined export settings that make the balancing of output quality easier. Here's how you can configure them based on destination:

For Web

1. **Export As:** Go to **File > Export > Export As**. The opened settings have been designed for web use.
   - **Format**: Select **JPEG, PNG**, or **GIF**, depending on the type of image.
   - **Image Size**: Change to the exact pixel size that is needed. Scaling down will reduce the file size, which is usually in need for web usage.
   - **Quality Slider**: This can be moved down to commit file size without showing quality reduction. In general, 70-80% quality is a good amount of balance for web usage.
   - **Color Space:** Put a check in the box that says "Convert to sRGB" for consistent color display across browsers.
   - **Transparency**: If your image requires it, enable transparency for PNGs.
2. **Save for Web (Legacy):** If you are used to old export options, then under **File > Export > Save for Web (Legacy)** allows for more granular options on web-specific settings.
   - **Lossy Compression**: Applied to PNGs to squash size even further.
   - **Metadata**: Also strip out metadata to reduce file size further.

For Print

1. **Export As PDF or TIFF:** Export your file as a PDF or TIFF for the best quality.

    *   **Image Resolution**: At least 300 PPI is recommended for good print clarity.

    *   **Color Space**: Under Color Management, check **Convert to CMYK** for printing compatibility.

    *   **Compression**: Do not compress files for printing to maintain high quality.

2. **Export to PSD for Collaboration**: When sending this to a designer or even a print house, it would be best to save this into a PSD format and not flatten the file. That way, if you or somebody else needs to make any more changes, that can be done without losing resolution or quality.

3. **Layers and Text Preparation for Printing**:

    *   **Flattening Images**: This might be helpful for some printing services regarding your image. First, duplicate the file before flattening it.

    *   **Embed Fonts or Rasterize Text**: This makes sure that text layers are rasterized and fonts embedded to avoid font substitution issues.

Tips for Quality Control

1. **Soft Proofing for Print:** Soft proofing in Photoshop 2025 allows viewing how the colors will look in print. Go to **View > Proof Setup** and select a CMYK profile to see the color shift.

2. **Use Adjustment Layers:** Make final adjustments for brightness, contrast, and sharpness with adjustment layers before exporting. It will finish your image for the medium it's being output to.

3. **Check File Size for Web**: If it is for a web image, try keeping it under 500 KB for optimal load time. Use Photoshop's Image Size and Quality sliders to balance quality and size.

4. **Save a Master File**: Always have a high-resolution master file. You can export web and print versions from it without compromising the quality of the original image.

Using Export As and Save for Web: Exporting for Different Platforms

The "Export As" Feature

The "Export As" feature is designed to make exports quick and easy across different platforms and devices. This gives you a set of options whereby you can export in multiple formats like JPEG, PNG, and SVG; you can set the dimensions, quality, and color space too. Here's how you can make good use of **"Export As"**:

Accessing "Export As"

1. Open your file in Photoshop and make any necessary adjustments.

2. Go to **File > Export > Export As**. This will open a new dialog box with export options.

Setting Up Export Options

The "Export As" dialog box provides a clean and intuitive interface with several options:

- **File Format**: Select the format in which you wish to export your file. Common choices include:
    - **JPEG**: Ideal for photos and images with gradients.
    - **PNG**: Best for images requiring transparency or high resolution.
    - **SVG**: Useful for vector graphics, especially for web and app design.
- **Quality**: For JPEGs, you can set the quality between 1 and 100, balancing file size and image clarity. A lower quality reduces the file size but can cause pixelation.

- **Scale**: Choose the scale of your export. Photoshop allows you to export at different resolutions, such as 1x, 2x, or even custom sizes. This is especially useful for responsive design, where different screen resolutions require various sizes of images.

- **Color Space**: Ensure your file is in the appropriate color space. For web-based images, **sRGB** is often the best choice as it provides accurate colors across different devices.

Multiple Sizes and Formats for Different Platforms

If you are preparing an image for different platforms (web and mobile), **"Export As"** allows you to export different versions of the same image with varying resolutions. Check **Scale All** to export different sizes all at once, say 1x, 2x, and 3x.

The "Save for Web" Feature

"Save for Web" is a legacy feature within Photoshop, yet it is one of the most used out there, especially among web designers who need to have full control of file size and how an image has been optimized. "Save for Web" contains some advanced settings that may make a huge difference when it comes to optimizing images for websites or applications with particular size restrictions.

Accessing "Save for Web"

1. **Go to File > Export > Save for Web (Legacy)**. This opens a different dialog box with more detailed optimization options.

2. **"Save for Web"** is especially useful for GIFs, JPEGs, PNGs, and BMPs for online use.

   ### Key Options in "Save for Web"

   - **Image Format and Presets**: You can select formats such as JPEG, GIF, PNG-8, or PNG-24. Choose the best format based on the image content:
     - **JPEG** is generally best for photographs and complex images.

- ○ **GIF** works for simple graphics with few colors and is commonly used for animations.

- ○ **PNG-8 and PNG-24** are ideal for images that require transparency.

- **Compression and Quality**: The compression settings in "Save for Web" allow you to adjust the quality. For JPEGs, you can adjust the quality level between Low, Medium, High, and Maximum. There is also an option for **Progressive JPEG**, which loads the image in multiple passes, improving the user experience on slower connections.

- **Image Size and Resolution**: You can resize your image directly in this dialog box by adjusting width, height, and resolution, making it convenient for web designers who need smaller versions.

- **Preview and Optimize for File Size**: The "Save for Web" feature shows an estimated file size, giving you a clear picture of the final output size. This is especially useful for optimizing web pages where smaller file sizes lead to faster loading times.

Choosing "Export As" vs. "Save for Web"

Understanding when to use "Export As" or "Save for Web" can help streamline your workflow:

- **Use "Export As"** if you are preparing images for multiple platforms (such as responsive images for both desktop and mobile) or need a simplified interface.

- **Use "Save for Web"** if you require detailed control over image optimization, such as for animations (GIFs) or images needing specific color profiles.

Practical Tips for Exporting

Exporting for Social Media

For each of the different social media platforms - Instagram, Facebook, and Twitter, there are suggested sizes and formats of images. While JPEG is a common format for photographs, PNG is the clearer export option when there is a need for transparency. Images can be exported at 72 dpi, where the resolution will still be good yet load times are quick.

Exporting for Web and Mobile Apps

With sites and applications, there is a constant give-and-take between file size and image quality. Larger, high-resolution files will display significantly crisper but can slow page load times. For instance:

- In cases where your work involves photography or highly detailed images, JPEG is generally better.

- If your job requires you to create images that need transparency, PNG is the better choice.

- If you are doing vector-based designs, SVG is perfect since it never loses resolution.

Exporting for Print

While both **"Export As"** and **"Save for Web"** are designed to be primarily for digital outputs, they can be used to create files for print, if you're saving in high resolution. Make sure color profiles are set to CMYK, and then select a higher resolution. Generally, 300 dpi will work.

Save As and File Types: PSD, TIFF, JPEG, PNG, and More

Understanding the different file formats available to work with in Adobe Photoshop can help in the development of the best quality and compatibility for projects. The

"Save As" function in Photoshop 2025 uses a range of file types that have different strong points concerning their use. Here is a close look at some of the common file types used: PSD, TIFF, JPEG, and PNG among many others.

PSD (Photoshop Document)

PSD is the native file format within Photoshop and becomes necessary when you want to retain all of your layers, masks, adjustments, and other features that are editable. Here are some reasons why a PSD is best for working files and project archives:

- **Full Editability:** A PSD file retains every element of your design, including layers, adjustment layers, smart objects, and vector shapes, which makes it fully editable for future modifications.

- **High Quality:** Since PSDs do not compress the image, they are lossless, meaning they will not affect quality.

- **Large File Size:** The PSDs store every bit of data from your project, and thus they inflate when you have a lot of layers or high-resolution images.

  Save as PSD if you will revisit to edit your project. In the case of collaboration, either with other designers or when preparing files for printing, saving in PSD format provides the most flexibility.

TIFF (Tagged Image File Format)

TIFF is indeed one of the most versatile and widely used formats in the pictorial world of printing and archiving, given its quality way of storage that allows different types of compression.

- **Lossless Compression:** TIFFs can be saved with either the lossless LZW or ZIP compression. This maintains quality within an image and does not shrink the file size too much.

- **Layer Support:** You could save a TIFF file in Photoshop with layers, and if one were to reopen the file in Photoshop, it would open with all its layers intact.

However, many other programs may not view a TIFF file that contains layers. So, use it at your own risk when sharing.

- **High-Quality Output for Printing**: TIFF is uncompressed or losslessly compressed when it is the best quality, so very adequate for professional printing.

  TIFF does not give troublesome moments while dealing with printing, especially in cases where these are high-quality large-format prints, magazines, etc., or when using such prints for vocational purposes.

JPEG (Joint Photographic Experts Group)

Probably, JPEG is one of the most used file formats, especially in web and digital media. The main characteristic of a JPEG format is to compress an image by losing some information to reduce the file size; this makes the format suitable for image distribution and storage.

- **Lossy Compression**: This format reduces the file size by disposing of some information in the image, which lowers its quality. However, you can change the levels of compression in Photoshop to balance quality with file size.

- **Small File Size**: JPEGs are lightweight, hence easily usable for online sharing and usage on websites and social media.

- **Low Editing Capability**: JPEG doesn't support layers, transparency, or high bit depth, and hence it is not good for ongoing editing.

  JPEG will be ideal for final output files meant for web use or when the file size needs to be as minimal as possible, such as in emails and web content.

PNG (Portable Network Graphics)

PNG is a lossless format, and it supports transparency, hence highly versatile for both web and graphic design projects.

- **Lossless Compression:** PNGs do not lose quality on saving, something that makes them quite appropriate for images where quality is critical.

- **Transparency Support:** PNG is one of the limited formats that support transparency; this is essential for logos, icons, and graphics that need to be placed over other backgrounds.

- **Optimized for Web Use**: PNG file sizes are larger compared to those of JPEGs; this, however, is optimized for the web, giving an effective preview of images across multiple devices.

PNG is widely used for logos, and icons, among other graphics that involve transparency and quality. Ideally, it suits web graphics that require either transparency or high-quality and lossless storage.

GIF (Graphics Interchange Format)

GIFs are known for their ability to save small, looping animations and become prevalent in social media and web graphics. Here are some key features of the GIF:

- **Limited Color Range**: GIFs only show 256 colors, which makes it a poor choice for photographs and any images that need smooth color gradations.

- **Supports Animation**: GIFs can include multiple frames for animated sequences;

- **Transparency Support**: GIF format supports transparency in a rudimentary fashion, without the fine edges around the subject that PNG allows.

  GIF does great for animations and low-color graphics, which is very poorly suited for high-quality image storage.

PDF (Portable Document Format)

Adobe's format for PDFs is versatile for document sharing and printing, especially when multiple pages or vector-heavy designs are involved.

- **Cross-Platform Compatibility**: PDFs have identical formatting across different platforms; therefore, these are great to use when sharing and for professional print projects.

- **Layer and Vector Support**: PDFs exported from Photoshop can retain text and vector layers, which keep your logos and other illustrations razor-sharp.

- **Multi-Page Projects:** PDFs have multi-page capability, which makes them great for use with documents, e-books, and portfolios.

  PDF is good to be used when you share documents that need to retain layout integrity, for example, printing or distribution.

BMP (Bitmap)

The BMP format is high-quality and uncompressed. The systems of the early computer graphics era widely adopted it. In general, it is usually less efficient for modern applications, since it requires very large file sizes.

- **Uncompressed Quality**: In general, BMPs don't store image data in compression, so they normally have huge file sizes.

- **Limited Compatibility for Modern Use**: They are well-supported by Windows applications but are less common in web and graphic design.

  BMP usually serves only for some niche applications or when working with really old applications since all modern formats have the same or even better quality with more compression possibilities.

SVG (Scalable Vector Graphics)

SVG is a vector format that supports scalable graphics and hence is very useful for logos and icons.

- **Resolution Independence:** Since SVGs are vector-based, they can be scaled infinitely without loss of resolution.

- **File Size Efficiency**: SVGs are normally smaller and web-optimized against pixel-based files.

- **Design Software Editability**: SVGs will be entirely editable within vector applications and with some web design programs; thus, they are useful when designs need to be dynamic and responsive.

  SVG is perfect for applications involving logos, icons, and other vector elements that are supposed to look different on different platforms.

Choosing the Right File Format

Understanding these file types and their uses can help you maximize quality, compatibility, and efficiency in your projects. Here's a quick summary:

- **PSD:** For working files with layers and high editability.
- **TIFF:** For print-ready files with high quality and minimal compression.
- **JPEG:** For web and sharing with adjustable compression.
- **PNG:** For web images requiring transparency and high quality.
- **GIF:** For simple animations and graphics with limited colors.
- **PDF:** For documents, multi-page files, and print layouts.
- **BMP:** For legacy or specialized high-quality needs.
- **SVG:** For scalable vector graphics on the web.

Batch Export and Automation

Understanding Batch Exporting: The Basics

Batch exporting is a process in which one exports multiple files or layers at once. This capability is quite useful in cases where the essence of one's work involves redundant exports, such as image resizing for multiple platforms, saving web assets, or exporting files in many formats. Adobe enhanced both Export As and Generator features to make batch exporting in Photoshop 2025 more intuitive and flexible.

- **Export As:** Export As in Photoshop 2025 offers the facility of selecting multiple layers, artboards, or groups and then exporting all of these in a single go in various formats such as JPEG, PNG, and SVG. This is indeed a very useful option when one is working on projects where files need to be saved in different resolutions, color profiles, or even file sizes. New in Photoshop 2025, the "**Export As**" feature also introduces a "**Batch Mode**" that allows users to define specific export settings for various layers and automate this process. To do this, go to **File > Export > Export As**, select multiple files, make any adjustments you would like, and click on "**Export**" to apply your configurations.

- **Generator Feature**: The generator in Photoshop allows the facilitation of exporting by naming the layers or groups with specific suffixes. For instance, adding "**.png**" or "**.jpg**" to the end of a layer name automatically exports the layer in that format within Photoshop. It has been further extended in Photoshop 2025 by directly specifying sizes and formats within the layer name, such as "**100px_icon.jpg**." This feature will prove powerful for designers working with numerous assets or platforms that demand different sizes or formats. To activate Generator, go to **File > Generate > Image Assets**, then name your layers accordingly.

Automating Repetitive Tasks Using Actions

Actions in Photoshop are a series of steps that can be recorded and, when applied to other files, can be run with just one click. This can be worth its weight in gold when repeating edits of resizing images, color adjustment, or adding watermarks.

- **Recording Actions:** To record an action, the Actions panel is opened via **Window > Actions,** and the **Create New Action button** is clicked. Anything done in Photoshop from that point forward, whether applying filters, cropping, or adjusting contrast, will be recorded step-by-step. Save this action to later be replayed on other images for consistency and to save time.

- **Enhanced Actions in Photoshop 2025**: Now, conditional actions can have various actions running based on the conditions. Say, if the image is a portrait, it runs an action, and if in a landscape, it performs another. That is great in many workflow scenarios to offer flexibility between different file types, orientations, or dimensions.

- **Actions and Batch Processing**: Once an action has been created, you can apply it to multiple files in bulk. In the menu, select **File > Automate > Batch**. Then, select the action you want to use along with the source folder where your images are located. You can export batch-processed files with Photoshop 2025 to a folder of your choice, making things much easier when organizing files.

Applying Advanced Automation with Scripts

For more complex tasks that fall outside what Actions could do and for larger and more expansive tasks, Photoshop has the option for scripting through JavaScript, VBScript, and AppleScript. Through scripting, any range of automation tasks-from specific filter applications to layer manipulation and even interaction with Photoshop through other applications can be enabled.

- **New Scripting Features in Photoshop 2025:** This release includes an extended JavaScript API that offers more detailed control over additional Photoshop functionality, making it easier to create customized automation solutions. Second, Adobe has provided several scripts, which were prebuilt for common tasks, such as "**Export Layers to Files**" or "**Image Processor.**" To access these scripts, head over to **File > Scripts**.

- **Custom Scripting Examples**: For instance, when one needs to perform some set of actions over and over again, save the files, and then upload them to a server, a custom script will automate the whole workflow for you. Working with cloud storage or an FTP server is part of the extended API in Photoshop 2025; it means a script can apply edits and transfer the files directly to their destination.

Working with Droplets of Photoshop for Quick Automation

Another powerful feature of automation allows users to enable the creation of small executable files from Actions that can be dragged and dropped onto other files or folders; these are called Droplets.

- **Droplet Creation:** To create a droplet, follow the path **File > Automate > Create Droplet**. Choose any action desired, choose where to save that droplet, and specify droplet file handling options (save options, error handling). Once created, all that needs to be done is drag-and-drop files or folders onto the droplet icon, and Photoshop will apply the specified action to each one.

CHAPTER EIGHTEEN

ESSENTIAL PHOTOSHOP TIPS, SHORTCUTS, AND WORKFLOW TECHNIQUES

Essential Keyboard Shortcuts for Efficiency: Mastering Commonly Used Commands

Adobe Photoshop is a strong tool for designers, photographers, and digital artists. Using all of its functionalities, though, can be time-consuming once you have to go through a lot of menus. Keyboard shortcuts speed up your work and thereby save not only time but also lots of effort.

Selection Shortcuts

- **V – Move Tool:** Quickly switch to the Move Tool to reposition layers or selections.

- **M – Marquee Tool:** For rectangular or elliptical selections. Use **Shift + M** to toggle between the rectangular and elliptical options.

- **L – Lasso Tool:** Freely select areas by drawing custom shapes. Press **Shift + L** to switch to the polygonal or magnetic lasso tools.

- **W – Quick Selection/Magic Wand Tool**: Automatically select areas with similar colors. Shift + W toggles between the Quick Selection and Magic Wand tools.

- **Ctrl/Cmd + A – Select All:** Select the entire canvas.

- **Ctrl/Cmd + D – Deselect**: Clears the current selection.

  These shortcuts help you quickly select specific areas for edits without interrupting your workflow to open menus.

Layer Management Shortcuts

- **Ctrl/Cmd + J – Duplicate Layer:** Quickly duplicates the current layer or selection.

- **Ctrl/Cmd + Shift + N – New Layer:** Adds a new layer above the currently selected layer.

- **Ctrl/Cmd + G – Group Layers:** Groups selected layers for better organization.

- **Ctrl/Cmd + Shift + G – Ungroup Layers:** Breaks apart grouped layers.

- **Ctrl/Cmd + E – Merge Layers**: Merges selected layers into a single layer.

- **Ctrl/Cmd + Shift + E – Merge Visible Layers**: Merges all visible layers, helpful when you're ready to finalize edits.

Organizing layers efficiently keeps your workspace clean, especially when working with complex projects involving multiple elements.

Brush Tool Shortcuts

- **B – Brush Tool**: Activates the Brush Tool instantly.

- **[and] – Increase/Decrease Brush Size**: These square brackets resize the brush diameter quickly.

- **Shift + [and] – Adjust Brush Hardness**: Decreases or increases brush hardness without navigating the settings.

- **D – Reset Colors to Default (Black & White):** Switches your color palette to black and white, useful for masking and erasing.

- **X – Swap Foreground and Background Colors**: Quickly toggles between two colors without opening the color picker.

These brush shortcuts are essential for painting, retouching, and other tasks requiring precision and speed.

Color Selection Shortcuts

- **I – Eyedropper Tool**: Selects a color directly from the image to make it your active color.

- **Alt/Option + Delete/Backspace – Fill Selection with Foreground Color:** Fills the selected area or layer with the current foreground color.

- **Ctrl/Cmd + Delete/Backspace – Fill Selection with Background Color**: Fills the selection with the background color.

- **Shift + Alt/Option + Backspace/Delete – Fill with Foreground or Background Color while Preserving Transparency:** This is helpful for selective recoloring within transparent areas.

Using these shortcuts, you can quickly manage color applications, making painting and retouching faster.

Navigation Shortcuts

- **Z – Zoom Tool**: Quickly zooms in and out. Press **Alt/Option** and scroll the mouse wheel to zoom without switching tools.

- **Spacebar + Drag – Hand Tool:** Pan around your image by holding down the spacebar while dragging.

- **Ctrl/Cmd + 0 – Fit to Screen**: Resizes your image to fit within the workspace.

- **Ctrl/Cmd + 1 – Actual Pixels (100%) View**: View your image at 100%, which is essential for detailed editing.

Navigating efficiently within your workspace makes it easy to access different areas of your canvas without losing focus.

Undo and History Shortcuts

- **Ctrl/Cmd + Z – Undo/Redo:** In Photoshop 2025, this toggles between your last action and the one before it. Use **Ctrl/Cmd + Alt/Option + Z** for multiple stepbacks.

- **Ctrl/Cmd + Shift + Z – Redo (Step Forward):** Steps forward in your history to reverse previous undos.
- **F12 – Revert:** Reverts your image to the last saved version, helpful if you want to start over with your last save state.

  Quick access to undo and redo commands allows you to experiment confidently, knowing you can step back if needed.

Transform Shortcuts

- **Ctrl/Cmd + T – Free Transform:** Resizes, rotates, skews, and warps layers or selections.
- **Ctrl/Cmd + Shift + T – Repeat Last Transform:** Repeats the last transformation you applied, useful for multiple objects that need identical adjustments.
- **Shift + Alt/Option + Drag – Uniform Scale from Center:** When transforming, this shortcut keeps scaling centered and proportional.

  Transforming objects accurately speeds up compositional adjustments and helps achieve symmetry and balance.

Blending Mode Shortcuts

- **Shift + Plus (+)/Minus (-) – Cycle through Blending Modes:** Toggles through different blending modes for the selected layer.
- **Shift + Alt/Option + O – Overlay Mode:** Applies the overlay blending mode directly to the active layer.
- **Shift + Alt/Option + M – Multiply Mode:** Applies the multiply mode directly.

  Blending modes offer creative ways to adjust color, light, and contrast, making it easy to achieve unique effects.

Masking and Layer Effects Shortcuts

- **Alt/Option + Click on Mask Icon – Create Layer Mask and Hide All**: Instantly creates a mask that conceals everything.

- **Ctrl/Cmd + I – Invert Layer Mask**: Inverts the current layer mask, which is helpful for selective masking effects.

- **Shift + Click on Mask – Disable/Enable Layer Mask:** Quickly toggles the layer mask to see the effect before and after masking.

  Masks give you nondestructive editing capabilities, allowing you to hide or reveal specific areas with precision.

File Management Shortcuts

- **Ctrl/Cmd + N – New Document**: Opens a new project window.
- **Ctrl/Cmd + S – Save**: Quickly saves your current project.
- **Ctrl/Cmd + Shift + S – Save As**: Allows you to save a different version of the project, useful for creating backups.
- **Ctrl/Cmd + Alt/Option + S – Save for Web**: Saves an optimized version for the web, reducing file size for online use.

  Efficient file management means your work is regularly saved and prepared to be exported in whatever format may be required.

Using Libraries for Asset Management: Managing Colors, Text Styles, and Graphics

Introduction to Photoshop Libraries

The Libraries panel in Photoshop 2025 is one central location that holds all reusable creative assets, colors, text styles, graphics, images, and many more. These Libraries are sharable across the Adobe suite, including applications such as Illustrator and InDesign, which may make them especially useful for teams working on several platforms. This saves a lot of time and reduces the amount of creation over and over again or cut and paste between projects, especially on big campaigns or multi-faceted projects that have very strict design guidelines.

Creating a New Library

To start using Libraries, you first have to open the Libraries panel via **Window > Libraries**. You can click **Create New Library**. It is a good practice to name your library by project, brand, or client to maintain the organization of your asset files. For example, if working on a redesign of a brand, you would want it to name the library after the brand where it would store all its color schemes, logos, and text styles.

Managing Colors in Libraries

Color is essential to the continuity of any brand, and Libraries are a fantastic way to manage them and use them within Photoshop. To add color to your library:

- Select the **Eyedropper Tool** and sample the color of your canvas, or using the Color Picker, select a new color.
- Click the **+** icon in the Libraries panel, then select **Color**. This will save the color as a swatch in your library.
- You can also name the color for quick identification, such as "**Brand Blue**" or "**Accent Green.**"

  Photoshop 2025 allows you to drag and drop colors directly onto objects from the Libraries panel to easily apply brand colors. Also, if you share your library with a team, everyone will have access and use the same color swatches to keep all deliverables consistent.

Organizing Text Styles

Text styles in Libraries make applying consistent typography across projects quick and easy. Here's how to create text styles:

- Open a new type layer with your preferred font, size, weight, and color, then lock in those settings from the Character panel.

- Once you have landed on a combo you like, click the **+** icon in the Libraries panel, choose **Text Style**, and the settings are saved.

  It saves the style of your text into the library and allows you to apply it on any text layer in just one click. This feature is especially useful when working on projects with strict typographic guidelines, as it allows not having to input font settings manually each time. For example, if you work over some publication, you may store and reuse repeatedly the styles of all headers, subheaders, and body text.

Storing Graphics and Logos

Logos and graphics are other valuable assets that utilize the storage facility of the library. Photoshop 2025 allows you to import vector graphics, logos, icons, and other graphical assets into your Libraries panel:

- Highlight the graphic element in your document, then click **Add Graphic** in the Libraries panel.

- If the graphic contains linked layers or smart objects, those remain intact so it becomes particularly easy to update these across all uses.

  This will be super beneficial for logo variations, brand icons, and other graphical elements that may be repetitive. You can further organize your graphics by naming them descriptively or by categorizing them into folders within the Libraries panel.

Using Adobe Stock and Libraries Together

With Photoshop 2025, Libraries will integrate well with Adobe Stock. You will be enabled to browse Adobe Stock right inside the Libraries panel, licensing or downloading assets directly into your library. That would be great in cases when you need high-quality stock images or vectors that you want to have easy access to and reuse. Depending on the needs of the project, Adobe Stock assets can be used either as placeholders or final assets, and these can be added to the canvas without having to leave Photoshop.

Collaborating Shared Libraries

One of the most powerful features of Libraries in Photoshop 2025 is that you're able to share them with coworkers. This will ensure that everyone on your team is using the same assets and, therefore, reduce the chances of any inconsistencies happening for this reason alone:

- To share a library, click **Share Library** and then invite collaborators via email. You can also update permissions where required ("**Can View**" or "**Can Edit**.") Shared libraries encourage collaboration, and you'll also not have to go through the hassle of asset handoffs again, since it keeps contributors up to date with the latest assets directly within Photoshop. If you work with clients, you can even share libraries to receive feedback on assets regarding color schemes or graphic elements.

Synchronizing Assets Across Devices

By default, Adobe Creative Cloud synchronizes your Libraries across multiple devices. This means that wherever you sign in, you will have access to your libraries. It is great in cases when you work on several devices, say, on your desktop and tablet, or in case you travel a lot. Libraries will make sure that your assets are available at any time, and in case a library is updated on any device, changes will appear on all other devices.

Some Tips on Efficient Library Management

To maximize your productivity with Libraries, here are some extra tips you could use:

- **Categorize Assets**: Since sometimes projects get very big, it's necessary to separate them into folders or name them descriptively to avoid confusion.

- **Archive Old Libraries:** Keep your workspace tidy. If you have completed a project, you know you will never touch that library again, so you'd better archive it.

- **Use Library Templates**: Adobe provides a multitude of library templates right in the Creative Cloud that you can download and then adapt for various purposes.

Troubleshooting Common Issues (Solutions to Frequent Problems and Errors)

1. **Photoshop Crashes on Launch**

   If the 2025 version of Photoshop is crashing on opening, then probable reasons can be outdated software, hardware conflicts, or corrupt preferences.

   Solution:

   - **Update Photoshop and System Software**: First of all, ensure that you have installed the latest updates available for Photoshop and your operating system. Many times, Adobe releases patches that fix stability problems.

   - **Check Graphics Card Compatibility**: Often, this might be caused by a card incompatible with or an outdated driver of the graphics card. Go to **Preferences > Performance** in Photoshop and check the **'Use Graphics Processor'** option. If this resolves it, update the GPU driver from the manufacturer's website and try reenabling it.

   - **Reset Preferences:** Crashes can also be caused by corrupted preference files. To reset the preferences, hold **Alt+Ctrl+Shift** for

Windows and **Option+Command+Shift** for Mac while opening Photoshop and confirm any prompt to reset preferences.

2. **Lagging or Slow Performance**

Photoshop can lag or perform very slowly, especially in handling big files or when there are several layers on it.

Solution:

- **Adjust Performance Preference Settings**: Go to **Edit > Preferences > Performance**. In the Performance Preference window, choose the **Memory Usage** percentage, allocating about 70-80% of the total RAM to Photoshop.

- **Optimize Scratch Disks**: Scratch disks are used by Photoshop for virtual memory. Once the scratch disk is almost full, performance will slow down. Thus, under Preferences > Scratch Disks, a drive that contains plenty of free space needs to be chosen. Preferably, an ultra-fast SSD drive is used for better performance.

- **Close Unwanted Tabs and Files**: Having too many open files entails a resource crunch, therefore potentially making it slow. Ensure that you close those tabs that you are not in use to free up that memory.

- **Clear History and Cache:** Too much undo state or history may lead to Photoshop slowing down. You can choose histories, clipboards, or all caches to purge from the **Edit > Purge** menu for better performance.

3. **Brush Lag or Jittery Lines**

You find that instead of smooth strokes, either delays or creating jagged lines are experienced while using brushes.

Solution:

- **Disable Smoothing**: Smoothing set too high causes lag with the brush. Lower the smoothing value on the brush toolbar or disable it.

- **Optimize Brush Settings**: Go into the Brush Settings panel and adjust **Spacing**. Higher spacing gives a more jittery stroke whereas lower spacing gives smoother lines.

- **Update Graphics Drivers**: The graphics card driver may be outdated. Make sure your graphics driver is updated.

4. **Photoshop Freezes When Saving Files**

Saving big files, especially in complex formats like PSD or PSB, sometimes hangs or takes a long time in Photoshop.

Solution:

- **Using File > Save As Instead of Save:** Sometimes saving a new copy can bypass the freeze.

- **Disable Compression**: Most of the time, Photoshops compress big-sized files that delay the save option. Disable the compression of PSD and PSB files in that regard. Go to **Edit > Preferences > File Handling**. The important thing is that disabling it will increase the size but the file will be saved rapidly.

- **Save in a Different Format**: Try saving in a much simpler format such as PNG or JPEG in case complications arise.

- **Set Ample Space on Your Disc**: Photoshop caches data in your disc during its saving process. Ensure you have ample free space on your selected drive.

5. **"Scratch Disk Full" Error**

This error pops up while working with Photoshop, which indicates that there is not enough scratch disk virtual memory to operate.

Solution:

- **Free Some of Your Disk**: Clear the irrelevant files from your main scratch disk. If possible, try moving larger files onto an external drive to allow space.

- **Change Scratch Disk Location:** Go to **Edit > Preferences > Scratch Disks** and then allocate scratch space to another drive with higher storage.

- **Clear Temp Files:** Sometimes, after a crash, among other reasons, Photoshop leaves temporary files. Look for temp files and clear them.

6. **Missing or Garbled Fonts**

   Photoshop, at times, does not detect fonts or fonts appearing garbled.

   Solution:

   - **Reinstall Fonts:** Reinstall such fonts that are problematic, so they can be correctly registered in your system.

   - **Clear Font Cache**: The corrupt cache of fonts may display issues. Quit Photoshop, and delete the font cache files found in (~/Library/Caches/Adobe/Font on Mac and C:\Users\YourUsername\AppData\Local\Adobe\TypeSupport on Windows).

   - **Use Adobe Fonts**: If the problem persists then use the fonts of Adobe Fonts for better compatibility.

7. **"Could Not Complete Your Request" Errors**

   The vague error message can be due to a set of underlying issues, usually relating to corrupt files or memory allocation.

   Solution:

   - **Reset Photoshop Preferences:** Very often, the error gets fixed just by resetting the preferences. As pointed out, start Photoshop with the

Alt+Ctrl+Shift keys for Windows and **Option+Command+Shift** keys for Mac pressed.

- **Open the File in Another Program**: If the problem happens in one particular file, try opening it in another program for corruption. Saving a new copy from another program often fixes it.

- **Increase Available RAM:** Go to **Preferences > Performance** and increase Photoshop's allocated memory.

8. **Color Profile Mismatch Issues**

Photoshop has different ways of showing color, which may be problematic when importing images.

Solution:

- **Set a Consistent Working Color Space**: Go to **Edit > Color Settings**, and set a constant color workspace such as sRGB or Adobe RGB. This reduces color drift across multiple devices.

- **Convert on Import**: If there is a warning upon opening an image, select "**Convert**" over "**Preserve**" to make your imported image match your workspace profile.

- **Disable Monitor Profile for Older Displays**: A corrupted or improper monitor profile can further cause color inaccuracy. Go back to your system's default monitor profile through **Control Panel > Color Management** (Windows) or **System Preference > Displays > Color** (Mac)

9. **Plug-ins and Extensions Issues**

Some of the plug-ins further can cause problems with instability and slow performance, especially if they are outdated or incompatible with Photoshop 2025.

Solution:

- **Disable and Isolate Problematic Plug-ins:** If any recently installed plug-ins or unfamiliar ones exist, go to **Help > Manage Plug-ins** and disable them. Relaunch Photoshop and re-enable plug-ins one at a time to identify the problem.

- **Update or Reinstall Plug-ins:** Ensure each plug-in is updated to the most recent version. If any can't be updated, uninstall and reinstall to clear up any installation problems.

- **Use Adobe-Approved Plug-ins Only**: Use only those plug-ins that have been vetted by Adobe, as they undergo careful testing about compatibility with recent versions of Photoshop.

CONCLUSION

Adobe Photoshop 2025, has again, set the bar high with its exciting digital creativity, seamlessly integrating the best of advanced technology with user-friendly enhancements. The AI-powered tools enable you to work with more precision and speed while making advanced editing both simpler and more accessible for professionals and beginners alike. From automated masking to the latest in generative fill, Photoshop keeps streamlining what's complicated with absolutely no compromise on quality, allowing users to push their creative envelope.

Notable in this version, too, are the extended capabilities for compatibility and sharing that envision a closer creative community. That is to say, users can edit, store, and share their projects online with ease across devices. It also contains new collaboration features to accommodate team editing in which real-time feedback and contributions to creative projects can be made more dynamic and interactive.

In a nutshell, Adobe Photoshop 2025 is not a photo editing tool but an extended creative suite that meets the challenge of ever-growing and changing demands from digital artistry. By integrating advanced tools with easy and intuitive interfaces and collaborative features, it provides a solid base for artists, photographers, and designers in every step of their work. With digital creativity ever-evolving, Photoshop 2025 leads the way to show how serious Adobe is about innovation and boundless visual expression.

INDEX

A

Access the Selective Color Tool, 202

Accessing and Navigating Channels, 289

Accessing the Color Balance Tool, 194

Accessing the Shape Tools, 117

Add and Format Your Text, 276

Adding and Removing Anchor Points, 284

Adding Depth with Gradient Maps and Color Fill Layers, 150

Adding Dimension and Lighting for Impact, 279

Adding Dimension with Gradient Maps, 281

Adding Text Effects with Layer Styles, 265

Adjusting Brush Settings for Control, 223

Adjusting Color Temperature with Color Balance, 195

Adjusting Hue, Saturation, and Lightness, 198

Adjusting Image Brightness/Contrast, 171

Adjusting Opacity, Blending Options, and Linking Layers, 61

Adjusting the Shape of the Brush Tip, 99

Adjusting Tone and Contrast with Curves, 155

Advanced Effects with Combined Opacity and Fill, 144

Advanced Gradient Map Techniques, 212

Advanced Masking Techniques, 175

Advanced Retouching Techniques: Content-Aware Fill for Complex Edits, 218

Advanced Techniques for Fine Details, 219

Advanced Techniques for Polygons, 120

Advanced Techniques with Smudge Tool, 115

Advanced Techniques with the Mixer Brush, 113

Advanced Techniques: Combining Channels for Complex Selections, 291

Advanced Techniques: Working with Curved Paths and Complex Shapes, 285

Advanced Texturing with Displacement Maps, 152

Advanced Tips for Brush Customization, 101

Advanced Tips for Hue, Saturation, and Lightness Adjustments, 201

Advanced Tips for Professional Results, 231

Advanced Workflow Efficiency in Using Content-Aware Fill, 221

Anchor Points and Segments, 282

Apply Fill Options, 128

Applying a Gradient Overlay, 260

Applying Adjustment Layers, 79

Applying Advanced Automation with Scripts, 307

Applying and Saving Custom Adjustment Presets, 79

Applying Blending Modes, 62

Applying Blending Modes to Adjustment Layers, 82

Applying Filters in Photoshop 2025, 236

Applying Filters to Smart Objects, 65

Applying Gradient to Change Layer Styles in Photoshop, 260

Applying LUTs for Quick Color Grading, 205

Applying LUTs in Photoshop 2025, 206

Applying Textures Using Layer Blending Modes, 150

Auto Color: Adjusting Color Balance, 166

Auto Contrast: Bringing Out Detail Without Changing Colors, 166

Auto Tone, Color, and Contrast: Utilizing Photoshop's Automated Adjustments, 164

Auto Tone: Let Depth Loose, 165

Automating Repetitive Tasks Using Actions, 306

Avoiding Repetition with Texture Variations, 224

B

Balancing Color Using Histograms, 172

Balancing Filters for Optimal Results, 245

Basic Elements of the Selective Color Interface, 202

Batch Export and Automation, 305

Best Practices for Realistic Color Temperature, 197

Blending Mode Shortcuts, 312

BMP (Bitmap), 304

Brush Settings Panel, 98

Brush Tool Settings: Flow, Opacity, Smoothing, and Pressure Sensitivity, 107

Brush Tool Shortcuts, 310

C

Changing Layer Opacity, 61

Choosing the Right File Format, 305

Choosing the Right File Types, 293

Clone Stamp Tool: Manual Cloning for Precise Corrections, 222

Collaborating Shared Libraries, 316

Color Balance Adjustment Layer, 75

Color Balance for Temperature Adjustments, 194

Color Balance: Its Role in Temperature Adjustments, 194

Color Selection Shortcuts, 311

Color: Accurate Color Corrections Without Affecting Luminance, 140

Combining Gradients with Other Layer Styles, 262

Combining Layer Styles for Advanced Text Effects, 275

Combining Paths and Shapes, 287

Common Filters Used in Photography: Blur, Sharpen, Noise Reduction, 241

Common Mistakes to Avoid, 232

Common Use Cases for Layer Masks, 176

Conclusion, 323

Contrast/Brightness Adjustment Layer, 159

Convert a Layer to a Smart Object in Photoshop, 64

Converting Layers to Smart Objects for Non-Destructive Editing, 64

Converting Paths to Selections and Masks, 287

Converting Text to a Selection, 276

Correcting Perspective Distortions, 91

Correcting Skin Tone and Texture: Techniques for Portrait Retouching, 225

Creating a Custom Gradient, 210

Creating a Gradient Overlay, 254

Creating a Layer Mask in Photoshop 2025, 173

Creating a Levels Adjustment Layer:, 72

Creating a New Brush from Scratch, 102

Creating a New Library, 314

Creating and Editing Paths: Vector-Based Selections and Editing with the Path Tool, 122

Creating and Saving Custom Brushes, 101

Creating and Saving Custom Gradients, 262

Creating Balance Through Composition, 161

Creating Basic Shapes, 130

Creating Complex Composites with Masks: Masking for Multi-Layer Composites, 185

Creating Curves with Direction Handles, 283

Creating Double Exposure and Light Leak Effects, 145

Creating Frequency Separation in Photoshop 2025, 229

Creating Gradient Overlays and Backgrounds, 253

Creating Light Leak Effects in Adobe Photoshop 2025, 147

Creating Paths Using the Pen Tool, 285

Creating Selections from Text, 275

Creating Shapes with Shape Tools, 286

Creating, Organizing, and Managing Layers, 57

Creative Applications of Distort Filters, 246

Creative Applications of Pattern Fill Layers, 259

Creative Applications of Render Filters, 248

Creative Effects by Using Blending Modes with Adjustment Layers, 82

Creative Effects with Blending Modes on Adjustment Layers, 81

Creative Effects with Distort, Render, and Stylize Filters: Effects for Digital Art, 245

Cropping for Composition and Specific Resolutions, 83

Cropping to Specific Resolutions, 85

Curves Adjustment Layer, 73, 159

Curves for Tone and Contrast Control, 154

Curves vs. Levels and Brightness/Contrast, 158

Customizing Automated Adjustments, 168

Customizing the Workspace, 20

D

Density Adjustments, 183

Designing a Gradient Background, 254

Detailed Overview of Each Blending Mode Category, 133

Difference: Unique Effects and Fine-tuning Alignment, 140

Double Exposure Using Adobe Photoshop 2025, 145

Dual Brush, Scattering, And Texture Usage in Realism, 105

E

Edge Detection, 180

Editing a Smart Object, 64

Editing Brush Tips, 98

Editing Paths with the Direct Selection Tool, 286

Editing Polygon Properties, 120

Editing the Layer Mask, 174

Ellipse Tool, 118

Essential Keyboard Shortcuts for Efficiency: Mastering Commonly Used Commands, 309

Experimenting with Texture Blending Using Opacity and Fill, 152

Exploring Key Brush Settings, 103

Exporting for Print, 300

Exporting for Social Media, 300

Exporting for Web and Mobile Apps, 300

Exporting for Web and Print: Choosing File Types and Optimizing Quality, 293

F

Feathering, 182

Feathering Tips, 183

File Management Shortcuts, 313

Fill and Stroke Options: Color, Gradient, and Pattern Fills for Shapes, 127

Fill Pattern, 128

Final Touches, 149

Final Touches and Adjustments, 225

Final Touches with Adjustment Layers, 153

Fine-Tuning Brightness with Curves, 156

Fine-Tuning the Gradient Settings, 261

Finishing and Saving Your Edits, 252

Free Transform Tool, 89

Frequency Separation: Advanced Technique for Professional Skin Retouching, 229

G

Generative Expand with the Firefly Image 3 Model, 23

Getting Started with Brush Settings, 105

GIF (Graphics Interchange Format), 303

Glow Effects (Outer and Inner Glow), 274

Glow Effects Tips, 275

Gradient Fill, 128

Gradient Types and Presets, 210

Gradients with Selections, 212

H

Healing Brush, Spot Healing, and Patch Tool: Removing Imperfections and Blemishes, 214

How Density Adjustments Work, 184

How Edge Detection Works, 180

How Feathering Works, 182

How It Works, 214

How Skew Works:, 90

How to Access, 256

How to Achieve Contrast and Balance, 158

How to Add a Stroke:, 272

How to Apply an Adjustment Layer, 71

How to Apply Camera Raw as a Filter, 250

How to Apply Component Blending Modes, 136

How to Apply Smart Filters in Photoshop 2025, 239

How to Change Brightness and Contrast, 163

How to Create your First File, 44

How to Download and Install the New Adobe Photoshop 2025, 11

How to Effectively Apply Drop Shadows:, 272

How to Enter the Brightness and Contrast Adjustments, 162

How to Feather a Mask, 182

How to Find and Remove Distractions with the Remove Tool, 21

How to Get Acquainted with Adobe Photoshop Workspace, 15

How to Insert Files Using Place Embedded, 49

How to Insert Files Using Place Linked, 52

How to Insert Images Using Drag & Drop, 48

How to Know the Toolbar, 36

How to Lock and Hide Layers, 65

How to Open Files with the Open Command, 46

How to Reset your Workspace, 27

How to Set Up a Clipping Mask in Adobe Photoshop 2025, 177

How to Understand the Menu Bar, 31

How to Use Free Transform:, 89

How to Use Lighten Blending Modes, 134

How to Use Mixer Brush Tool, 110

How to Use Perspective:, 91

How to Use Quick Mask Mode in Photoshop 2025, 190

How to Use Selective Color, 203

How to use the Mixer Brush and Smudge Tool, 110

How to Use the Puppet Warp, 93

How to Work with Inversion Blending Modes,
136

I

Interpreting the Histogram, 170

Intro to Vector-Based Selections and Paths, 122

Introduction to Photoshop Filters, 234

Introduction to Photoshop Libraries, 313

Introduction to Smudge Tool, 113

J

JPEG (Joint Photographic Experts Group), 302

K

Key Stylize Filters:, 248

L

Layer Management Shortcuts, 310

Layer Opacity and Fill Adjustments: Differences
and Effects of Opacity vs. Fill, 141

Layer Styles for Text Effects: Drop Shadows,
Strokes, and Glows, 270

Layer Styles: Adding Inner and Outer Shadows,
280

Layering Techniques for Texture and Tone
Blending, 149

Levels Adjustment Layer, 159

Linking Layers, 63

M

Major Components of the Photoshop Workspace,
16

Managing Colors in Libraries, 314

Managing Shapes and Paths in the Layers Panel,
132

Mask Areas Using Selection Tools, 78

Mask Refinement Tips, 185

Mask Refinement: Edge Detection, Feathering, and
Adjusting Density, 180

Masking and Layer Effects Shortcuts, 313

Minimum and Recommended Specifications, 9

Multiple Sizes and Formats for Different Platforms,
298

Multiply: Darkening Images and Adding Shadows,
137

N

Navigating New Features in Adobe Photoshop
2025, 19

Navigation Shortcuts, 311

New Features in Photoshop 2025 for Color
Balance, 196

New Features of the New Adobe Photoshop 2025, 3

New Filters Features in Photoshop 2025, 237

Noise Reduction Filters, 244

O

Opacity, 108

Opacity Adjustment: Full Transparency Control,
142

Opening Histograms within Photoshop 2025, 169

Optimizing Export Settings, 295

Organizing Layers with Groups, 58

Organizing Multiple Smart Filters, 240

Organizing Text Styles, 314

Overlay: Adding Contrast and Boosting Color, 138

Overview of Adjustment Layers: Types and Uses of
Each Adjustment Layer, 68

P

Path Creation and Editing: Manipulating Paths and
Shapes, 285

Path Operations and Combining Shapes, 130

PDF (Portable Document Format), 303

**Performing Non-Destructive Editing with
Adjustment Layers**, 59

Perspective Tool, 91

PNG (Portable Network Graphics), 302

Practical Application of Clone Stamp Tool, 225

Practical Applications of Blending Modes: Using
Multiply, Screen, Overlay, and More, 137

Practical Applications of Clipping Masks, 178

Practical Applications of Mask Refinement
Techniques, 184

Practical Applications of Selective Color, 204

Practical Applications of Smart Filters, 241

Practical Temperature Adjustment Tips, 196

Practical Tips for Exporting, 300

Pressure Sensitivity (for Pen Tablet Users), 109

PSD (Photoshop Document), 301

Q

Quick Mask Mode: Temporary Masking for Precise
Selections, 189

R

RAM:, 10

Rectangle Tool, 117

Refine Edge, Quick Mask, and Object Selection, 289

Refining Texture on the High Frequency Layer,
231

Refining the Adjustment with the Layer Mask, 77

Refining the Edit with Layer Masking, 224

Refining the Selection, 278, 290

Resizing Shape Layers, 124

Resizing, Rotating, and Warping Shape Layers, 124

Retouching with Frequency Separation, 230

RGB, 201

Rotating Shape Layers, 125

S

Save As and File Types: PSD, TIFF, JPEG, PNG, and
More, 300

Saving and Exporting Text Layers, 267

Saving and Exporting Your Combined Shapes,
132

Saving and Managing Custom Brushes, 100

Saving and Managing Paths, 124

**Saving and Reusing Selections with Alpha
Channels**, 291

Saving Custom Adjustment Presets, 80

Saving Custom Brushes, 104

Saving Your Custom Brush, 100

Saving Your Edited Image, 164

**Scattering: Adding Organic Randomness to
Brush Strokes**, 106

Screen: Lightening Images and Adding Glow, 138

Selecting and Modifying Brush Tips, 97

Selection Shortcuts, 309

Setting Smoothing for Accuracy, 101

Setting the Foundation with Layers and Smart
Objects, 279

Setting Up for Content-Aware Fill Success, 218

Setting Up the Workspace, 122

Setting Up Your Clone Source for Precision, 222

Setting Up Your Document, 275

Setting Up Your Layers for Blending, 149

Shape Fill and Stroke Options, 127

Smart Filters: Non-Destructive Application of
Filters on Smart Objects, 238

Smoothing, 109

**Smoothing Skin Tone on the Low Frequency
Layer**, 230

Soft Light: Subtle Contrast and Gentle Effects, 139

Some Tips on Efficient Library Management,
316

Step-by-Step Guide, 217

Steps to Adjust Mask Density, 184

Storing Graphics and Logos, 315

Straightening an Image Using Content-Aware Crop,
87

Stroke and Fill Adjustment, 132

Stroke Key Settings:, 273

Stroking and Filling Paths and Shapes, 288

SVG (Scalable Vector Graphics), 304

Synchronizing Assets Across Devices, 316

T

Text Transformation and Warping: Creating
Dynamic Text Shapes, 267

Texture: Adding Realistic Surface Detail, 106

Texturing with Layer Masks for Precision, 151

The "Export As" Feature, 297

The Basics: What are Opacity and Fill?, 142

The benefit of Smart Filters in Photoshop 2025, 238

The Healing Brush Tool, 214

The Role of Gradients in Layer Styles, 260

The Spot Healing Brush Tool, 215

TIFF (Tagged Image File Format), 301

Times to Apply Quick Mask Mode, 190

Tips and Tricks for Working with Clipping Masks,
179

Tips for Adjusting Density, 184

Tips for Best Results, 215

Tips for Choosing the Right Source Area, 223

Tips for Edge Detection, 182

Tips for Effective Filter Use, 237

Tips for Effective LUT Use in Photoshop 2025, 208

Tips for Gradient Maps in Photoshop 2025, 212

Tips for Maintaining an Organized Workspace, 30

Tips for optimum usage of Selective Color, 205

Tips for Quality Control, 296

Tips for Using Quick Mask Mode Effectively, 193

Transform Shortcuts, 312

Transform Tools Overview: Free Transform, Skew,
Distort, Perspective, 89

Transformations and Adjustments with Shape Tool,
121

Transforming Images, 85

Transforming Paths and Shapes, 288

Troubleshooting Common Issues, 221

Troubleshooting Common Issues (Solutions to
Frequent Problems and Errors), 317

Troubleshooting Common Path Issues, 124

Types of Adjustment Layers and Their Uses:, 68

Types of Photoshop Filters, 235

U

Understanding Adjustment Layers, 81

Understanding Automated Adjustments in
Photoshop, 164

Understanding Basic Clone Stamp Tool Principles,
222

Understanding Batch Exporting: The Basics, 305

Understanding Blending Modes, 81

Understanding Brush Basics, 101

Understanding Brush Basics in Photoshop 2025, 97

Understanding Channels in Photoshop, 289

Understanding Clipping Masks in Photoshop, 176

Understanding Color Temperature and White
Balance, 194

Understanding Content-Aware Fill in Photoshop
2025, 218

Understanding Contrast and Balance, 158

Understanding Curves: The Basics, 154

Understanding Export Needs: Web vs. Print, 293

Understanding Fill Layers in Photoshop, 256

Understanding Frequency Separation Layers, 229

Understanding Hue, Saturation, and Lightness, 198

Understanding Layer Masks: Basics of Masking and
Transparency Control, 173

Understanding Layers and Layer Stacks, 54

Understanding Masks in Photoshop, 185

Understanding Paths and Shapes in Photoshop,
285

Understanding the Basics of the Pen Tool, 282

Undo and History Shortcuts, 311

Using Adjustment Layers to Modify Histograms,
170

Using Adobe Stock and Libraries Together, 315

Using Camera Raw as a Filter for Enhanced Editing,
249

Using Clipping Masks: Linking Layers for Targeted
Effects, 176

Using Clone Sources for Complex Edits, 223

Using Content-Aware Fill for Complex
Backgrounds, 219

Using Edge Detection, 181

Using Export As and Save for Web: Exporting for
Different Platforms, 297

Using Fill: Content-Only Transparency Control,
143

Using Gradient Maps for Advanced Effects, 255

Using Histograms to Guide Adjustments, 168

Using Levels, Curves, and Color Balance, 72

Using Libraries for Asset Management: Managing
Colors, Text Styles, and Graphics, 313

Using Masks with Adjustment Layers, 76

Using Multiple Gradient Maps, 212

Using Opacity and Fill Creatively in Designs, 144

Using Path Operations through the Options Bar,
130

Using Select and Mask, 290

Using Selective Color for Targeted Edits, 201

Using Shape Dynamics, 99

Using the 3D Lighting Effects Tool, 279

Using the Content-Aware Crop Tool, 86

Using the Custom Shape Tool, 120

Using the Pen Tool for Precision Selections: Paths,
Curves, and Anchor Points, 282

Using the Polygon Tool, 119

Using the Selection, 277

Using the Smudge Tool, 114

Using Your Custom Brushes, 104

Utilize Photoshop 2025's Neural Filters:, 231

W

Warping Shape Layers, 126

What are Layer Masks?, 173

What are Photoshop Filters?, 234

What is a Gradient Map?, 209

What is a Histogram?, 168

What is a LUT?, 205

What is Camera Raw?, 249

What is Quick Mask Mode?, 189

When and Why to Use Automated Adjustments, 167

When to Use Fill Adjustments:, 144

When to Use Opacity Adjustments:, 143

Why Use a Histogram?, 168

Why Use Camera Raw as a Filter?, 250

Why Use LUTs in Photoshop 2025?, 206

Why Use Quick Mask Mode?, 189

Working with Adjustment Layers for Contrast, 158

Working with Channels for Selections, 289

Working with Color Channels in Curves, 156

Working with Curves in Photoshop 2025: Some Practical Tips, 157

Working with Droplets of Photoshop for Quick Automation, 308

Working with Gradient Maps, 209

Working with Gradient Masks, 174

Working with Gradients: Linear, Radial, and Custom Gradients, 253

Working with Layer Visibility and Opacity, 58

Working with Paragraph and Character Panels, 266

Working with Path Options: Creating, Editing, and Saving Paths, 284

Working with Pattern Fill Layers, 258

Working with Reflections and Shadows, 220

Working with Shape Tools: Rectangle, Ellipse, Polygon, and Custom Shape Options, 117

Working with Solid and Pattern Fill Layers, 256

Working with Solid Color Fill Layers, 257

Working with Stroke, 273

Working with Text Layers: Adding, Editing, and Formatting Text, 263